Learn to
Garden

Learn to Garden

EDITOR-IN-CHIEF GUY BARTER

PHOTOGRAPHY PETER ANDERSON

A DK PUBLISHING BOOK

LONDON, NEW YORK, MUNICH,
MELBOURNE, AND DELHI

CONTRIBUTORS
Guy Barter   Lia Leendertz
Philip Clayton   Alan Toogood
Andi Clevely   Dr. Daphne Vince Prue
Dr. Isabelle Van Groeningen   Matthew Wilson

NORTH AMERICAN CONSULTANT
Trevor Cole

SENIOR EDITOR   Helen Fewster
PROJECT ART EDITOR   Murdo Culver
PROJECT EDITOR   Zia Allaway
EDITORS   Letitia Luff
                       Candida Frith-Macdonald
US SENIOR EDITOR   Jill Hamilton
US EDITOR   Mary Sutherland
US ASSISTANT EDITOR   John Searcy
PROJECT DEVELOPMENT   Pamela Brown
ART EDITORS   Elly King
                       Rachael Smith
                       Helen Taylor
MANAGING EDITOR   Anna Kruger
MANAGING ART EDITOR   Lee Griffiths
DTP DESIGNER   Louise Waller
MEDIA RESOURCES   Lucy Claxton, Richard Dabb
PICTURE RESEARCH   Carolyn Clerkin
PRODUCTION CONTROLLER Mandy Inness

First published in the United States in 2005
by DK Publishing,
375 Hudson Street, New York, New York 10014
05 06 07 08 09 10 9 8 7 6 5 4 3 2 1

DK books are available at special discounts for bulk purchases for sales
promotions, premiums, fund-raising, or educational use. For details,
contact: DK Publishing Special Markets,
375 Hudson Street, New York, NY 10014 or SpecialSales@dk.com

A CIP catalog record for this book is available from
the Library of Congress
ISBN 0-7566-0916-X

Color reproduction by Colourscan, Singapore
Printed and bound in China by Toppan

Discover more at
www.dk.com

Contents

1 How plants work
14–31

Gardening from the plants' point of view. What plants need to survive and how evolution in the wild has equipped them for life in the garden.

2 Soil and climate
32–51

The importance of looking after your soil and recognizing how weather affects plant growth, helping you plant and manage the garden successfully. What you can do to improve the natural conditions, and how to reap the benefits of composting.

3 Know your garden
52–73

Assessing your own garden, plotting sun and shade, and finding out how you can take advantage of the good points and improve the bad. How to recognize the best plants for particular areas within your garden.

INTRODUCTION

If you are new to gardening it may come as a surprise to learn that experienced hands envy you. You are about to embark on an enthralling and satisfying pursuit, which may prove as rewarding to you as it is to those who have gardened for years. And the adventure lies before you.

Gardeners once learned their skills from their parents, friends, or neighbors. Today, a wealth of books, magazines, and television programs offer help and advice, but trying to piece together all of this disparate information can be time consuming and confusing.

Learn to Garden brings together everything you need to know to begin gardening and breaks the information down into straightforward, easy-to-follow steps. Through every step of this journey, you will obtain practical experience and get tips to help with every problem and uncertainty. We will guide you through the basics, so that you can get to understand your soil and site, choose good plants and look after them properly, and ultimately how to make new plants for free by propagation. As your skills, experience, and knowledge increase, this book will remain a valued companion, always available to give a quick and to-the-point answer. In fact, you don't even have to be a beginner to find it useful.

WHERE TO START?

Possibly you already have a vision of how you want you garden to look. This book will give you an outline of practical steps you can take to achieve it, starting perhaps with containers or by improving the lawn, and working up at your own pace to flowerbeds and borders, trees,

Simple drifts and traditional borders are achievable, once you get to know your garden conditions and understand how to put plants together. Then experiment with the colors you most enjoy.

However small your garden, you can use a single, carefully chosen container plant to provide a focal point or, as here, a woodland landscape in miniature.

shrubs, and hedges. You won't find recipes for makeovers or grand designs; the aim is to help you make various improvements now and develop the know-how to create the garden of your dreams. Better to start small than to risk lots of money in what may turn out to be a discouraging and costly disappointment.

Instead, take the time to look at your garden through the seasons; observation is at the heart of successful gardening, and this book will help you assess what you've got. Established trees, shrubs, or hedges can cast deep shade but might provide privacy, shelter, or beautiful features in other seasons with bark, berries, or blossoms. You will learn how to renovate them if they need it, and to enhance them with flowering climbers, a scattering of bulbs, or a surrounding border.

A few pots quickly transform parts of the garden, while you take the time to think through your long-term plans.

GETTING A PLANT'S-EYE VIEW

Choosing plants that grow well in your soil, site, and locality is the key to gardening success. It follows that knowing a little bit about the plants themselves—how they work, what they need to survive, and how they have adapted to different amounts of sun, shade, heat, or drought—will help you match them to your own garden conditions. A brief guide explains how plants, soil, and climate

Making new plants can become an addictive hobby. You can gain a real sense of satisfaction from seeing your own seedlings thrive, and watching apparently lifeless seeds develop into healthy plants.

work—giving you enough to help you fathom what is going on behind the scenes and, equally important, to recognize plants and planting combinations that are never going to work the way you want.

Just an inkling of these amazing invisible processes can give you that bit of extra confidence so helpful in making the leap of faith involved in choosing plants, sowing seeds, or pruning a shrub. For example, knowing how plants respond to having bits removed will help you anticipate the consequences of when and where you make a pruning cut. Without this, you are literally making a stab in the dark.

Of course there will be setbacks. That (within reason) is part of the fascination. You may discover problems that are of your own making, and learn how to remedy

Watching the garden change with the seasons helps you understand how it has evolved and gives you the opportunity to assess the pros and cons of all its features.

them, but you can also take comfort in knowing that some things really are beyond your control.

Time spent gardening should be a pleasure. It is often best done in spurts; a relaxed, daily wander through the garden with pruners and a trowel allows you to deal with minor problems before they get out of hand, and warns you when more drastic remedies are needed. But be warned: keep a notebook handy because you never know when inspiration will strike!

You won't just get a beautiful garden Learning to garden is healthy exercise, reduces stress, and is immensely satisfying.

Garden jargon explained

Acidic Refers to soil with a *pH* of less than 7 and determines the range of plants that can be grown.

Aerate Digging or forking the soil or spiking a lawn to allow more air in.

Alkaline Refers to soil with a *pH* of more than 7 and determines the range of plants that can be grown.

All-purpose fertilizer See *Fertilizer*.

Alpine A plant that grows above the tree line in mountainous areas; often used to describe rock garden plants that grow in lower altitudes.

Annual A plant that germinates, flowers, sets seed, and dies in one growing season. "Hardy annuals" can be sown the autumn before; "marginally hardy" ones in spring.

Aphids Greenfly or blackfly.

Architectural Buzzword used to describe plants with a strong outline or bold leaf shape.

Aspect Which way a garden, a wall, or a plant faces.

Bare-root Nursery-grown trees and shrubs dug up and sold without a pot or any soil around their roots.

Bedding Temporary planting for seasonal displays.

Biennial A plant that grows one year, flowers the next, and then dies.

Biological control Deliberate release of a tiny organism that kills certain garden pests.

Bleed To lose sap freely through a cut or wound.

Blind A shoot or a bulb that fails to flower.

Blood, fish, and bone See *Fertilizer*.

Bract A modified leaf at the base of a flower or cluster of flowers. Bracts may be colorful like petals.

Brassica A member of the cabbage family.

Broadcasting Scattering seed or fertilizer evenly over the soil, rather than distributing it in *drills* or furrows.

Bulblet A baby bulb produced from the base of a mature bulb, and easily separated from it.

Cell tray See *Module*.

Cloche A low clear plastic or glass dome, tunnel, or box used to protect young garden plants, or to warm the soil.

Cold frame A glazed, boxlike, unheated structure with a lid used to protect plants from the elements.

Coir Recycled outer fibers of coconuts, used as an ingredient in potting mixes.

Compost A homemade organic material formed from plant waste and other organic matter, used to improve soil or as a mulch.

Compacted soil With all the pockets of air that plants need squashed out of it, e.g., after heavy use of a lawn.

Composted bark By-product of the lumber industry that makes a good soil conditioner. Not to be confused with chipped bark, a mulching material. Bark chips dug into the soil rob it of nitrogen and may take years to decay.

Containerized A plant raised in the open ground and potted up for sale.

Coppicing To prune back a tree or shrub close to the ground to stimulate the growth of young stems.

Corm An underground bulblike body. When mature, baby "cormels" or "cormlets" form around it (see also *Bulblet*).

Crocks Shards of broken terracotta pot sometimes placed at the bottom of containers to improve drainage.

Cross-pollination When pollen from one plant fertilizes the flower of another.

Crown The base of an herbaceous plant where the stems join the root system, from where new shoots grow.

Cultivar Cultivated varieties of plants selected for desirable characteristics, such as flower or leaf color. Their names are written within single quotes.

Cuttings Parts of a plant—e.g., sections of stem or root—that can be grown to form a new plant.

Damping off A very common disease that causes small seedlings to keel over at soil level and die.

Deciduous Of trees and shrubs that drop their leaves every year in the autumn.

Division A method of increasing perennial plants by dividing them into sections, each with roots and one or more shoots.

Dormancy When growth temporarily ceases or other plant functions slow down due to the seasonal effect of low temperatures in winter, or other adverse conditions, like excessive heat or drought. Seed dormancy prevents *germination* until conditions are favorable.

Double-digging Deep digging, turning the soil over to a level equal to two spade-blades ("spits") in depth.

Drill A narrow, straight, shallow furrow or groove into which seeds are sown or seedlings planted.

Ericaceous soil mix Acidic potting soil mix, suitable for growing lime-hating plants, like rhododendrons, in pots.

F1 hybrid Plant bred for uniformity and desirable flowers or other characteristics. Seed from F1 hybrids will not come *true*.

Fertilization Successful *pollination* resulting in the formation of seed.

Fertilizer A source of plant *nutrients*. Organic fertilizers include blood, fish, and bone; pelleted chicken manure; and seaweed-based products. Inorganic fertilizers are chemical formulations. "General," "all-purpose," or "balanced" fertilizers serve most purposes. May be in granular, powder, pelleted, or liquid formulations. Controlled-release fertilizer, in pellets or granules, releases its nutrients into the soil over several months.

Fleece A light, woven, translucent or transparent fabric that can be used to protect plants from cold or from pests.

Frost pocket A low area of land where cold air collects.

Geotextile A man-made water-permeable material (membrane) that is used to suppress weeds.

Germination Chemical and physical changes that take place when a seed starts to grow into a plant.

Glaucous A blue-green, blue-gray, gray, or white bloom on leaves or other plant parts.

Glyphosate Type of herbicide, or weedkiller, that is absorbed through the leaves to kill the plant.

Graft union The point where a bud or stem is joined to a rootstock of a different plant when being grafted.

Green manure Fast-maturing crop, such as clover, winter rye, or alfalfa, grown and then dug into the soil before it flowers to raise the soil's fertility.

Growing season Usually from spring to fall when temperatures are above 43°F (6°C).

Hardening off Gradually acclimatizing plants that have been raised indoors to cooler conditions outside.

Hardiness How resistant to cold a plant is.

Hard landscaping Anything in the garden that is not living plants, hedges, or lawn, e.g., paths, walls, gravel.

Hardy Plants that can withstand outdoor conditions year round and temperatures below freezing without protection.

Heavy soil With a high clay content, hard to work.

Heeling in Temporary planting to protect a plant until it can be placed in its permanent position.

Herbaceous A nonwoody plant with upper parts that usually die down to a *rootstock* in the winter, usually applied to *perennials*, or borders planted with perennials.

Herbicide A chemical that kills plants.

Horticultural grit A fine, washed grit added to potting soil mixes or heavy clay soil to improve its drainage. Also used as a mulch. Sold in bags by garden centers.

Horticultural sand Fine washed sands are used as a top-dressing for lawns and for propagation benches. Coarse washed sand can be added to soil and potting media to improve drainage. Builder's sands may contain materials harmful to plants and soils.

Humus The residue of organic matter in the soil that helps improve it.

Integrated pest management The practice of using natural predators, organic methods of pest control, tolerating an acceptable level of pests, and resorting to chemical controls only when this level is exceeded and plant health is severely threatened.

Landscape fabric See *Geotextile*.

Lateral A sideshoot or root.

Layering Method of *propagation* involving encouraging a stem to grow roots where it touches the ground, while still attached to the parent plant. Useful for climbers.

Alpine

Green manure

Seed leaf

Marginal plant (iris)

Green bracts above flowers

Acid-loving rhododendron   Sucker   Pollinator   Pricking out   Succulent

Leader, leading shoot The main or central shoot of a branch or a young tree.

Leaf mold Rotted-down, fallen (i.e. dry) leaves. It is a good soil conditioner.

Legume Member of the pea or bean family, e.g., sweetpea.

Lime Horticultural product added to soil to raise the *pH*.

Limy soil Alkaline—e.g., chalky—with a *pH* above 7.

Light soil With a high sand content, fast-draining.

Loam Soil comprising ideal amounts of sand, clay, and silt. Easy to work, water-retentive and free-draining.

Marginal A plant that can grow equally well in shallow water or in moist soil at the edge of a pond or stream.

Marginally hardy A plant that will not survive temperatures much below freezing.

Microclimate Spot in the garden with conditions that differ slightly from the norm, e.g., a sheltered sunny wall.

Mixed border With both shrubby and *herbaceous* plants.

Module or cell trays Used for sowing seeds in, consisting of separate compartments, or cells.

Mulch A material spread over the soil surface to suppress weeds and conserve moisture.

Mushroom compost The spent growing medium used by mushroom farmers; a useful soil conditioner and mulch but contains lime.

Native Plants originating in the country or area you live in.

Naturalistic Informal, imitating nature.

Naturalized Introducing plants so that they look as if they are growing naturally—e.g., snowdrops in grass.

Neutral soil With a pH of 7, neither acidic nor alkaline.

NPK Chemical abbreviations of the major plant *nutrients*, nitrogen (N), phosphorus (P), and potassium (K).

Nursery bed A small area of the garden set aside for sowing seeds, propagation, or growing on young plants.

Nutrients Minerals needed for healthy plant growth.

Offset A baby plant produced alongside a larger one, easily detached from the parent.

Organic matter Anything derived from plants or animals that is dug into or spread over the soil to improve it. May be the result of recycling—e.g., garden compost—or leaf mold, manures, or chipped bark.

Overwintering Moving nonhardy plants into a protected, frost-free place, such as a greenhouse or conservatory, to spend the winter months until late spring or early summer when danger of frost is over and temperatures have risen.

Peasticks Twiggy branches ideal as supports for tendril climbers, such as peas.

Peat Partially decayed, organic plant matter formed on the surface of waterlogged soils. Peat moss or sphagnum peat is used in soil mixes.

Peat substitute Container media, such as *composted bark*, that provides similar conditions to peat.

Perennial A plant that lives for at least three growing seasons; usually applied to *herbaceous* plants.

Pergola A linked series of arches over a path or patio, either open at the top or with a roof.

Pesticide A substance used to kill pests.

pH A measure of acidity and alkalinity on a scale of 1 to 14: 7 is *neutral*, below 7 is *acid*, and above 7 is *alkaline*. You can buy pH testing kits from garden centers.

Photosynthesis The complex process by which green plants manufacture their own food in the form of carbohydrates.

Pinching out Nipping out the tips of shoots with finger and thumb to make the plant bush out lower down.

Pollarding The regular or annual pruning back of stems to a short trunk to form a small, lollipop-shaped tree.

Pollination Transfer of pollen from one flower to another.

Pollinator The pollinating agent, e.g., bees, the wind.

Potbound A plant with crowded roots that has grown too big for its container.

Potting on Moving a plant from one pot to a larger one.

Pricking out The transfer of recently germinated seedlings that are growing closely together into containers where they have more room to grow on.

Propagation Making more plants by raising seed, rooting cuttings, grafting, or other means.

Propagator A device with a glazed cover and the means to regulate humidity and temperature for seed germination and the growth of young seedlings and cuttings.

Rain shadow The dry ground next to a wall or fence that is sheltered from prevailing winds and rainfall.

Reverted When the leaves of a *variegated* plant go back to being all green.

Rhizomes Branching stems with buds and roots growing close to soil surface. Sometimes fleshy, e.g., bearded irises.

Ripe/ripening Used to describe a shoot of a shrub or tree when it has become mature and firm over the course of a summer.

Rootball The roots and soil or potting mix that surrounds them in a container or in the soil.

Rootstock 1. The roots of a plant used in grafting. 2. The root system of an *herbaceous* plant that survives over winter while the top growth dies down.

Runners Stems that lie on the soil surface and root at the tips—e.g., strawberries.

Scarification The removal of debris from a lawn using a rake or other tool.

Seed leaves The first leaves a seedling develops.

Seep hose (or soaker hose) a hose pierced with holes to allow water to dribble out very slowly along its length.

Self-seeding The unaided natural scattering of seeds that produces seedlings around the parent plant.

Sheet mulch See *Geotextile*. Also, a plastic sheet spread over the soil to warm it up before sowing seed. Black plastic sheeting can be laid over soil for up to a year to clear the ground of perennial weeds.

Shelter belt Trees or shrubs planted to protect the garden from wind, but taller and wider than a hedge.

Soil mark The dark mark on the stem(s) of an uprooted tree or shrub that shows where it originally met the soil.

Sour Foul-smelling soil or potting mix that lacks oxygen and contains stagnant water, resulting from waterlogging.

Specimen Plant with a striking shape that looks good planted on its own, e.g., a tree in a lawn.

Spit The depth of a spade blade, usually 10–12in (25–30cm).

Stress Plants under stress cannot function properly, start to wilt, and become more vulnerable to pests and diseases. The cause is usually lack of water due to dry (or frozen) soil, but may also be waterlogging or physical damage.

Subsoil The layers of soil beneath the *topsoil*: often paler and less fertile than the topsoil above it.

Succulent A plant with thick fleshy leaves and/or stems that is adapted to store water, e.g., sedum.

Sucker 1. A shoot that grows from a plant's roots or an underground stem. 2. On grafted plants, a sucker is any shoot that grows from below the graft union, and should be removed.

Tamp To firm or pack down soil to bring it into contact with plant roots or newly sown seeds.

Tap root One main downward-growing root, e.g., a carrot.

Tender A plant that will not survive temperatures below 41°F (5°C).

Thatch A layer of dead material that accumulates on the surface of lawns.

Tilth A fine, crumbly layer of soil ideal for sowing seeds.

Top dressing 1. A mix of compost, *topsoil*, and/or *fertilizers* applied around a plant or on a lawn to replenish nutrients. 2. A decorative layer spread over the soil.

Topsoil The upper layer of soil, darker and more fertile than the *subsoil*.

True Resembling the parent plant. Seed that will not "come true" results in plants that may look different from their parent.

Variegated Usually referring to leaves that are splashed or margined with a different color, often cream or yellow.

Variety Commonly used word to describe a variant of a plant (cultivar).

Vermiculite A lightweight mineral that retains water well and, mixed with potting soil mix, improves its texture.

Wall shrub Any shrub trained and tied in to a wall.

Weed-suppressing membrane See *Geotextile*.

Whip A young tree, yet to grow any side branches.

Understanding plant groups and names

The plant world is infinitely varied, from tiny mosses to giant trees, and flowering plants to plumed grasses. To bring order to this diversity, plants are classified into groups on the basis of shared characteristics, such as the structure of the flowers and fruit, or the arrangement of the leaves.

Plant names are an important part of the classification; you may think them unwieldy, but botanical names are used world-wide as a means of precise identification, which is not possible with common names. Common names are often very local: one plant may have several names, or one common name may refer to a few different plants; for example, the name "marigold" could be describing a *Calendula*, *Tagetes*, or *Caltha*.

What's in a name?

The plant name tells you the genus, and if it is a species, cultivar, or a hybrid (*see below*). Italics distinguish the genus and species. If repeated references are made to a few plants of the same genus, the genus is often abbreviated – so *Helianthus annuus* becomes *H. annuus*.

(1) Genus (2) Species

Helianthus × *multiflorus* 'Meteor'

(4) Hybrid sign   (3) Cultivar

Family

ROSE (*ROSACEAE*)

LILY (*LILIACEAE*)   DAISY (*ASTERACEAE*

Plants with similar characteristics are grouped into families, eg. daisy- or asterlike plants are in the daisy family (*Asteraceae*). Members of the same family are then broken down into smaller groups to reflect their differences.

1 Genus (pl. genera)

TAGETES

ASTER   ACHILLEA

The genus is like a surname; eg. the genera in the daisy family (*Asteraceae*) include *Aster*, *Achillea*, *Tagetes,* and *Helianthus* (*shown left*). But within each genus are plants with different characteristics, so further division is needed.

2 Species

Helianthus annuus

This is like a first name, but it follows the genus; here, *Helianthus annuus* is the annual sunflower. There can also be some variation within a species that may have occurred in the wild or as a result of plant breeding.

3 Cultivars

Helianthus annuus 'Teddy Bear'

Cultivar names are given to plants that have been bred or selected for decorative or useful characteristics. *Helianthus annuus* 'Teddy Bear', for instance, has been bred from the annual sunflower for its large, double flowers.

4 Hybrids

H. × *multiflorus*

You may come across names with an "x." This means the plant is a hybrid, the result of two different species cross-pollinating (in this case *H. annuus* and *H. decapetalus*). This occurs both in the wild and in cultivation.

Subdivisions of species

In addition to cultivars (from the words *cultivated* and *varieties*), see 3, which are the result of plant breeding or selection, there can also be variations within a species that occur in the wild. These result in minor differences in appearance, such as the height of the plant, flower form, or leaf shape. Further subdivisions are used to take account of them:

- **subspecies (subsp.):** usually a distinct geographical population of plants.
- **variety (var.):** usually a less significant degree of variation than a subspecies.
- **forma (f.):** occurs sporadically and involves one variation, such as flower color; for example, a white-flowered plant in a normally pink-flowered species.

Botanical names explained

In addition to understanding how a plant is grouped and identified, the name, or part of the name, offers clues about it, too. Botanical names can be derived from Latin, Greek, or native terms, and may describe, for example, the flower color, leaf texture, or plant size. The names may look off-putting, but they can be useful. Here is a selection of the most common.

Botanical terms used in plant names

Plant parts

baccatus	berrylike
coccifera	bearing berries
florus	refers to flowers
folius, or phyllus	refers to leaves

Shape and habit

arboreus	treelike
compactus	compact or dense
contortus	twisted, contorted
elatus	tall
elegans	elegant
fruticosus	shrubby
humilis	small or low-growing
nanus	dwarf
pendulus	weeping
procumbens	prostrate
repens, or reptans	creeping
scandens	climbing

Color

albus	white
aureus	golden
bicolor	two-colored (may apply to flowers or foliage)
brunneus	brown
caeruleus	blue
coccineus	scarlet
croceus	yellow
glaucus	bloomed
niger	black
purpureus	purple
ruber	red
tricolor	three-colored (may apply to flowers or foliage)

Leaf shape and form

acerifolius	maplelike leaves
angustifolius	narrow leaves
argutifolius	sharply toothed leaves
buxifolius	leaves similar to boxwood (Buxus)
coriaceus	leathery
heterophyllus	leaves of variable size
ilicifolius	similar to holly (Ilex)
integrifolius	leaves without teeth
latifolius	broad leaves
macrophyllus	large leaves
marginatus	margined
parvifolius	small leaves

General descriptions

armatus	thorny
barbatus	bearded (usually of flowers)
campanulatus	bell-shaped
cordatus	heart-shaped
dendroideus	treelike
edulis	edible
floridus	free flowering
fulgens	shining
grandis	large
hirsutus, or hirsutissimus	hairy, or very hairy
lanatus	woolly
macro–	large
micro–	small
mollis	soft
nervosus	veined or ribbed
officinalis	medicinal
plumosus	feathery
pubescens	downy
pungens	sharply pointed

rotundus	rounded
rugosus	wrinkled
setaceus, setifer, or setosus	bristly
scaber	rough-textured
spinosus	spiny
variegatus	variegated
villosus	softly hairy
zebrinus	striped

Fragrance of flowers and leaves

anisatum	scented like anise
citriodorus	lemon-scented
foetidus	bad smelling
foetidissima	very bad smelling
fragrans, or fragrantissima	fragrant, or very fragrant
graveolens	heavily scented
moschatus	musky scent
suaveolens	sweet-scented
suavis	sweet
odoratus, odorifer, or odoratissimus	sweetly scented

Area or country of origin

africanus	from Africa
alpinus	from alpine regions
australis	southern
campestris	from plains or fields
canadensis	from Canada
canariensis	from the Canary Islands
capensis	from the Cape (South Africa)
chinensis, or sinensis	from China
europaeus	from Europe
japonicus	from Japan
occidentalis	western
orientalis	eastern

Euphorbia mellifera

Malus baccata

Escallonia rubra

Helleborus argutifolius

How plants work 1

What plants need to make them grow • How garden plants have evolved
Controlling plant growth • Light, temperature, and the greenhouse effect

Plants from the global garden

The plants that we grow in our gardens come from all over the world. They evolved to succeed in their native homes, whether tropical or arctic, desert or wetland, so knowing where a plant originally came from can often give you a good clue as to its needs. Plants from the desert will grow well, albeit slowly, in hot, dry conditions. Trees from the far north can withstand harsh winters but may not thrive in warmer climates, whereas plants from the tropics may be killed at low temperatures—even when these are above freezing. Although alpine plants from high mountains can withstand freezing, they cannot tolerate winter moisture. Choosing plants that naturally thrive in a climate similar to your own is an important step toward gardening success.

The garden habitat

Conditions found in the garden are very different from those in the wild, largely due to our gardening activities—the garden is a managed habitat. In the wild, plants compete with one another for water, nutrients, and light, and their success depends on winning this struggle. For instance, in a desert only those plants that are particularly efficient at gathering, storing, or using water will live. In the garden, plants have no need to fight for survival because we provide the essentials by watering, feeding, and pruning, which improves air circulation, increases light levels at the plant's center, and maximizes flowering. We also take away

Adapted by man

Some of the plants found in gardens are grown in their original wild form. However many, and probably most, garden plants have been altered by selection (when gardeners save only the seed of their best specimen) or by professional plant breeders to develop desirable characteristics: a longer flowering season; larger, showier blooms; fragrance; greater tolerance of frost or drought; compact growth, or better resistance to disease. The cultivation requirements of these plants often differ from those of their wild ancestors, which makes it more difficult to select plants purely on the basis of their origins.

Wild roses have single flowers and are unkempt, scrambling shrubs. Popular cultivars such as Iceberg, with double blooms and a compact habit, are the result of intensive breeding.

competition by removing weeds and taming plants that threaten to grow too large or spread too far. Our attempts to control damaging pests and diseases give garden plants a further boost. But plants don't get it all their own way; by deadheading to prolong flowering (a form of pruning), we prevent plants from producing seeds.

Pampering in gardens makes it possible for most plants to survive, but it will be easier to look after those suited to your local environment. It is important to select plants that are the right size and form and give them enough space to grow. This guarantees that the extra care you provide is channeled into strong prolific flowering, rather than helping an unsuitable plant cling to life.

Cacti are perfectly tailored to their environment. They can store lots of water and are covered with sharp spines to stop passing animals stealing the moisture. Although the adaptations of other plants may not be so obvious, all plants have evolved to suit conditions in their native range and the niche they inhabit there.

Plant types and their place in the garden

Gardeners divide plants into categories according to their appearance and their use in the garden. It is wise to pick those that will enjoy your local climate, but also make sure that they are the shape and size you want. If, for example, you try to keep a large shrub small by pruning, it will throw up lots of new, strong shoots in an attempt to restore its natural balance.

Ferns

Ferns are deciduous or evergreen plants that do not flower. Most ferns prefer shady areas, where the large architectural foliage of these plants often provides welcome interest.

Trees, shrubs, and climbers

These types of plants provide long-lived, structural elements in your garden. They come in all shapes and sizes, are deciduous or evergreen, and may have attractive bark, flowers, foliage, or fruit.

Trees have a single, woody, main trunk and a branched canopy. They bring height into the garden. Large trees are unsuitable for small gardens and can cause dry shade—check the expected dimensions before you buy them.

Shrubs are also woody plants, but with more branches coming up from ground level. They provide a framework and foliage at a lower level than trees and come in all shapes and sizes. Some can be trained against walls or fences.

Climbers can be woody or herbaceous, and scramble over plants, or anything else, to get to the best light. You can make use of this ability to disguise any eyesores in the garden, as well as to brighten up dreary walls and fences.

Flowers

Although many trees, shrubs, and climbers also produce flowers, gardeners use the term "flowers" to describe herbaceous (non-woody) plants whose blooms are the major component of color in the garden. They are conveniently divided into further groups depending on how they grow, because this is a major factor in deciding what plants to put where.

Bulbous plants store food so plants can shoot up fast after dormancy. Bulbs like daffodils (*Narcissus*) flower, replenish their energy reserves, then die back to survive adverse conditions, such as drought or cold, underground.

Herbaceous perennials, like golden rod (*Solidago*), live for several years and usually flower each year, although not always the first year after sowing. Many, but not all, die back completely in winter and regrow the following spring.

Biennials, such as teasel (*Dipsacus fullonum*), produce only foliage in their first year while they build up the energy to flower spectacularly in the next year, following a period of winter cold. They are often used for early displays.

Grasses are annual or perennial plants with tough, narrow leaves that grow at the base, which is why they can tolerate being mown or grazed. Turfgrasses are used for lawns, and ornamental grasses are increasingly popular in borders.

Annuals complete their life cycle in less than a year so they can survive cold winters or dry summers as seed. They are useful for short-lived and colorful displays, such as that provided by the deep blue cornflower (*Centaurea cyanus*).

What do plant roots do?

Roots are the parts of plants that anchor them in the soil. Without secure anchorage, plants are exposed to damage from "wind rock," so it is important when planting to firm the soil around the roots and to stake young plants where necessary.

Gardeners are often unaware of how much of the plant consists of roots; they are often forgotten because they are out of sight. For example, the roots of lawn grass can descend to 5ft (1.5m) if the soil is deep enough—which means that beneath each 10 square feet (sq m) of lawn you would find about 25 miles (40km) of roots.

An absorbing job

The most important function of a plant's roots is to absorb water and minerals from the soil and transport them to the shoot. Unlike animals, which obtain food in the form of carbohydrates, fats, and proteins, most plants make their own, using a process called photosynthesis (*see box above*), and many of the raw materials required are gathered below ground by the roots. Some roots also act as food stores, like those of root vegetables such as carrots and parsnips.

Healthy roots are vital for the plant's well-being and need as much, if not more, care and attention as the plant above ground. They continue to grow throughout the plant's life,

exploring the soil in search of water and minerals. Like animals, plants rely on oxygen to convert their food into the energy needed to fuel this growth.

Normally, oxygen for the roots is absorbed from air spaces found in the soil. However, when soil is compacted or flooded there is no air in the soil. The roots are starved of oxygen, and this ultimately leads to root death. Maintaining the soil structure and drainage is therefore one of the most essential tasks in gardening (*see pp.36–49*). This also explains why overwatering can drown and kill plants, especially those in containers. This is a particular

How photosynthesis works

Green plants make their own food from air and water. The raw materials for this manufacturing process—known as photosynthesis—are gathered by the roots, which obtain water and minerals from the soil; and the leaves, which absorb carbon dioxide (CO_2) from the air. The energy needed to combine the water and carbon dioxide comes from sunlight, collected by a mineral-based green pigment in the leaves called chlorophyll (*see p.20*). Water (H_2O) from the roots is then split into its components of hydrogen (H) and oxygen (O). The oxygen is released, and the hydrogen is combined with carbon dioxide from the air to form energy-rich carbohydrates to fuel plant growth.

How do the roots grow?

A growing root has a root cap at its tip, which streamlines and protects it as it travels through the soil. Behind the root cap is the growing zone, where cells divide and expand to push the root cap forward. Thin root hairs branch out from this region, increasing the area through which nutrients and water enter.

Provided there is close contact between the roots and soil, water and some nutrients, like nitrogen and potassium, can be taken up along the entirle length of the root. However, calcium and iron enter mainly near the tip. This is why it is important to firm well and water in when planting. Inside the roots are transport pipes ("xylem") that take water and mineral nutrients up to the leaves and shoots where photosynthesis takes place. Other pipes ("phloem") bring energy-rich carbohydrates made in the leaves back underground to fuel root growth.

Fine root hairs collect water

Large roots help transport water upward

Roots can account for about a fifth of the plant's total weight

Special roots are sometimes needed. Aquatic plants, such as waterlilies (*far left*), have long, air filled channels between their roots and leaves to get oxygen below ground so their roots don't drown. The roots of some plants don't grow in soil at all: many orchids (*left*) live on tree branches. Their roots have an outer layer that can absorb moisture from the air.

problem in winter, when most plants grow very slowly so lose very little water. You should usually water container plants only when the soil is dry to the touch.

Salt of the earth

Fourteen minerals are considered to be essential for healthy plants, and green plants usually obtain them from the soil. Most of these nutrients are needed in tiny quantities, so you'll rarely have to add them to your garden. But the minerals that plants require in the greatest amounts— nitrogen, phosphorous, and potassium—often need to be topped up, which is why these three minerals are the usual components of compound fertilizers; despite its abundance, nitrogen from the air is not available to green plants.

In the wild, plants have developed their own ways of supplementing their mineral intake. Almost all plants form mutually beneficial relationships with fungi, known as "mycorrhizal fungi." These fungi appear to help plants by extracting phosphorus from the soil, but they probably also increase the uptake of other nutrients. In return, fungi obtain the carbohydrates needed to sustain their own growth from their host. In poor soils or heathlands, where heathers and other tough plants grow, plants depend on mycorrhiza. In gardens, fertilizers make these plants independent of mycorrhiza; in fact, they actually suppress beneficial fungi.

Finding the right chemistry

Some plants have evolved on soils with particular characteristics and consequently are better suited to some soils than others. For instance, rhododendrons have adapted to grow on acidic soils. If they are grown in alkaline, chalky conditions, their roots find it difficult to take up enough iron—which is needed to make green chlorophyll—so the young leaves of acid-loving plants grown on the wrong soil often look quite yellow. This is why it is helpful to find out more about your soil (*see pp.36–39*). Don't despair if you discover. however, that you have alkaline soil; a good range of plants, such as clematis, have evolved on these soils too, and can thrive because they have adapted to cope with the problem (*see pp.38–39*).

Although green plants are unable to take nitrogen from the air, some bacteria in the soil can do just that. Some of these live harmlessly in nodules on the roots of certain plants like those in the legume family: peas, beans, clover, and lupines. Inside the nodules, bacteria convert nitrogen gas into the nitrogen-containing compounds plants need. In return, the bacteria receive food from their host.

Nodules on plant roots

Why plants have green leaves

Photosynthesis mainly occurs in plant leaves, but it also takes place in the other green parts of plants, for example in the green stems of some cacti, or in the stems of many bulbs such as daffodils, which continue to photosynthesize if just the flower is nipped off after it has faded. The carbohydrates created by photosynthesis are extremely versatile. They are transported around the plant to where they are needed, and can either be used immediately, or stored as starch—as they are in the overwintering roots of carrots, for example. When the plant needs energy to fuel growth, the stored carbohydrates are broken down and their energy is released in a process called respiration. It is then used to fuel the reactions that make fats, proteins, and other materials that the plant requires in order to grow and reproduce.

It's difficult to overstate the significance of photosynthesis. It doesn't just generate food for the plant itself; photosynthesis by green plants provides the food source for almost all animals, via complex food chains, and for many fungi, via decompostion. Plants also maintain the atmosphere we breathe by consuming carbon dioxide and releasing oxygen. About half of the world's photosynthesis occurs on land, mainly in tropical rain forests, and the rest in oceans, lakes, and rivers.

Photosynthesis in the garden

Provided there is enough light, the rate of photosynthesis increases with the amount of carbon dioxide in the atmosphere. In greenhouses, cold frames, and cloches that are crammed with foliage, carbon dioxide levels often drop below those in the air outside because the plants use it up faster than it can be replenished. This is why it is important to open the vents as early as possible on a bright sunny day to allow air to circulate and maintain carbon dioxide levels. This also prevents overheating.

Making light work

All green plants depend on receiving enough energy from sunlight to carry out photosynthesis. Just as plants have adapted to different types of soil, they have also evolved a number of ways to use the light levels in their natural

The importance of being green

Using water, air, and a few minerals from the soil, plants generate the energy required to sustain most other living things. They do this by being green.

Plant leaves act like solar panels to capture light energy from the sun and convert it into chemical energy in the form of carbohydrates. This process—photosynthesis, from the Greek meaning "using light to place together"—is possible due to the presence of light-absorbing pigments in the leaves. The most important of these is green chlorophyll. Chlorophyll absorbs blue and red light—which are then used to drive the process of photosynthesis—and reflects green light, which is why plants appear green.

Red and blue light are absorbed by green chlorophyll

Green light is reflected

Organisms with no cholophyll are unable to carry out photosynthesis so they are ultimately dependent on green plants. Fungi break down plant matter to get their energy, while animals either eat plants—or eat an animal that has eaten them.

Yellow or orange pigments in the leaves also contribute to photosynthesis but are usually masked by green chlorophyll. You can see them most clearly in autumn, after the chlorophyll in deciduous plants has been broken down for recycling before leaf fall.

habitat efficiently, and therefore prefer to be grown in similar conditions in the garden.

Shade-loving plants, such as ferns, originated in moist, sheltered, woodland habitats. Their leaves tend to be thinner than those of sun-lovers because the weak, shady light in these conditions cannot penetrate as deeply. To compensate for this, the leaves of these plants tend to be larger, to increase the surface area that is available to capture light, and a darker green because they have more chlorophyll packed into their cells, which increases the amount of light the leaf can absorb. Many shade-loving plants do not tolerate full sunlight—their leaves are easily scorched, and they are also very prone to drying out.

Good ventilation is important in greehouses, cold frames, and cloches, especially on sunny days. This is not just to get rid of excess heat but also to allow carbon dioxide levels to be replenished as they are used up by the plants to make food.

Shade plants have leaves that are generally large, thin, and dark green to allow them to catch and use the dim light found beneath trees efficiently. They also tend to enjoy the damp soil and sheltered atmosphere typical of a woodland habitat.

Sun-loving plants, for example, Mediterranean herbs like rosemary, generally have smaller, thicker, and tougher leaves to resist desiccation. Because the sun is so strong, it penetrates deeply into the thicker leaves and provides enough light for photosynthesis over a much smaller surface area. However, this makes photosynthesis inefficient when these plants are grown in shady conditions. If sun-lovers find themselves short of light, they divert their energy into fast, energetic growth in an attempt to outgrow their neighbors and reach better light conditions, a tactic best described as "shade avoidance." This is an undesirable response, as it results in leggy plants with weak stems. You will often find areas of shade in your garden, whether from trees or from nearby buildings; it is important to choose plants that will thrive under these conditions.

Plants that have been shaded to conserve water during germination, or as cuttings (*see p.24*), should be gradually exposed to stronger sunlight over a period of about 10 days; otherwise, the leaves may become scorched.

Leaves and water loss

Why do plants need so much water? Only a very small proportion of water absorbed by roots—about 2 percent—is needed for photosynthesis. Some water is used to fill cells so they stay firm, like a water bed, and prevent wilting. But most water just passes through the plant and is lost from the leaves. As a rough rule of thumb, an area of continuous vegetation, like a lawn or a fully planted border, loses about 5½ gallons per sq yd (25 liters per sq m) of water every 7–10 days. This is influenced by weather: both wind speed and sunshine increase water loss. The problem is photosynthesis—leaves must open their pores for carbon dioxide to enter, and the pores let water out too.

"Catch 22"

The lives of plants are always balanced on a knife edge. Plants are weakened by water stress, a common condition caused by an insufficient supply of water to the roots, or by losing water too rapidly from the leaves. If the plant loses too much water through its pores, it will wilt, but the pores must remain open in order to get enough carbon dioxide. To make matters worse, in order to use light energy in photosynthesis, the pores must be kept open in daylight, when higher temperatures result in the greatest water loss. If the pores stay closed to save water, photosynthesis stops, and the plant will ultimately die from starvation.

Plants often suffer from water shortages in their natural habitats. Regions that have Mediterranean climates, such

How do plants lose water?

Leaves are covered with tiny pores that open to let carbon dioxide in and get rid of oxygen, but they also allow water to escape.

Just as liquid finds its own level, so water vapor moves from where it is concentrated to where it is less concentrated. Inside the leaf there is 100 percent relative humidity, so vapor escapes via the pores and spreads out into the surrounding air: the drier the air outside the plant,

Pores on a leaf

the faster the plant loses water. Even if the outside air is very humid, leaves can still lose water quite quickly: hot air carries more water vapor, therefore the air inside plant leaves that have been heated by the sun will hold more water vapor than the surrounding atmosphere.

as southern California, experience seasonal summer drought, and rainfall occurs almost exclusively in winter. Water is permanently scarce in arid regions, where rainfall is low all year, especially in deserts. Fortunately, plants have adapted in many different ways to survive under these conditions. An understanding of their strategies will help you choose plants with the ability to survive periods of drought that may affect your garden.

Reducing water loss

Normally, the first defense of plants running short of water is to close their pores. This prevents carbon dioxide from getting in, and photosynthesis grinds to a halt. Plants from constantly dry areas have therefore developed methods of reducing the amount of water they lose without shutting down photosynthesis. The leaves of drought-tolerant plants often have features that you can easily spot:
• Small leaves, or even green spines like gorse, expose a smaller surface

Plants wilt and become limp when their cells lose water. Although they may seem to revive quickly, either on their own or with watering, normal cell functions take much longer to recover, so water plants regularly in dry spells.

Leaves are surrounded by a "boundary layer" of slow-moving air, which is increasingly humid in still air, reducing water loss. Wind can sweep this humid air away, causing "wind scorch," especially on young leaves vulnerable to drying out.

Plants have adapted to survive in habitats short of water. In Mediterranean regions, for example, plants grow during the damp winter, then whole hillsides bloom in spring (*left*) before summer drought begins. In grasslands (*above*), wildflowers also make the most of the damp spring, setting seed and dying down before the dry summer, when grasses hog most of the available water.

area to the sun's heat, and also reduce the area through which water is lost.

• Sunken pores and thick, waxy cuticles, like those on conifer needles, help protect against drying winds.

• Hairy leaves, like those of sage, trap an extra-thick layer of moist air and slow the rate of water loss from the leaves. The hairs also prevent this layer from being blown away by wind.

• Some plants have pores only on the undersides of their leaves, which keeps them out of the sun.

• Shiny or silvery-gray leaves, like those of lavender, reflect heat, keeping leaves relatively cool and reducing water loss.

• Rolled-up leaves is a strategy used by some grasses. This keeps the leaf pores out of the sun and the wind and creates a humid microclimate inside the roll.

Plants that cannot cope without water are likely to respond by shedding their leaves altogether and halting growth until conditions improve. Many lose only some of their leaves, especially the older ones, which results in unsightly plants with only a few leaves remaining at the tips of the shoots.

How can plants survive without a drink?

Plants originating from more extreme environments have had to develop additional tactics to survive water shortages. Some plants only have to tolerate seasonal droughts, but others come from deserts that are parched all year round.

Drought avoiders survive dry periods by retreating beneath the ground. Seeds, corms, and bulbs like tulips (*above*) all lie ready to spring back to life when the rains arrive.

Tolerance of dehydration allows some plants to withstand losing a considerable amount of water. The "resurrection" plant, *Selaginella*, can dry out almost completely without harm.

Water collectors store water for their personal consumption during periods of drought—succulents and cacti, such as *Echinocereus*, survive desert conditions in this way.

Water savers have developed ways to reduce the amount of water lost from their foliage. Their leaves may be small, like heather's, hairy, reflect heat, or be dropped in times of drought.

Water spenders, like prairie grasses, have very deep root systems that can obtain water from a large surrounding area. This ability makes them less susceptable to drying out.

Protecting young plants from water shortages

Cuttings use and lose water in the same way as whole plants, because their leaves still actively carry out photosynthesis. However, these young plants are at an obvious disadvantage because they don't have roots to collect replacement moisture. This makes them extremely vulnerable to drying out. Some cuttings benefit from an application of hormone rooting powder (*see p.26*) to speed up root development so they can get their own water, but there are a number of other steps you can take to reduce the amount of water lost by your cuttings.

Shading (here with mesh) reduces the temperature inside a propagator, which helps prevent cuttings from drying out.

A plastic bag over the pot increases the humidity around the leaves, so water does not move through the leaf pores as quickly.

Misting uncovered rooted cuttings helps avoid stress in the transition period by cooling the leaf surface, thereby reducing water loss.

Conserving water by photosynthesis

Many plants have reduced water loss from their leaves by evolving special foliage (*see previous page*). Some species have gone even further, and have developed a different type of photosynthesis. With global warming possibly leading to higher summer temperatures, these plants may become increasingly important in gardens.

Most plants need to have their pores open during the hours of daylight to allow photosynthesis to take place (*see p. 18*). However, two groups of plants have clever ways of avoiding this. In areas where water is always scarce, some plants reduce water loss by opening their pores only at night, when temperatures are cooler. They absorb carbon dioxide during the night and store it temporarily. During the daytime, the leaf pores close so no water is lost, and the stored carbon dioxide is released inside the leaves. Photosynthesis then continues normally. This type of photosynthesis is less efficient than the normal kind, and these plants, such as agaves, often grow quite slowly.

North American prairie grasses, famous for their drought-tolerance as well as their beauty, have a different method of photosynthesis. They have had to adapt to arid and subtropical regions with strong sunlight and periods of water shortage, rather than constant drought. Again, carbon dioxide is temporarily stored, but instead of happening overnight this occurs very rapidly during the day, even though light intensities and temperatures are high and the leaf pores are open. If water runs out and the pores close, the stored carbon dioxide can be released inside the leaf and the plants can continue as normal.

Choosing drought-tolerant plants, such as Spanish broom, is by far the most effective way of coping with gardens prone to dry periods and reduces the need for watering, which is both wasteful and time consuming.

Helping save water

The best policy in a dry garden, or in climates prone to periods of drought, is to choose plants that will happily cope with the conditions, such as those with the adaptations described above. But don't forget to check plant hardiness as well – although some drought-tolerant plants will survive cold winters, many are unused to them and may be damaged or even die.

Although plants have devised a range of ways to help themselves survive drought, in the garden there are many ways you can give a helping hand. The most obvious is through watering, but water is an increasingly scarce resource. Also, plant roots grow toward water, so if you constantly provide water at the soil surface, the roots may not grow deep down to the parts of the soil that rarely dry out. It is better to boost your plants' natural defenses against drought by watering them only in emergencies. This will give them time to establish.

Plants, like animals, lose more water when it is hot, so one way to decrease water loss is to cool them down. In nature plants have small or reflective leaves to achieve this effect (*see below*). In the garden, one obvious solution is to shield a plant from the sun. This is useful in hot weather, especially for plants that you've just put in the ground, which haven't had a chance to develop deep, spreading root systems. You can use just about anything to provide shade – even a sheet of newspaper draped over the vulnerable plant will suffice. Shade is especially important in greenhouses, where

temperatures can soar. However, if you are shading plants to keep them cool, don't forget that low light levels can limit photosynthesis. Make sure that you remember to remove shading as soon as conditions allow.

Another way to cool leaves is to spray them with water. This draws out heat as the water evaporates—in the same way as sweating cools people. Evaporating water has the additional benefit of making the surrounding air more humid, which helps slow water loss even more (*see p.22*). This is particularly useful in enclosed environments, such as greenhouses, cold frames, or propagators where the humid air cannot immediately escape. But be especially careful if the plants are growing in full sun, because droplets of water can act like tiny lenses, focusing the sun's rays and causing small scorch marks to appear on the leaves.

Mediterranean plants often have small, silvery, hairy leaves to help them conserve water in the fierce summer heat. In cooler climates they will thrive in the extra reflected warmth of a gravel garden or patio.

Drought-tolerant plants often need very good drainage, so if you have damp soil you could create raised beds (*left*). When they thrive, drought-tolerant plants are among the most freely flowering plants.

Prairie grasses not only have narrow leaves that reduce the surface through which water can be lost but also use a special kind of photosynthesis that makes them very resistant to drought.

What controls plant growth?

Plants can grow only within the constraints of their genes, which are a kind of blueprint for growth. A dwarf shrub, for instance, will always grow slowly, even with ideal quantities of water, light, and nutrients. Messenger substances—the plant hormones—also play a major role. Hormones directly control aspects of a plant's growth, such as whether it will flower, produce a structure such as a bulb or tuber, or go into a dormant period. Hormones are organic compounds that act in very low concentrations to bring about a specific response. Hormones are usually made in one part of the plant, then transported to a distant site of action.

Which way up?

Perhaps the most important plant hormones—as far as gardeners are concerned—are auxins. Naturally occurring auxins move through plants in only one direction, from the tip of the shoot down; this downward movement means that the auxins used to control shoot and root growth have different levels of concentration throughout the plant. For example, roots form in response to high concentrations of auxins. In propagation, hormone rooting powders are used to mimic this property, but they should be used sparingly because large amounts will be counterproductive.

Hormone rooting powder mimics natural plant hormones to aid rooting.

When a cutting is made, plant hormones called auxins accumulate at the base of the cutting and promote the formation of new roots. Rooting powders boost natural hormone levels.

The direction in which auxins travel is not reversible, so if you are taking cuttings (*see p.244*), make sure that you plant them the right way up. If you are making leafless hardwood cuttings, take precautions to make sure you remember which end of the cutting was nearest the shoot: the usual method is to make a slanting cut at the shoot end and a flat cut at the base where the new roots will form.

It is thought that auxins are responsible for making plants bend toward the light. Auxins accumulate on the shady side of the stem, stimulating growth on that side and causing the stem to bend. This light-influenced bending is known as "phototropism." If you grow houseplants or seedlings on a window sill, it is important to rotate them to redistribute the auxins if you want them to grow straight.

Plants also respond to gravity, which causes directional growth known as "geotropism." Gravity causes horizontal roots to bend downward (positive geotropism) because the lower part of the root grows more slowly than the upper half. Horizontal stems bend upward (negative geotropism) because the lower part of the shoot grows more rapidly than the upper part—probably due to the redistribution of auxins toward the lower part under the influence of gravity.

Unnaturally high levels of auxins result in distorted growth and ultimately the plant's death. This is exploited in

Genes and inheritance

Genes control potential size, shape, color, and more, in some cases using plant hormones as their messengers. They pass from one plant to another by sexual reproduction (*see pp.28–29*). Plant breeders can use this to produce new cultivars by crossing two different plants. New plants also arise from mutations, a genetic change that gives rise to new characteristics such as those seen in this range of conifers.

Conifers of all sizes, shapes, and colors

hormone weed killers, which contain synthetic auxins that can be applied at higher concentrations than natural ones.

How pruning works

On many plants, the topmost, or "apical," bud of a shoot is dominant. It controls the development of other branches by preventing or slowing the growth of the lateral buds below it, so the plant grows tall and leggy. It is thought that this is caused by the production of auxins at the shoot tip. If you remove the end of an apical shoot, the buds below will be released from its dominance and begin to grow so that the plant will become more rounded. Standard "lollipop" bay trees are trained into their distinctive shape by exploiting this. The dominant shoot is left while the plant grows a tall, straight stem. Once the stem has reached the desired height, the top shoot is removed and the bushy head is slowly formed by pinching out the shoot tips.

How plants detect shade

Plants need to know whether or not they are in the shade so they can grow in the appropriate way (*see p.21*). They can detect shade cast by foliage because red light is trapped by leaves, whereas infrared light will pass straight through—a special light-absorbing pigment called phytochrome enables plants to distinguish between red and infrared light. So, if phytochrome detects lots of red light, the plant is in sun; if it detects little red and lots of infrared light, it is in shade.

Shade from buildings, or anything that isn't a leaf, does not alter the relative amounts of red and infra light, so the phytochrome system doesn't detect it. This type of shade is probably identified by a pigment that is sensitive to blue light and the total amount of light reaching the plant.

Plants detect gravity, a mechanism known as "geotropism." Roots grow downward toward gravity, while stems grow upward away from gravity. A decorative result of the response of plant stems enables climbers, such as clematis, planted by a tree to scramble up unaided.

Dominant shoots
If the topmost bud is removed by pruning, wind, or grazing animals, the lateral buds begin to grow out. Eventually the strongest shoot will become dominant, so if you want a plant with a bushier shape, keep pinching out the top of each shoot.

Ripening gas

Fruits ripen in response to a sudden increase in the plant hormone ethylene, a gas. The ethylene produced by ripe fruit can also cause the ripening of other fruit nearby. This explains why ripe and unripe fruits should not be stored together, and is the reason you should always keep fruit in a well-ventilated area—unless, of course, you want to trigger ripening. For example, a ripe apple put with green tomatoes in a drawer or a paper bag will speed up the ripening process because the gas is trapped and concentrated. Bananas are picked and transported while they are green and unripe, and then ripened by a controlled release of synthetic ethylene when they get to their destination.

Flowers and seeds

Many of the plants we select for our gardens are chosen for their colors and scents. In the wild, the shapes, colors, and scents of flowers have evolved to assist pollination, which is essential for reproduction. Plants that are pollinated by the wind, like many grasses, have small, green, and usually unscented flowers, but other plants must attract their animal or insect pollinators by stimulating their sense of vision and/or smell.

The most common pollinators are insects, which have a highly developed sense of smell and excellent vision. Insects see things differently from us: bees, for example, can see ultraviolet patterns on flowers, known as honey guides, that are invisible to the human eye. Some butterflies have distinct color preferences; for instance tortoiseshells prefer yellow, while swallowtails are attracted more by blue and purple. Flowers pollinated by insects that feed at dusk, such as moths, are normally a paler color so they are easily visible in poor light, and blooms that have evolved to attract night-flying creatures are

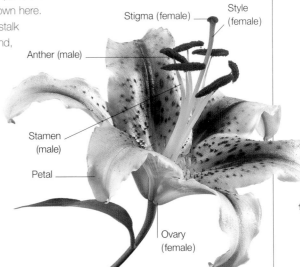

The pollination process

Flowering plants need male and female organs for reproduction. These organs are sometimes found in different flowers growing on the same plant (as for birch or hazel); sometimes they are in different flowers growing on different plants (as in many hollies); and sometimes male and female parts are found within the same flower, as in the lily shown here.

The male organs consist of a stalk (stamen) with an anther at the end, where pollen is produced. Male pollen grains are deposited, by insects or wind, on the female "stigma," held on a "style." There, the pollen grains germinate and produce long tubes, which grow down through the style to the ovary at the flower's base. When a pollen tube reaches the ovary, it fertilizes the ovule inside, transferring its genes, and a seed is formed.

Stigma (female)
Style (female)
Anther (male)
Stamen (male)
Petal
Ovary (female)

often highly scented—a signal that can be followed in the dark. Some flowers prefer flies as pollinators; you can usually identify these by their unpleasant scent. Flower shape can also be significant: the bee orchid (*Ophrys apifera*) not only looks like a female bee but smells like one too, so male bees try to mate with them, and spread pollen in the process.

The next generation

To produce seed, male pollen must reach a female stigma (*see box, above*). Some plants can pollinate themselves ("self-pollination"), but others need pollen from another plant of the same species and are "cross-pollinated." If you have plants in your garden that require cross-pollination, and you want them to produce fruit or seed, you will need to grow more than one plant. Garden center labels will usually indicate if this is the case. Plants raised from any seed you save from cross-pollinators are likely to be quite variable—some might be exceptionally high quality, but others may disappoint. If you raise seed from self-pollinated flowers, the new plants will be much the same as the old but may become less vigorous over the years.

Pollen is distributed with efficiency by insects like butterflies and bees, which collect energy-rich nectar in return. It can also be carried by the wind, but this can be more hit and miss, so wind-pollinated plants like grasses compensate by producing lots of pollen.

Many of our garden plants are the result of generations of selection and hybridization with other species which have produced desirable forms and colors that are quite different from those of their wild parents. These plants rarely breed true—if at all—from seed, and consequently are best multiplied by other means, such as by division or from cuttings (*see pp.238–45*). Your new plants will be exact genetic copies of their parent, or "clones."

Plant catalogs may describe some seeds as being "F1 hybrids," which are produced by crossing two highly selected inbred parent plants. F1 hybrid seeds produce very uniform and often vigorous plants, but they themselves do not breed true, and plants raised from their seeds are highly variable.

Squirrels store seed by burying nuts for winter food. However their stores are often forgotten, and will germinate in spring.

Germinating seeds

As seeds ripen, they lose water and are ultimately shed by the plant. Under natural conditions it is not only desirable for seeds to be dispersed as widely as possible (*see box, below*) but it can also be advantageous for plants to spread the germination of their seed over time. From a gardening perspective, this is often a disadvantage—we usually want seeds to germinate at the same time, in the pot or ground.

Some plants overwinter in the ground as seeds, which are

Ferns and spores ferns and mosses are different from other plants in your garden—they don't have flowers or seeds but instead produce spores on the undersides of their leaves.

less vulnerable to cold than seedlings and won't germinate until they have experienced a period of low temperatures. Others will not germinate in the dark, and remain dormant in the ground until the soil is disturbed. You can get around both these mechanisms by sowing light-requiring seeds on the surface of the soil, and by keeping seeds requiring exposure to cold in a refrigerator for a period (usually several weeks) before sowing. However, seeds are not sensitive to cold when they are dry, so make sure you allow them to absorb some water before refrigerating them.

How seeds spread

Seeds are cleverly designed little packages that are easily transported to colonize new places. Some seeds can survive for years before germination occurs, if conditions are bad. Each seed contains a tiny plant—an embryo—together with enough stored food to support it during germination until it has developed shoots and leaves that are able to photosynthesize and produce food for itself. All this is wrapped in a protective coat, and in many cases enclosed within a fruit to aid dispersal.

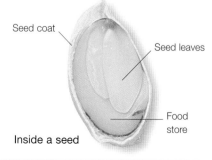

Seed coat
Seed leaves
Food store
Inside a seed

Naked seeds are not encased in a fruit. They are produced by conifers, a group of plants called gymnosperms, which means "naked seed." Each seed sits on a cone scale.

Fleshy fruits such as blackberries, surround some seeds to make them tasty to eat. They later pass out of the animal in another place and germinate unharmed.

Dry seeds have no tasty cover and are usually dispersed by the wind. Many have ways to help dispersal, such as the wings, or keys, of maple trees and the parachutes of dandelion seed.

Gardening through the seasons

As we have seen, plants have several stages in their life cycle, and will germinate, flower and fruit, lay down food stores in bulbs or tubers, shed leaves, and enter dormancy to prepare for different conditons in each season of the year. But how do they know what time of year it is?

Long and short days

Plant leaves are sensitive to day length, which varies predictably throughout the season, and send messenger signals to the parts where the response—flowering, or bulbing—occurs. Day length influences flowering in many plants. Long-day plants flower in summer, when light and temperatures are at their optimum levels. Short-day plants flower in spring or autumn, often because summers in their native habitats are too dry, or to avoid shade from deciduous trees. Short-day plants from the tropics, such as poinsettas, won't flower in

The long or short days of the seasons in temperate climates can influence flowering. Rudbeckias (*left*) need long, summer days to convince them to flower and are known as "long-day plants." Late-flowering chrysanthemums, such as 'Talbot Jo' (*far left*) are "short-day plants," which means they bloom when the nights begin to draw in during late summer and autumn.

Plants in deciduous woods often flower in the spring, before the leaf canopy unfolds above them and reduces the available light. They are able to do this by detecting the seasons.

the garden because low temperatures kill them before the days are short enough to initiate flowering.

Freezing temperatures

In temperate climates, freezing winter temperatures provide plants with another dramatic seasonal marker. We have seen that plants from areas that regularly experience freezing temperatures have devised ways of surviving: some die back and overwinter as seed, which can usually withstand very low temperatures; others huddle up inside storage organs like bulbs, corms, or tubers, and stay underground where

Frost damage to marginally hardy shrubs, such as *Garrya*, is likely to occur if thawing happens too fast. Plants on east-facing walls are particularly at risk from the early sun and will suffer more damage than in a position that thaws more slowly.

frost doesn't penetrate. Trees and shrubs can't retreat in this way, so they make changes in their cells to prevent damage.

Surprisingly, the worst damage that plants experience at low temperatures is not caused by freezing solid, but is due to the loss of water from their cells. When temperatures approach zero, hardy plants protect their tissue cells by moving water out of the cells and into the cell walls, where it freezes. The highly concentrated liquid left inside the cell has lots of chemicals dissolved in it and doesn't easily freeze. As temperatures rise, the ice melts and water moves back into the cell; damage occurs only if the ice melts before the cell is ready to reabsorb the water. Plants exposed to direct, early-morning sunlight are therefore more likely to suffer frost damage than plants that thaw slowly through the day.

The ability of some plants to develop frost resistance, or hardiness (*see pp. 48–51*), is quite remarkable. Some trees have been found to withstand temperatures as low as −58°F (−50°C) when dormant, and yet, when actively growing, the same plants can be killed by just a light frost. In woody plants, winter hardiness develops as the plants become dormant in autumn. Herbaceous plants typically develop frost hardiness during exposure to low temperatures (usually about 41°F/5°C); this is why plants grown indoors must be gradually "hardened off" before they are planted outdoors.

What about the "greenhouse effect"?

Climate change caused by greenhouse gasses is likely to have a number of effects on plants. Some them will be good and others not so good, but they will almost certainly result in differences in our gardens. It is thought that changes will probably include an increase in carbon dioxide, milder temperatures, and higher rainfall.

According to some estimates, the amount of carbon dioxide in the atmosphere could double, which should let plants photosynthesize—and therefore grow—faster (*see p.20*). Milder winter and spring temperatures may increase the range of plants that can be grown in temperate gardens because the growing season will be longer and frost-damage to less hardy species will be reduced.

But the benefits are likely to be far outweighed by the negative impact. Potentially, one of the most serious effects of climate change would be on soils, as increased rainfall washes nutrients, especially nitrates, away, causing more soil compaction and erosion. Waterlogging is likely to increase in frequency. Storm damage is also likely to occur more often.

Summer drought could become common. Even short periods of hot, dry weather coupled with a shortage of water can weaken plants and even kill them. Hardy plants that require winter cold to break dormancy or initiate flower buds may suffer (*see box below*). Warmer temperatures, especially during winter, may also increase pests, diseases, and weeds. Lawns in particular may become a thing of the past, as they suffer from drought one day and heavy rainfall the next, and require mowing all year if winters are milder.

A chilling experience

Some plants, most obviously biennials, must experience a period of chilling at temperatures just above freezing before they are able to flower. Most hardy trees and shrubs also need exposure to winter cold in order to break dormancy so that they can resume growth the following spring. Many seeds need to be chilled before they are able to germinate. This prevents them from germinating in summer so the seeds can ride out freezing winter temperatures that young plants just would not survive. If you want to sow seed in spring, you can overcome this by sowing seed in moist soil mix and keeping the pot in a refrigerator for a few weeks.

Cotoneaster frigidus seed, like that of many other hardy species, must experience a period of cold before it will germinate, so it is best sown in autumn.

Digitalis grandiflora, the foxglove, is an example of a biennial that usually needs a period of chilling to trigger flowering early in the next year.

Soil and climate 2

How soil and climate work • Understanding your soil • Dealing with different types • Improving your soil • All about compost • Plant hardiness explained

What is soil and what does it do?

Far from being mere "dirt," soil is the raw material with amazing properties out of which you create your gardening dreams. Plant roots find moisture and food in the spaces between soil particles, and the soil's job is to hold enough moisture to sustain the garden in dry spells but allow surplus water to drain away in wet weather. It also protects roots from heat and cold. Soil is just a thin skin on the planet's surface, but all life on land depends on it.

What is soil made of?

Soil may be remarkable stuff, but it is made of mundane materials. The main ingredient is mineral particles, found in a range of sizes and in varying proportions in different soils, and at different depths (*see pp.36–37*). Chalk and limestone soils contain particles of calcium carbonate; these are alkaline and make the soil unsuitable for some plants (*see pp.38–39*).

Soil usually has two layers that gardeners need to know about: topsoil and subsoil. Topsoil contains organic matter, which gives it its dark color and fertility. Subsoil, which

Soil as an anchor Roots penetrate spaces between soil particles in search of sustenance. In doing so they also hold plants firmly in the ground.

has little organic matter, is usually paler than topsoil and often has a different texture. The depth of these two layers can vary considerably.

Working with your soil

You should aim to make your soil the best medium for holding nutrients and water, and allowing seeds to germinate and roots to explore. There is no recipe for this—you have to make your own judgment. Don't worry if you are new to gardening, because soil is forgiving if you don't do anything too drastic.

To grow healthily, plant roots need oxygen, so be sure that your soil doesn't become compacted (with soil particles so tightly packed that air is squeezed out) or waterlogged. Avoid digging up plants to move them in cold, hot, or dry spells; this makes their roots susceptible to damage, or cultivating soil when it is dry, as precious moisture evaporates. Choose plants that suit your site and soil, so you can work with nature rather than taking on a constant, often unsuccessful struggle.

Where does soil come from?

Soil is formed by the weathering of rocks. This is caused by water erosion, frosts that crack the stone, the chemical action of acid rainwater, and biological activities, such as burrowing worms and expanding and contracting plant roots. Soil may remain lying on top of its parent rock, but more usually it is carried to another site by rivers, glaciers, and even the wind. Rivers, for example, carry and deposit gravels, sands, and finer particles of silt. Some soils were formed by deposits that were laid down on the seabed in times when the sea level was higher. This means that gardeners have to deal with a wide range of soils with very variable properties. Soil has taken thousands of years to form and, since it is not feasible to make new soil, as a gardener you need to look after what you have. Buying soil is an expensive business and best avoided if possible.

The life of soil

Minerals make up the bulk of soil but do not make it fertile. For that, organic matter is essential. Organic matter is animal and plant material, and many gardening activities help accumulate it in the soil. It is vital to remember that soil is a living material. Just a pinch is estimated to contain millions of beneficial bacteria, as well as microscopic plants, animals, and fungi. When plant matter, such as falling leaves, comes into contact with the soil, bacteria break it down to use in their life cycles. Although much of it is lost to air as the bacteria respire, it leaves a residue of valuable, dark-colored material called "humus." Humus forms

only about 2–12 percent of most garden soils, yet it has a significant effect. Even small amounts improve soil. Humus holds moisture like a sponge, reducing the risk of drought and increasing the nutrient-holding capacity of the soil, making sandy and clay soils behave like desirable soil. It prevents particles from packing down under the influence of rain, watering, or your own gardening activities, even on soils prone to compaction. In the garden, adding manure, compost, or leaf mold contributes to the formation of humus. Organic matter disappears quickly, but the resulting humus is more resilient and decays very slowly.

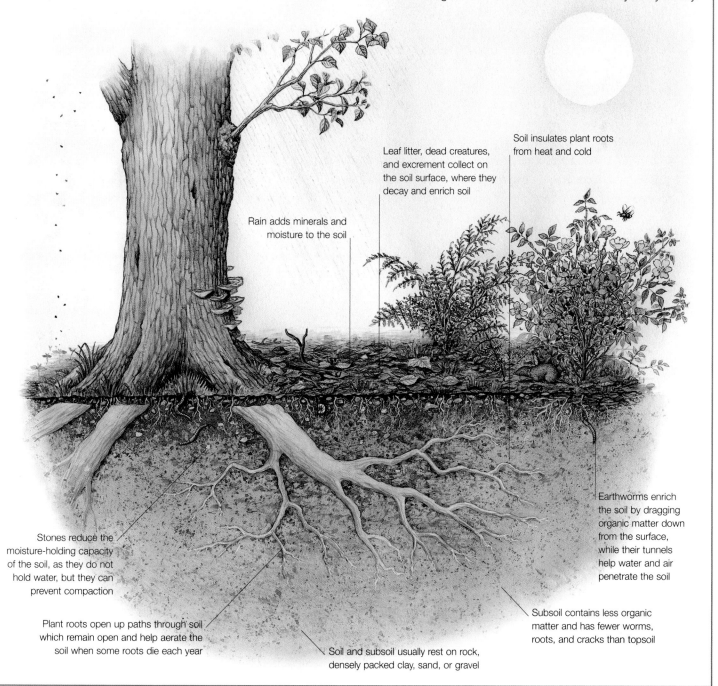

Soil insulates plant roots from heat and cold

Leaf litter, dead creatures, and excrement collect on the soil surface, where they decay and enrich soil

Rain adds minerals and moisture to the soil

Earthworms enrich the soil by dragging organic matter down from the surface, while their tunnels help water and air penetrate the soil

Stones reduce the moisture-holding capacity of the soil, as they do not hold water, but they can prevent compaction

Subsoil contains less organic matter and has fewer worms, roots, and cracks than topsoil

Plant roots open up paths through soil which remain open and help aerate the soil when some roots die each year

Soil and subsoil usually rest on rock, densely packed clay, sand, or gravel

What kind of soil do I have?

Knowing what type of soil you have is absolutely essential for successful planting, because some plants tolerate a range of soil types, but many have definite preferences. The best way to find out what you have is to dig an inspection pit; ideally dig pits at different times of the year and in different parts of the garden. Inspection pits tell you several things:

• More about the soil's texture, which can vary from sandy to loam, to clay, and all types in between.

• The depth of your topsoil, which could be as little as a smear on the surface or, if you are lucky, quite deep.

• The type and perhaps the depth of the subsoil. Glaciers shifting soil in the last Ice Age have caused some surprising combinations, such as gravely soil over clay, or even acidic loam over chalk. If your topsoil is shallow, the subsoil is more important, particularly for trees and larger shrubs that need to make deep roots for stability.

• Your soil's moisture content and the depth of the water table. Different soil types have different water-holding capacities; a little rain may drain through sand quickly, while the same amount can make a clay soil quite wet.

Digging an inspection pit

Take a spade and two plastic sheets and dig a hole about 24in (60cm) square and deep. Place the darker-colored topsoil and paler subsoil on separate sheets as you dig.

Fertile topsoil becomes degraded and poorer if it is mixed with infertile subsoil, so it is important to keep the two separate and replace them in the right order.

Note how deeply you can see roots and earthworm tunnels penetrating the side of the pit. The deeper you find them the better—the soil is in poor shape if they are confined to a narrow band at the top, and you must find out the cause. If the topsoil is shallow or absent, you will need to bring some in before you can garden successfully, unless you want to make a wildflower meadow (*see pp. 186–89*).

When you reach soil that looks much paler, generally after about 8–10in (20–25cm), with far fewer worms, roots, and cracks, you are down to the subsoil. Continue digging, putting the soil on the second plastic sheet, but there is no need to go deeper than 24in (60cm). Soil below this level is of less importance to gardeners. At some stage you may meet impenetrable rock, densely packed clay, or some other barrier, or the subsoil may peter out into sand, gravel, or rubble: this means you have reached the limit of the soil.

Soil particles

Clay particles are about 100 times smaller than fine sand and 2,000 times smaller than coarse sand. They have a huge surface area and pack together, holding water in the minute spaces between them. Water is held so tightly by capillary action that plants may not be able to extract it. Clay is usually most abundant in subsoil.

Assessing your soil
Compare the size of the two piles. A small pile of topsoil means it is shallow, and you may have to add more if it is to be deep enough for vegetables, fruit, or flowerbeds. Alternatively, gathering all the available topsoil into raised beds may provide sufficient depth and is a useful design device. A small pile of subsoil means that underlying rock is close to the surface, limiting the area roots can search for water and food and to find anchorage.

Topsoil rich in organic matter is dark in color. Sandy and chalky topsoils are paler because organic matter is washed out of them.

Subsoil is paler than topsoil—it contains less organic matter. It usually has more stones. Although subsoil has little nutritional value, its depth and water-holding qualities are important.

Testing soil texture

The size of the particles in soil determines its texture and what grows best in it. Texture is hard to change on a large scale, so you need to adapt your gardening to fit your soil. Take a cupful of moist topsoil in your bare hand and shape it into a ball. Try to work it into a sausage shape, and rub it between your fingers. The "ideal" soil is loam, which will hold together in a ball and show finger impressions without being sticky. Most soils, however, will tend toward either clay or sand.

Clay soil feels smooth and sticky, will roll into a sausage and bend into a loop, and is shiny when rubbed. The tiny particles pack together so water does not easily drain, and air spaces are minute. The high water content makes clay slow to warm up in spring and sticky to work.

Smooth to the touch

Holds together extremely well

Sandy soil feels gritty and falls apart as you try to mold it into a ball. Sand grains are the largest soil particle, with big air spaces through which water can drain freely. With their low water content sandy soils warm up fast in spring but dry out quickly in droughts.

Gritty texture

Crumbles when squeezed

If your house is recently built, you may find that building and landscaping work has mixed the topsoil and subsoil, obliterating the distinction between the two. Watch out for building waste in the soil, and dark topsoil below pale subsoil. This is bad news for a gardener, and although builders may place a layer of better quality soil over their works, it is sometimes thinner than it should be (*see p. 73*).

Counting stones

Check your two piles of soil for stones. A few small stones help prevent the soil from packing down, but too many hinder digging and planting, and reduce the water-holding capacity of the soil. Trees and shrubs take stones in their stride, but if your soil is full of stones it is worth removing some for demanding plants, such as herbaceous perennials, or fruit and vegetables. Collect up all surface stones before making a lawn or they will catch mower blades; you can use them for path foundations. Soft, white stones may be chalk, and other porous stones could be limestone. If a small stone bubbles when placed in a tumbler of vinegar, this suggests limestone, and alkaline or "sweet" soil (*see pp. 38–39*).

Water table and drainage

The water table is the natural level at which water rests in the soil. Leave your inspection pit empty for at least 24 hours in dry weather to determine the depth of the water table. If there is no water in the pit, the water table is below its floor. Now fill the pit with water, cover with wood or plastic to keep out any rain, and leave overnight. If all the water does not drain away, the soil is likely to be prone to waterlogging in wet weather, limiting the range of plants

Testing for drainage

you can grow. Draining away excess water can be tricky. The water has to go somewhere; gardeners seldom have access to streams or ditches, and pumping surplus water into public drains is often prohibited. You may need to make raised beds, or plant trees and shrubs on low mounds.

Is my soil acidic or alkaline?

You need to know if the soil in your garden is acidic or alkaline because this has an effect on what plants you can grow. Some, like rhododendrons, do not grow well in an alkaline soil, while others, such as clematis, thrive in alkaline, or "limy," sites.

Understanding the pH scale

The term pH is just a way of expressing how acidic or alkaline a substance is: the lower the pH number, the more acidic the soil. Acidity and alkalinity depend on how much calcium is present in the soil. Acidic soils lack calcium and alkaline ones have it in excess, while neutral soils—7 on the pH scale—have just enough calcium to mop up acidity.

Why pH matters

The pH controls how readily trace elements found in soil are available to plants. In acidic soil, manganese and aluminim are too readily available and can poison lime-loving plants. In alkaline conditions, manganese and iron are locked away so that acid-loving plants cannot obtain them, causing yellowing leaves, or "chlorosis."

Altering the soil pH

You can raise the pH of acidic soil to make it more alkaline by adding lime—a dusty material containing calcium carbonate, often called "ground" or "garden" lime. This reduces acidity for about five years, but think carefully before using it. Most plants will put up with some acidity, and you can grow a wider range in mildly acidic soils.

In theory, you can add acid material to limy soils to lower the pH, but acidifying materials, such as sulfur dust, act slowly, are needed in very large amounts. It may be worthwhile on a neutral or mildly limy soil, but the quantity of sulfur needed to to turn an alkaline soil acidic would be enormous and costly.

Plants for acidic or alkaline soil

Alkaline soils

Soils with a pH of 7–8 are alkaline. There is no practical way of making them acidic in the long term, and acid-loving plants will certainly fail if you try growing them in these conditions. The good news is that limy soil is often well drained and quick to warm up in spring. Incorporate plenty of organic matter, and a very wide range of plants will thrive. Organic material helps to make nutrients more accessible, boosts water availability, and feeds the plants. However, beware of overfertilizing, as this results in tall, floppy plants. One advantage of an alkaline soil is that plants are often sturdy enough to grow without staking.

Pulsatilla vulgaris Pasque flowers need fast-draining soil and full sun; they're good for rock gardens, but will grow elsewhere. A little tricky, but worth trying.

Campanulas There are many reliable forms, with tall plants for borders, like this *C. lactiflora*, and low types for raised beds, gravel gardens, and edging.

Clematis These are happy on most soils but do well on limy soil. Grow climbers, like this *C. montana*, or the herbaceous *C. heracleifolia* and *C. integrifolia*.

Dianthus Pinks, such as *D. deltoides* (above), *D. armaria*, and *D. barbatus*, are compact, brightly-colored gap-fillers which grow well in sunny spots.

Scabiosa Cottage garden favorites, scabious combine well with a range of plants. Try 'Butterfly Blue' (above) and *S. caucasica* 'Miss Wilmott'.

Sorbus aria Whitebeam is one of the best trees for limy soil, but *S. aria* grows large. 'Lutescens', here, is more compact at 30ft (10m) tall and 24ft (8m) wide.

Syringa Lilacs are great in spring, but less so in summer; liven them up with roses or clematis. *Syringa meyeri* 'Palibin' is good in small gardens.

Verbascums Grown for their felted leaves and dramatic, usually yellow, flower spikes. *V. bombyciferum* and *V.* 'Helen Johnson' are both good choices.

Over pH7 Alkaline or "sweet"; not for lime-haters but suitable for lilacs, pinks, clematis, and wallflowers.

pH 7 Neutral; suits most plants

Testing soil for pH level

You can get a good idea of your garden's pH using a testing kit from a garden center or hardware store. Kits come with full instructions, are simple to use, and are usually more reliable than the meters sold for home use.

1 Take samples from different parts of the garden, since soil is seldom uniform. Make a note of where each sample comes from so that you can exploit any variations, such as an acid patch, when you draw up your planting plan. Add the soil to the chemical solution in the test tube and shake to mix.

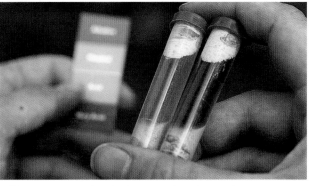

2 Match the colored solution against the pH chart to assess what kind of soil you have. Dark green indicates alkaline soil, bright green is neutral, and yellow or orange indicates acid.

Acidic soils

A wide range of plants tolerate acidic soils, but acid-loving or "ericaceous" plants are almost impossible to grow elsewhere. If your soil is not acidic you can grow them in containers filled with ericaceous soil mix.

Pieris Refined shrubs with interesting foliage for acidic soil in shade. 'Forest Flame', shown right, has burning red young shoots and white flowers.

Calluna vulgaris The many cultivars of this heather are ideal for beds or groundcover, with red, pink, purple, or white summer flowers.

Camellia Elegant, evergreen shrubs for sun or shade, as long as soil is moist. Most have pink or red blooms; 'Cornish Snow' has unusual white flowers.

Erica carnea Small heathers with many cultivars that flower at different times. Ericas bear pink, purple, or white flowers; some have yellow foliage.

Exochorda The arching branches of these striking, compact shrubs are laden with white, cup-shaped flowers in spring and summer.

Hamamelis Many witch hazels have attractive flowers in late winter. *H. x intermedia* 'Pallida', shown here, is a reliable and very fragrant yellow favorite.

Magnolia x soulangeana Cultivars grow to just 18ft (6m). Magnificent goblet-shaped flowers appear in spring before and as the new leaves unfurl.

Pachysandra terminalis Useful groundcover with glossy, toothed foliage. 'Variegata' is less vigorous and more easily controlled in small gardens.

Skimmia Robust evergreen shrubs with attractive foliage and flowers; for fruits, male and female plants usually need to be grown together.

pH 6.5 Slightly acid; ideal for most plants. Some acid-lovers, like camellias, can put up with this pH.

Under pH 5.5 Very acid or "sour"; ideal for acid-loving ericaceous plants, such as rhododendrons and heathers; other plants will be satisfactory but lime-lovers will not thrive.

Cultivating the soil

Wild plants get along perfectly well without any digging, but in gardens some cultivation is useful. It loosens packed down or "compacted" soil, improving both aeration and drainage, and at the same time buries or loosens weeds, making them easier to pull out. When cultivating the soil, you can also incorporate any organic matter, fertilizer, or lime you apply far more quickly than rain, worms, or other natural agents can. An inspection of your soil should give you an idea of what is needed (*see pp. 36–39*).

Digging, where you lift out and turn over the soil on a spade, is quite slow and heavy work, especially on clay soils, so you may want to do it in stages, tackling a small area at a time. Sometimes it is enough to loosen, rather than turn over, the soil with a fork or large hoe to mix in fertilizers or lime. This is a good technique for sticky clay soils, where a fork breaks the soil up along naturally forming fracture lines to create clods rather than slicing it as a spade does. Forks and hoes are also useful for working around existing plants, and teasing out the roots of persistent weeds.

Once you have dug the ground you may not need to dig again for two or three years, and you can often avoid it altogether by keeping off the soil, and only working it in

What is "single digging"?

Single digging is when you turn over the soil to the depth of the spade blade, to loosen soil, bury weeds or debris, and mix in manure, fertilizer, or lime. Dig a trench across one end of your plot, take the soil to the other end, and dump it outside the area you're digging. Take out a new trench next to the first, turning the soil from the new trench into the original one. Repeat this process until you have turned over the soil on the whole plot, then use the soil from the first trench to fill the last one.

Keep the spade upright as you drive it into the soil, to make sure you dig to a uniform depth.

1 First, dig out the soil from the first strip. Work from the front to the back of the strip, and create a trench one spade or "spit" deep and one spade's width. Place the excavated soil on the surface at the end of your plot.

2 Add organic matter, such as well-rotted manure or garden compost, to the bottom of the trench. Then dig out the second strip as in step 1, but place the soil into the first trench, on top of the organic matter.

3 Add organic matter to the second trench, using a fork to break it up if necessary. Fill in this second trench using the soil dug out from the first. You can dig larger plots in the same way, dividing them up into several strips.

Digging is not compulsory

Beds and borders do not have to be dug each year. If your soil is well structured and you dig it thoroughly at the start, mixing in plenty of organic matter and a moderate dressing of fertilizer, and amending any shortage of lime, there is often no need to dig again. Living organisms thrive better in undisturbed soil than they do in cultivated ground, and although digging lets in air so organic matter breaks down faster, it can also damage soil structure. Combining a "no-dig" approach with organic mulches will lead to improved soil, but it does mean that you have to plan your garden carefully to minimize the need to turn over the soil.

Walking on the soil will undo all your good work. Lay paths and work from planks laid on the soil to preserve its structure and prevent compaction.

Raised beds help reduce labor. Be sure to make them narrow enough that you can tend them from the path without having to tread on the soil.

Stepping stones positioned in beds and borders will allow you to keep off the soil while you weed, which helps prevent soil compaction and reduces the need to dig.

dry weather. If soil sticks to your boots when you walk on it, then it is too wet to work. You should also avoid digging in summer, when the soil is at its driest. The ideal time to dig clay and loam is autumn; winter frosts will help to break down any clods on the surface. Sand is best dug in spring.

Benefits of organic matter

Organic matter is essential for fertile and well-structured soil (*see p.35*). "Organic" gardeners aim to feed the soil with organic matter, rather than feed plants with fertilizers, arguing that a soil rich in living organisms that feed on a generous supply of organic matter is the ideal growing medium for healthy plants. Even if you use fertilizers, which are generally helpful, it is good practice to feed soil with as much organic matter as you can lay your hands on. As it breaks down, organic matter provides plants with nutrients, especially nitrogen, which can be lost from the soil through the action of bacteria or washed out by rain. Organic material releases nitrogen gradually, so some will be present in the soil whenever your plants happen to need it most.

The other advantage of incorporating organic matter is that it helps improve soil structure. Well-structured soil retains nutrients and moisture well, allows excess water to drain away, and contains the air needed to allow roots to breathe. The humus in organic matter bonds together fine clay particles into crumbs, creating larger spaces between them, and thereby improving drainage. Humus improves sandy soils, increasing both their water- and nutrient-holding capacity. If you apply organic matter every year you will soon reap these rewards.

Liming the soil

Add lime to the soil in the amounts recommended by the results of pH test kits. Sandy soils need less lime to change the pH than clay soils. Take care not to overdose because too much lime will reduce plant growth and once it has been added, it can't be easily countered. Plants may be scorched if lime reacts with the nitrogen in fertilizer—fork lime into the soil well before planting and don't add fertilizers within two weeks in the same year.

Dealing with different soil types

Gardeners were growing wonderful gardens long before the complexity of soil was properly understood. Today, we can use "soil science" as a shortcut to the knowledge that was previously acquired over years of observation and disappointment. Once you know your soil, you can give it the best possible treatment. You might have the impression that applying feeds or fertilizers is the most important factor in raising plants, but the capacity of the soil to provide water is more important. A moderate amount of a general-purpose fertilizer to supplement, but not replace, organic matter usually provides your garden with all the nutrients most ornamental plants need. Fruit and vegetable plots, however, will probably need more generous fertilizing.

Loam soils

If you have dark brown soil with a crumbly texture, which usually denotes plenty of organic matter, you will have few problems. A loam soil contains roughly equal amounts of clay, silt, and sand, which means it has good reserves of nutrients and ample supplies of water accessible to roots.

Earthworms in topsoil live on organic matter, and thus are a good indication of its presence. Their burrowing actions further improve the soil structure.

Fruit crops, such as redcurrants, grow best on a deep, fertile soil that holds plenty of moisture. They will produce their heaviest crops on a rich loam soil.

Loam soil profile

Advantages
- A well-structured loam with plenty of organic matter supports the widest possible range of plants and needs the least work
- Holds plenty of moisture and nutrients, so plants need little or no extra watering or feeding

Disadvantages and solutions
- This is not the soil for a wildflower meadow, which needs poor soil (low in nutrients)
- The acidity or alkalinity of your soil will still limit the range of plants you can grow (see pp.38–39)
- Loam soils are usually fertile enough for most plants—use 60 percent of the usual fertilizer recommendations to avoid overfertilizing (see pp.160–161)

Best for growing
- A wide range of plants, including demanding fruits and vegetables

Sandy soils

Although light to work, sandy soils gradually settle and pack together. To prevent this, you may need to dig them in late winter, adding organic matter at the same time if possible, as well as in spring. Organic matter improves the soil's capacity to retain both water and nutrients that are otherwise washed out. Calcium is easily lost from sandy soils, making them prone to acidity; test the soil pH to see if you need to add lime.

Acanthus spinosus is a drought-tolerant plant suited to the dry conditions of sandy soil.

Lawns on very sandy, free-draining soils need regular autumn care in the form of raking and fertilizing (see p.176).

Sandy soil profile

Advantages
- Free-draining and light to work; may be worked at almost any time of year
- Quick to warm up in spring, encouraging plants to start growing earlier

Disadvantages and solutions
- Prone to drought, especially by late summer; mulch with organic matter in spring
- Low in nutrients, which are quickly washed out; apply general fertilizer, such as a rose fertilizer, every spring
- Organic matter breaks down quickly so don't dig unless you have to
- Often acid (see p.38); check pH and, if necessary, add lime every 5 years to counter this

Best for growing
- Annuals and drought-tolerant plants
- Trees, including conifers, are fairly drought-proof once established

Clay soils

Clay holds on to plant foods, keeping them within reach of roots and releasing them as plants require, but it is also prone to waterlogging and compaction. The key is to improve the soil structure. Add organic matter, which binds clay particles together into lumps, creating wider air spaces between them, and allowing roots to penetrate and extract water and food. The spaces also help excess water drain away and allow air into the soil. To improve drainage further, dig in grit or horticultural sand; never use building sand. Lawns on clay need special treatment (*see p.180*).

Moisture-loving plants grow well on clay soils that always remains damp. You could also create a natural pond, using the clay to line it.

Cracking occurs on clay soil when it dries out in droughts, but don't worry: cracks can actually help to open up the structure and bring more air into the soil.

Clay soil profile

Advantages
- Water retentive, moist, and fertile
- Suitable for a wide range of plants if it is prepared well

Disadvantages and solutions
- Hard to work, heavy, and sticky, clay should be dug when dry in late summer and early fall; working when wet will destroy the soil structure
- Cold, and slow to warm up in spring so there is a later start to the growing season
- Prone to compaction, so be prepared to add about a barrowful of compost or composted bark per square yard/square meter every few years
- Poor drainage is improved by digging in coarse sand, grit, or fine gravel to about a spade's depth
- Add lime, if necessary (*see pp.38–39*)

Best for growing
- Bog plants and moisture-lovers

Chalky or limestone soils

Organic matter breaks down very quickly in lime-rich soils, so it is vital to add plenty each year. Be generous when feeding and mulching. Don't even think about trying acid-loving plants—they will never really thrive, if they survive at all. You are likely to see many plants with yellowing leaves on chalky soil, and not just the acid-lovers—California lilac, for example, will also yellow. Help your plants by mulching and watering well, and add to the soil plenty of bulky organic matter and a generous application of a balanced, general-purpose fertilizer to feed them.

Clover grows well in poor, chalky soils; it is a pretty wild flower, and it can also be useful in a lawn because its roots increase the nitrogen in the soil.

Wildflower rich lawns and meadows are especially likely to be successful on a chalky soil. The best turf prefers mildly acid conditions but good lawns can be achieved with careful feeding and mowing.

Chalky soil profile

Advantages
- Can be fertile if the topsoil is deep and kept rich in organic matter.

Disadvantages and solutions
- Usually alkaline, these soils are not for acid-loving plants, and even lime-loving plants can suffer nutrient deficiencies, so feeding is essential
- Shallow chalk soils are very free-draining; apply a thick annual mulch of organic matter to help conserve moisture
- Quickly lose nutrients; be generous with feeds and leaf mold, rotted manure, or garden compost
- Treat deep, sticky chalk soils as for clay

Best for growing
- Lime-loving pinks and clematis (*see p.38*)
- Drought-tolerant plants (*see pp.64–65*)
- Wildflower meadows

Mulching to improve the soil

Wild plants grow in soil that is constantly receiving a surface addition of leaves, dead animals, and other organic debris. You might have noticed this thick, dark covering on the soil when walking in woods, and perhaps scuffed it aside to see the soil perforated with many holes and burrows, and the tiny creatures that made them scuttling for cover. This "biological rain" is incredibly effective in improving soil and plant growth, and you can imitate it in your own garden (never collect such material from the wild). When you can't mix organic matter into the soil, mulching (*see below*) will improve soils nearly as effectively, if a little more slowly.

What is mulching?

A mulch is a layer of organic or inorganic material spread thickly over the soil, where it performs several functions. Any mulch moderates soil temperatures, suppresses weeds, and helps reduce moisture loss from the soil. Inorganic mulches of gravel, stones, or pebbles, and sheet materials such as geotextiles suppress perennial weeds but do not improve the soil structure. Organic mulches, the most important for improving the soil, are broken down and carried beneath the surface by soil organisms. A depth of at least 2in (5cm) is needed, but 3–4in (8–10cm) is better.

Mulches are best spread in late winter, when they will seal in winter rain and prevent annual weeds from growing as the soil warms up in spring. As an organic mulch rots, feeding the soil life and ultimately your plants, it disappears and will need an annual repleninshing. Perennial weeds will thrust through organic mulches, so remove them before mulching.

Before mulching

If using a fertilizer, spread it when laying a mulch in late winter. This ensures that the fertilizer is washed down to the roots by the winter rains. You can also hide drip or seep irrigation (*see p.156*) beneath the mulch. Trying to water through mulches in summer requires very large quantities of water, so an irrigation system beneath the mulch can be helpful.

Seep hoses can be covered

Organic mulching materials

Good materials for organic mulches include garden compost (although it may harbor weed seeds), shredded prunings, lawn clippings, and leaf mold, but few gardens manage to produce enough of these materials to mulch all the soil thickly; you'll usually need to buy some material such as mushroom compost, bark chips, or locally produced yard waste (sometimes offered free from local recycling centers). Each of these has particular advantages and disadvantages (*see pp.158–59*). Another option is to use a layer of one of these store-bought, weed-free materials to top off your homemade mulch, which will provide both better weed suppression and often a more attractive surface.

A shredder will turn your own woody prunings into small fragments that can be used as a mulch without further treatment, but they are bulky, expensive machines. It may be better to rent one, or share one with friends. Try renting one to see how it works; you need a large machine to shred branches, or you can hire an arborist to shred large quantities.

Mulching and moisture When you pull back a thick organic mulch you can often see how it reduces evaporation and keeps soil moist. The worms you find beneath the mulch help work it into the soil, where it will also help hold water.

Making leaf mold

Autumn leaves are a gift for gardeners because they are a free source of one of the best soil improvers: leaf mold. Unlike compost, which is made by bacteria that work best in warm conditions, leaves are broken down by fungi, which are more active in cooler temperatures. For the best results, separate leaves from other garden waste. Use only leaves from deciduous trees; shred evergreen and conifer leaves and use as a mulch, or wherever you would use other shredded prunings.

Raking it in (*left*) Gather leaves before they smother lawns and borders. It should not take long with the right tools: a wide rake for lawns, a smaller flexible wire rake for beds or borders, and a big square of fabric to move the leaves.

Plentiful supply (*above*) Leaves from a woodland area can blow all over your garden. If you have large quantities, a vacuum that shreds and compacts leaves can be helpful, because this speeds their breakdown.

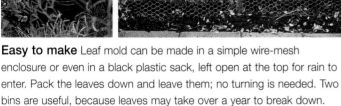
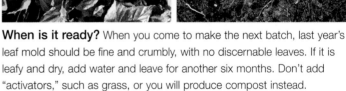

Easy to make Leaf mold can be made in a simple wire-mesh enclosure or even in a black plastic sack, left open at the top for rain to enter. Pack the leaves down and leave them; no turning is needed. Two bins are useful, because leaves may take over a year to break down.

When is it ready? When you come to make the next batch, last year's leaf mold should be fine and crumbly, with no discernable leaves. If it is leafy and dry, add water and leave for another six months. Don't add "activators," such as grass, or you will produce compost instead.

The power of composting

Compost is the gardener's secret weapon in making plants thrive. Materials like grass clippings can be used "raw" as a mulch, but will do limited good. They may be too dry, or become slimy, and take a long time to rot down and improve the soil. They are much more effective once they have been composted. Garden compost is a crumbly, dark, organic material, processed from waste materials from the kitchen and garden. It is made by harnessing soil bacteria and other microorganisms in the natural processes of breakdown and rotting. Garden compost is a good soil improver, easy to add to the soil or to use as a mulch. It is not sterile, and would make a poor potting medium.

Store-bought potting soil mix consists of blended ingredients, such as sand, loam, organic matter, and fertilizers. It is weed- and disease-free, often sterile, and not an effective soil improver. Nor is it cost-efficient: you would need large quantities of commercial soil mix to add to your soil.

Ingredients for the compost bin

Getting the right balance of materials is important in making good compost. The ideal mix is 20–50 percent green, leafy material, with the rest consisting of more fibrous, woody material. In practice you will have different materials at different times of year and seldom in amounts that allow careful blending and rapid filling of the bin. Make do with what is available and the results will be entirely usable, even if they do not constitute perfect compost; over time the materials will balance out. The main point is to try to prevent the bin from being dominated by one ingredient.

Leave it out

Citrus peel, rhubarb, and most other fruits, vegetables, and plants are safe to use, but do not add the following to the compost pile:
• material that is diseased, damaged, or contaminated with weedkiller
• weeds carrying seeds or with roots that might survive composting, such as dandelions or bindweed
• cat and dog droppings, which can harbor harmful organisms
• kitchen waste containing animal materials, such as scraps of meat, which can attract rats

Soft, green materials

Vegetable kitchen waste

Weeds that have not gone to seed yet

Grass clippings

Soft, green material, vegetable kitchen waste, and moderate amounts of grass clippings provide readily available nitrogen and other nutrients for microorganisms. However, they are wet and soft and tend to settle into a solid, airless mass. They must be mixed with fibrous material.

Fibrous, woody materials

Fallen leaves

Shredded paper or cardboard

Eggshells

Twiggy prunings

Spent bedding plants

Decaying stems of perennials

Carrot peelings

Shredded woody material, spent bedding plants, and trimmings from herbaceous plants provide tougher, carbon-rich material with less nitrogen. Fallen leaves are ideally used for leaf mold (*see p.45*) but, if you don't have the time or space, they can be included in compost.

Building the compost pile

Your role in making compost is to provide soil organisms with warmth, moisture, and a good mix of materials. Placing bins on bare soil allows organisms to get inside. Otherwise, add a spadeful of compost from an old pile, or soil, for every 12in (30cm) of material. In autumn there may be more material than you can deal with. Make a temporary bin of wire netting or scrap wood, such as old pallets, until you can transfer the contents to your bins, or dig in excess material on any bare soil; it should rot away during the year.

Ideally, you should fill your compost bin with a good blend of materials in as short a period as possible. In practice, it is more likely that the bin will take some time to fill up. This means that it probably won't generate enough warmth for speedy, thorough composting, and most weed seeds and roots will survive, as will any organisms in diseased material. Large-scale municipal composting should reach temperatures that eliminate these problems, but small volumes of homemade compost cannot match this, so be careful what you add to your own compost pile.

With the right blend of ingredients there should no need for "activators." These nitrogen-rich materials help break down woody materials and can be useful when you have too little soft, green material in your compost bin. Alternatively, you can add a thin layer of barnyard or stable manure, mushroom compost, or a sprinkling of nitrogen-rich fertilizer to every 6in (15cm) of woody material. Adding lime is sometimes recommended, but is usually unnecessary, unless you are composting lots of shredded conifer prunings or waste fruit, which can be very acidic.

Ready to use?

Once the bin is full it can be left until the compost is ready to use, but if you are energetic, turning the compost can speed up the process. Empty the bin and mix the contents, adding water to any dry material before returning it to the bin. This is where having two bins is an advantage: compost shrinks as it rots, so that two piles can be combined into one, leaving a bin free to fill with fresh material for a new supply.

To check the progress of your heap, pull back the upper layers to see if the fibrous material is breaking down. If not, it may be too dry and need watering, or it could need more soft, green material, such as lawn clippings, to add nitrogen. Solid, soggy, foul-smelling masses will improve if you add

Shredded materials rot down faster than unshredded ones. You can chop most stems and leaves up with a spade, but it may be worth renting a shredder in autumn to reduce heavier woody material and leaves.

Bad smells indicate compost that is too wet. To rectify this, turn it and add fibrous material. Alternatively, a layer of well-rotted compost from another bin or a layer of spent potting soil mix will help seal in odors and suppress flies.

some fibrous material. Eventually, only the twiggy material will remain recognizable, and you can use the compost as a mulch or soil improver. But if you have a small household or modest garden, your compost may not turn out to be the ideal, uniformly crumbly, brown material you had hoped for. Instead, it will probably have twiggy and semirotted parts mixed in with a more encouraging dark brown mass that smells like moist woods. Pick or sieve out the unrotted components, and add them to your next compost batch; even this woody material will rot down eventually.

Which kind of compost bin?

For small amounts of waste, a container or bin is best. The larger the bin, the faster it will work; aim for at least a cubic yard (cubic meter), but most bins are much smaller. Other options are to make your own bin using mesh or wood, or simply to pile material in a heap in a sheltered spot, although this can look unsightly and only works if you make a large heap. A pit is another possibility, but it will be hard to empty and may become waterlogged in the winter. Whichever type you use, it should have a lid to keep out the rain. Air vents dry out the ingredients, increasing the need to add water and are not needed if a good open mix of materials is used (*see opposite*). To speed up the rotting process you can increase the airflow by turning the contents of the bin.

Wire-mesh enclosures need to be large for good results. Insulate with straw between two layers of mesh (*above left*) or cardboard (*above right*).

Wood keeps the compost material warm, but will rot in time.

Plastic is inexpensive, rot proof, and the most common material for bins.

Climate and hardiness

Garden plants originate from many climates, and it is surprising how well plants from different places around the world grow together in our gardens. Because of this, you might think that knowing where a plant originates is irrelevant, but getting plants to grow in your garden is made easier if you have an inkling of their natural habitat.

The temperature is the most obvious factor affecting your garden. Climate also affects the length of the growing season and how much rain, light, and wind you can expect.

The growing season

This is the time of the year when it is warm and moist enough for plants to grow actively. The farther from the equator you go, the narrower the gap between the last frosts of spring and the first of autumn, and the shorter the growing season. If you live in an area prone to long, severe winters, you will be able to grow tender plants outside only between the last frost in spring or early summer and the first one in autumn, and tender plants that need a long growing season, such as cannas, are not likely to do well.

Plants grow rapidly in spring and early summer. Late summer and autumn are important times for the "ripening" of plants, affecting how well they ride out the winter, or their hardiness. Heat at the end of the season encourages plants to harden their cell membranes and accumulate food reserves that help them resist freezing damage. Cool, sunless summers may mean that plants go into winter without developing the necessary resistance to cold.

As winter approaches, plants shut down their activities by shedding leaves and retreating below ground into bulbs or

What is hardiness?

Hardiness is a plant's ability to withstand the local climate. In an area subject to frost, this means resistance to cold; elsewhere it means resistance to heat or drought. Knowing where a plant comes from does not automatically tell you if it will survive or be hardy in your garden. Lavender and rosemary grow naturally on well-drained land in a warm climate, but will thrive in moister conditions and cooler climates. Small variations can also make a difference: Eucalyptus are not very cold-hardy, but those raised from seed collected from high ground can be much hardier than those raised from seed collected in the hot, dry bush.

Hardy plants Hardy plants will survive the levels of frost in temperate areas. Most plants we call hardy make new growth when temperatures exceed 40–43°F (4–6°C); if temperatures stay around this point, there may be little or no growth. Some plants, such as *Sorbus commixta*, prove very hardy and grow in climates more severe than their own.

Tender plants The metabolism of tender plants runs poorly below 54°F (12°C), and if temperatures dip this low at night, plants such as *Hibiscus rosa-sinensis* may fail to thrive. These plants have no realistic chance of surviving periods of severe weather and need to be brought into shelter, such as a greenhouse, as soon as there is a threat of frost.

Marginally or half-hardy plants Unless you live in a warm climate, it is unlikely that plants like olives (*Olea europaea*) will make it through the winter. In a cool climate you can improve their chances by selecting spots with sheltered microclimates, mulching, providing good drainage and soil structure, and protecting them with straw or fleece in winter.

Hardiness zones

Large countries and continents are divided into hardiness zones on the basis of winter temperatures. In the United States and Canada, hardiness is indicated by a numerical zoning system that is based mostly, but not entirely, on minimum temperatures. These zones are published in map form in many gardening books, but the zone maps are different for these two countries and are not interchangeable. Plants will generally grow as far north as the zone number given, but in the US, summer heat also limits the area where a given plant will survive. The American Horticultural Society has developed a Heat Zone map that addresses this problem.

A **sunny wall** both stores and reflects heat. It can extend the growing season and help wood ripen in late summer.

hardy rootstocks, and wait it out until warmer weather. Unseasonably warm and rainy periods in winter can rouse plants from this dormant state and cause damage even in plants that have been "hardened" against cold.

The effects of cold

The length and severity of the winter often dictates what you can grow in your area. You can water in dry spells, or boost drainage where excess moisture is a problem, but it is much harder to keep temperatures above damaging levels. You can resort to special techniques to protect plants from winter cold (*see pp.166–67*), and make use of microclimates (*see pp.60–61*), but these only apply to some plants and situations. Hardiness is vitally important, and it is worth understanding the different ways cold can affect plants.

Frost can be of two types. Wind frosts occur when air with a temperature below freezing moves across the garden. These often happen in winter, and their effects are rapid freezing of plants and—if the cold weather goes on long enough—the soil. They are particularly damaging to evergreens. Their ill effects can be mitigated by deciduous hedges, fences, and other shelter.

Radiation frosts, on the other hand, occur on clear nights when objects, including vegetation and buildings, radiate heat into the night air and become colder. The cold air in contact with the cooling objects flows downward and collects at ground level. On a sloping site the cold air will flow to the lowest point of the garden, creating a frost pocket (*see p.56*). If the night skies are free of clouds or fog and there is little or no wind, the air temperature will often fall below the freezing point.

Frosts occur when air temperatures reach the freezing point, and if the air is moist, hoar frost forms on surfaces. In dry air no hoar frost forms, and the frost may be called a "black frost." Frost damage happens first and most severely at ground level, and the upper parts of plants may sometimes be unaffected. The ground is cooled by cold air collecting at ground level, and if cold air persists, soil freezes. A series of freezing winter nights often results in frozen soil, which damages roots, tubers, and other underground organs.

Dealing with cold

Keep an eye on temperatures by hanging an inexpensive minimum–maximum thermometer out of the direct sun to record the overnight lows. Even a small garden may have several "microclimates," so find and exploit them. You can reduce the effects of cold by creating shelter from wind, which alters the garden's microclimate, and by allowing cold, frosty air to drain away, so that you avoid frost pockets. A thick mulch of coarse organic material can help insulate roots from cold air (*see p.167*); a blanket of heavy snow can have the same effect in a colder climate (*see pp.50–51*).

Plants and climate

Climate is more than just how low temperatures fall in winter. It consists of how much rain, sun, and wind you get, and when you get it. Getting plants to grow in your garden is easier if you understand these details of their native climate.

For example, in continental climates winters tend to be dry and often very cold. It might seem that resilient natives of these regions would easily survive the milder winters of a maritime climate, which is moderated by the surrounding seas. But the winters in maritime climates tend to be wet. Continental plants that shut down for winter and retreat below ground into structures such as bulbs and tubers can survive deep, dry cold,

but they may succumb to fatal rots in mild, wet soils. As a result, some plants that can tough out the most rigorous alpine or continental winters, such as *Allium campanulatum*, are not fully hardy in milder climates and will never thrive there as they do in their places of origin.

Spring is also a critical time. In continental climates it arrives with a bang and does not last long, but in maritime climates it can be a tentative season with warm spells punctuated by frosts, chilly winds, and droughts. This can lead to continental plants starting growth too early only to be cut down by frosts and then, in autumn, failing to harden up for winter.

World climate map

The world can be divided into areas with similar climates in terms of the cold, rainfall, and seasons they experience. Despite being widely separated by geography, indigenous plants have adapted in similar ways.

Key

- Tropical with year-round rain
- Tropical with monsoon rain
- Tropical with seasonal rain
- Hot, dry desert
- Cool, temperate maritime
- Warm, temperate
- Cool, temperate continental
- Cold, arctic
- Mountain

Maritime

The ocean warms and cools more slowly than the land, giving maritime climates dry summers and wet winters that are not exceptionally cold. Many garden trees and shrubs originated in this climate in Europe, while New Zealand is home to phormiums and pittisporums, and eryngiums are found around the world. These can all struggle in areas with very cold, dry winters, or long, scorching summers. Between these extremes, they are often easy-going, reliable plants that withstand some drought once established and look after themselves through the winter.

Eryngium maritima (Sea holly)

Tropical

Plants from hot climates never experience frost, cannot tolerate cold, and have adapted to a long growing season. Many tropical plants are used as summer bedding, then discarded each year, or as house and conservatory plants that can spend summer outside (*see pp.206–207*). Despite the potential for year-round growth, you need to be ready to encourage plants into dormancy for winter by cutting them back, as for fuchsias and geraniums, or drying off the tubers of plants like dahlias and cannas for indoor storage (*see p.166*).

Dahlias

Mediterranean

This is a warm, temperate climate, with mild, fairly wet winters and hot, dry summers, found around the Mediterranean, and in areas of southern California, South Africa, Chile, and Australia. It is the source of many evergreens and plants that tolerate the dry shade underneath, as well as bulbs that escape summer heat underground, like cyclamen and tulips. Most like a well-drained soil and the sunniest spot in the garden.

Ceanothus (California lilac)

Continental

Hot summers and cold winters are typical in parts of North America and Asia. Plants from these regions, like flowering quinces, peonies, and echinaceas, will tough out cold but not a lack of summer moisture. They thrive on moist soils provided they are not waterlogged, but fail on dry, sandy soil, unless you water.

Chaenomeles x *superba* (Japonica)

Desert

These are dry climates with little rain. They are also generally hot; although nightime temperatures can be very low, sustained cold is unknown. Here cacti and desert succulents have adapted to resist drought, but cannot survive frost. Most are grown as houseplants in cooler climates, although hardier succulents, such as some sedums and sempervivums, can resist frost as long as they are grown in fairly free-draining conditions.

Euphorbia milii (Crown of thorns)

Cool and moist

These conditions are often found in lower mountain regions like the Himalayan foothills. These are home to the shade- and moisture-loving rhododendrons, which need plenty of water in summers to do well. Conditions in western China are less mild and moist, and a huge range of hardy garden plants originated here, including the more robust rhododendrons, bamboos, and camellias, which need reliably moist, free-draining soil to do best.

Rhododendron falconeri (tree rhododendron)

Mountain and alpine

Alpine plants tend to hug the ground and have deep roots to help survive extremely cold winters, and strong winds and intense light levels that dry them out. At lower altitudes, they may succumb to wet winters or be swamped by large plants. They need a low-nutrient soil or rooting medium that is always moist but well-drained. They can be grown in troughs, wall crevices, or gravel beds in gritty, free-draining soil mix.

Leontopodium alpinum (edelweiss)

Arctic

The tough plants from these cold regions can be surprisingly vulnerable to sudden cold snaps in milder climates. This is because they proof themselves against the cold using special mechanisms (*see pp.30–31*); in mild, temperate climates, there may be insufficient cold to initiate the process. Very few of our garden plants come from these climates.

Larix laricina (Larch)

Know your garden 3

Your local climate • Evaluating your garden • Monitoring sun and shade
Seasonal variations • Making the most of every niche

Your garden in close-up

Gardens come in all shapes and sizes, and in all types of locations. Where you live has a direct bearing on the types of plants you can grow. Are you in a cold, high rainfall area, or on a dry, windy hilltop? Does winter weather linger for weeks, or is it rare for the thermometer to drop below freezing? While your locality has a prevailing climate, your garden also has its own distinct microclimates (*see p.60*), influenced by a range of factors, including the direction your garden faces, the surrounding buildings, and features such as hedges, walls, or fences.

Soil type has a huge impact on what you can grow. No matter how much you want rhododendrons, if you live in a comparatively dry area with alkaline soil, you would be well advised to cultivate a passion for another group of plants. The good news is that over thousands of years plants have evolved and adapted to grow in a wide range of conditions, giving you plenty of choice for every site and soil type. Once you understand these adaptations you will be able to spot plants that can cope with specific conditions and those that won't.

Gardens perched on top of hills are exposed to the weather, and the plants you choose need to be particularly resistant to drying winds and high light levels.

Blank canvas or neglected chaos?

Brand-new gardens can be a bleak prospect, especially if the "topsoil" is little more than a token gesture to cover up builders' rubble, plastic bags, and broken tools. Plants can come to the rescue, since there are many that thrive in the wild in what can only be described as the natural equivalent of these conditions. If you have inherited a garden it can be a double-edged sword, depending on whether it is to your taste or not and how enthusiastically the previous owners gardened. An old, neglected garden can be just as daunting as a new one—what should stay, and what should go?

Getting what you want

There are other factors to consider, too. Who will use the garden, and what for? How much time can you realistically spend tending it? You don't want to start resenting the time it takes up. And what about encouraging wildlife to the garden? This can be enormously rewarding and enjoyable, especially if you want to help children learn about the natural world.

The better you understand your garden the better it will look and the happier your gardening experience will be, because you will be able to take advantage of all the garden has to offer. It will also help you avoid the most common pitfalls, which can be costly and discovering. Finding out

Your garden is as unique as you are, and even if it is one of many that are superficially similar in any suburban street, there will be subtle differences between them.

about your garden will take time, for there is no substitute for watching and learning as the seasons go by. The process never ends—gardens begin to grow and change from the moment the first plant is planted. What is a sunny spot today could become an area of dappled shade with the addition of a tree. And nature is always ready to change the rules just when you finally get everything "just so." If a storm topples a large old tree, it can have huge repercussions. In the longer term, climate change is expected to have a big impact.

Gardening is as large a subject as you want it to be, but learning about your own patch will stand you in excellent stead for the future. All gardeners make mistakes along the way—errors are one of the best ways of learning—but a good understanding of your garden will help make sure that your mistakes are small and, with luck, inexpensive.

Knowing your local climate

Most of us like to talk about the weather, often to complain about it, but how many of us really take note of the climate in our area? If we travel to work, our idea of the weather in our gardens may be based only on what we experience on weekends. And memories play tricks. It's amazing how easy it is to think of a summer as being particularly wet or especially dry when it was actually the opposite.

The climatic conditions that affect plants most are rainfall, extremes of temperature, wind strength and direction, and light levels. Knowing the local climate is the first step in understanding which plants grow best in your garden. While most gardens can be manipulated in one way or another to

Coastal gardens suffer fewer frosts because of the proximity of the ocean and the regular sea breezes; the northern East Coast, however, still gets some extremely cold winter weather.

overcome prevailing conditions, the predominant climate—the macroclimate—will always influence plant selection.

It can be interesting to find out the average annual rainfall and the maximum and minimum temperatures in your area. Local libraries often keep weather records, and various Internet sites also provide weather details, including historical data. Also, observe what is growing well in your area; a good place to look is in gardens open to the public where plants are clearly labeled. Make a note of any that catch your eye, and look them up in reference books to find out about the conditions they prefer and what levels of cold they will tolerate (*see pp. 48–49*). Talking to local gardeners is another good way to gain information and advice.

Armed with this knowledge, you can apply it to your own yard but, before planting, you need to take a closer look at some other factors.

In a valley it is usually damp because rivers can draw weather systems toward them, but hills also affect rainfall—one side of a valley is often wetter than the other. Cold or freezing air will often settle and persist in valleys and on flood plains.

Your garden environment

Wind is probably the most important factor in the garden environment. Gales and storms can cause substantial physical damage, but even normal breezes have an impact because they dry out leaves, and plants will need to be watered more often. Even in a small garden some areas may be more exposed to wind than others. Try to identify the windier or more turbulent parts of your garden and, if possible, reduce the problem by planting hedges or living screens (*see p.70*). Their sheltering effect extends up to five times their height.

The trouble with fences, hedges, walls, and windbreaks is the shade they cast. In small gardens they can seriously impair light levels. A barrier can also restrict views. In these cases consider growing plants such as heathers, which are native to exposed areas and are resistant to drying up. Drought-resistant plants often have small, needlelike or waxy leaves to help reduce water loss.

Plants and wind

Wind disturbs the moist air layer that naturally collects on the surface of leaves, making them lose water more quickly than on a still day (*see p.22*). As the plants begin to dry out, the leaves close their pores. This prevents carbon dioxide from getting into plants, and photosynthesis —and therefore growth— stops. This is why plants grow best in the shelter of hedges and fences.

Soil and moisture

After wind, soil moisture is the next essential factor for a garden's success. Too much in winter or too little in summer is a common complaint of gardening life. In addition to rain, walls, fences, and hedges also affect soil moisture by casting "rain shadows" (*see below*). Dig down to see to what depth the soil is dry, because this will determine what you plant. Many plants prefer good drainage (*see p.68*) and will thrive in dry soil, and even more can be grown if plenty of moisture-retentive organic matter is incorporated before planting.

It is much harder to improve damp soils, especially if the culprit is a high water table (*see opposite*). If your garden is very damp you can create well-drained spots by building raised beds or by planting on ridges and mounds. Otherwise, you should try to improve drainage as much as possible and choose plants that will tolerate wet conditions (*see p.67*).

Specific problems

Weather can be modified to a surprising degree by features in or around your garden to cause localized havoc. Once the problem is understood, it can often be fairly easily fixed. However, if it is your house that is creating a dry area, the best strategy is probably to improve the soil as much as possible and then choose plants that can cope.

Frost pockets form as chilly air sinks to the lowest point it can. Areas at risk include dips, valley bottoms, and places where cold air can collect behind a barrier.

Rain shadows occur at the base of walls, fences, and hedges, where rain driven by the prevailing wind never reaches the ground. They can be tiny or wide, depending on the height of the barrier and wind speed.

Wind turbulence is caused by solid walls, fences, and buildings as the wind tumbles over them and creates an eddying effect. You can reduce the problem by using barriers that let some air through.

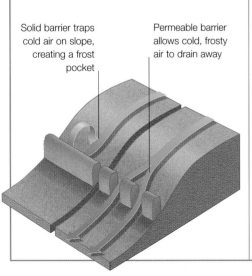

Solid barrier traps cold air on slope, creating a frost pocket

Permeable barrier allows cold, frosty air to drain away

Building intercepts slanting rain, creating an area of dry soil

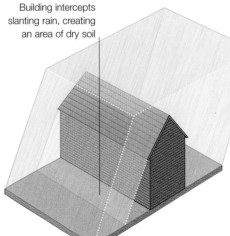

A semipermeable barrier filters wind and slows it down gradually

Wind accelerates and swirls over a solid barrier, often damaging plants

Wind damage caused by gusts and eddies swirling around solid barriers is nearly as bad as that of unchecked wind. Semipermeable barriers, such as trees and shrubs, hedges, trellis, or nonsolid walls and fences, give more effective shelter to the garden. They may also cast less shade and don't completely block your views.

Various shades

Gardeners are justified in regarding deep shade as challenging because few plants thrive with no direct sunlight. In addition, tall trees rob plants beneath them of moisture as well as light, leading to the dreaded dry shade. Buildings, especially if close together, create dry, shady areas by intercepting slanting rain and, to make matters worse, they channel wind into tunnels of fast-moving, gusty air. In such situations, add as much organic matter to the soil as possible, water plants well before and after planting, and mulch them generously. A drip or seep irrigation system will help (*see p.154*) by delivering water directly to plants before the tree roots can get hold of it and reducing evaporation.

Wind between buildings can be slowed by erecting a semi-permeable barrier, such as a trellis fence. You will still need really tough, shade-tolerant plants to populate such places.

Conifers cast the most deadly, year-round shade. Nothing can be reliably grown beneath them, but you may find these areas are useful to provide a sheltered, cool place for plants in containers that dislike intense summer heat, or for placing compost bins and storing stakes or spare terra-cotta pots.

Some areas have lesser degrees of shade, such as dappled shade beneath light vegetation, or where shade is cast for only some of the day. Here are opportunities for growing some of the many plants that develop best in what is often called "partial shade."

Finding out about the water table

In all soils there is a level at which water lies in the soil—the water table. It fluctuates according to the weather, similar to the water level in a lake or river, but will stabilize at a certain point. If parts of your garden remain constantly wet it may be that the water table is naturally high, making the soil wet. To check the depth of the water table, dig an inspection pit (*see pp.36–37*) in dry weather. If there is no water in the pit the next day, the water table is below 24in (60cm), and the problem is more likely to be poorly draining soil.

Waterlogged soil

Where there is dappled shade from open trees, or where the shade from buildings lasts for less than half a day in summer, plants won't grow as much as in the open, but they will be more sheltered, which can make up for the lower light levels.

Monitoring sun and shade

Because some plants are adapted to a sunny place, and some to shade (*see pp. 20–21*), knowing where the sun falls in your garden is crucial to success. The sun affects the amount of light and warmth, and therefore which plants you can grow. Find out which direction your garden faces—north, south, east, or west. This "aspect," or exposure, can be found by observing where the sun rises and sets and whether the back or the front garden receives the most sun. In general, south- or west-facing gardens are warmer and sunnier than north- or east-facing ones.

It is also worth taking time to observe the passage of the sun, not just through the course of the day, but throughout the seasons. This important information will allow you to build a picture of which areas are permanently shady—at the foot of a fence, for example, or beneath an evergreen tree—and which get most sun—nearest to the house, or in the middle of the lawn. Once you know where these areas are, you can begin think about what plants will thrive in them and plan your garden accordingly.

The seasonal variation can be quite wide—the trajectory of the sun varies from summer, when the it rises high in the sky, to winter, when it hugs the horizon. Clever use of plants can make the most of these changes: the low watery sunlight of midwinter, for example, will illuminate colorful stems, such as those of coppiced dogwoods and willows, and bring interest to the winter garden.

If you live in an urban area and your garden is surrounded by other buildings, the winter sun may barely peep over the rooftops and into the garden, although it will be quite sunny in summer when the sun moves through the sky directly above.

Your garden's exposure

To work out the aspect of your garden, stand with your back to the house. The direction you are facing, whether north, east, south, or west, is the same as your garden. If you are unsure, remember the sun rises in the east and sets in the west. East-facing gardens get the morning sun, and those facing west have sun in the afternoon. South-facing gardens can be bright for much of the day, but north-facing plots don't get much direct sun at all. East- and north-facing gardens can be unsuitable for tender plants, either because there is not enough warmth, or because the temperature rise after the nighttime cool is too rapid (*see p.31*). Remember though, each wall or fence in the garden also has an aspect, and can create its own sun-trap or shady area.

Morning in a garden facing northwest, and the summer sun has climbed high. A few shadows remain, and during the rest of the year there would be more shade until later.

Middle of the day and the garden is still sunny. Having been in full sun for over four hours, the soil will potentially be very warm and dry—the gardener has made use of drought-resistant plants such as grasses that can cope with this.

Afternoon shade is starting to creep in, cast by trees at the bottom of the garden, but because the plot is facing northwest it catches the afternoon sun. The shade will vary through the year, especially if the trees are deciduous.

Evening shade has come a long way into the garden although there is still a sun-trap near the house. The low evening sun brings out the warm yellows and oranges of the plants in the sunny bed to the right.

A season at a glance

The look of the garden can change considerably through the seasons. The light quality and brightness changes and patches of shade move. Deciduous trees and shrubs lose their leaves in winter, at the same time that most herbaceous plants die down. It takes some care to make sure a garden looks interesting and attractive throughout the year.

Spring (*right*) The bare branches of deciduous trees allow lots of light into the garden, which spring bulbs and early flowering perennials like hellebores and lungworts can take advantage of. Spring tree blossom provides a touch of color.

Summer (*far right*) Shade appears as the deciduous trees come into full leaf. In darker areas, grow shade tolerant plants such as heucheras or geraniums, including *Geranium phaeum* and *G. sanguinium*. Variegated shrubs, like the mock orange *Philadelphus coronarius* 'Variegatus' or *Choisya ternata* 'Sundance', or white-flowered shrubs such as hydrangeas, can brighten up gloomy corners.

Fall (*far left*) Enjoy the color that the leaves of many deciduous trees take on before they drop. Light levels are similar to those of spring time as the sun sinks lower, but the quality of the light is often more subdued.

Winter (*left*) This is the best time to observe the garden critically—if the structure works in winter it should work the rest of the year with the distractions of flowers and foliage. Sculptural evergreens are constant and will look good even covered with snow, but don't be tempted to include too many or the effect will be spotty. Areas under the trees have some protection from the worst effect of cold. Choose very hardy plants for east-facing walls because early morning sun can cause damage to spring flowers and tender shoots (*see p.31*).

Understanding microclimates

Microclimates are local variations in the general climate and can include soil type, and exposure or shelter, sun, or shade. Understanding microclimates enables you to exploit them to your advantage. Even across a small area, such as a garden, there will be enough variation to grow a broader range of plants than might at first seem possible. In addition to observing sun, shade, and wind, look for hidden variations by testing the soil in different areas for moisture levels, depth of topsoil, and its pH.

A tender azara exploits the conditions found in a very sheltered corner of the garden and helps brighten up a dark spot.

Just as microclimates may already exist, they can also be created. For example, when laying a patio leave a few gaps between paving slabs and fill them with gritty soil to make planting pockets. In a sunny spot, drought-tolerant herbs like thyme or oregano will thrive in the additional reflected heat and light from the paving and will make using your patio a truly sensory experience. Whatever the prevailing conditions, there will be plenty of suitably adapted plants to choose from. But some conditions may seem more challenging than most, so let's look at a few in closer detail.

Rain rarely reaches the foot of this wall—sun-loving plants will thrive, but they will need extra care while they establish.

What's in my garden?

Microclimates can provide opportunities for growing plants that might be difficult to establish out in the open. A warm, sunny wall can be the perfect spot for marginally hardy plants, even if the rest of your garden is cool and shady. An area that is always wet will suit bog plants. If you have a dry, south-facing garden, it may seem that nothing will grow there, but there are plants for this spot too.

1 **Soil type** can vary within your garden and may change from acidic to alkaline, or from sandy to clay, within short distances.

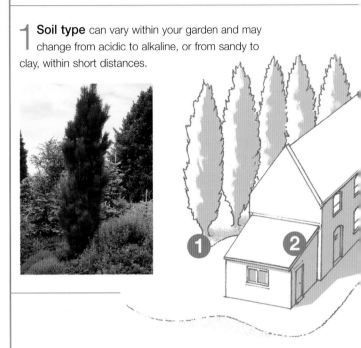

2 **Walls** and greenhouses will absorb heat in the sun, then release it slowly later. Walls can also create frost shadows, so placing containers against them during winter will help to keep plants frost-free.

3 **Slopes** are generally dry because water runs to the lowest-lying areas in a garden. Lower areas may also be more prone to frost, because cold air sinks. The combination of frost and wet soil is especially damaging, and only very hardy plants will tolerate such conditions.

4 **South-facing walls** reflect heat and so can provide the perfect planting opportunity for less hardy plants. They are traditionally used for growing and ripening fruit like peaches and plums, and for ornamentals such as roses, which may flower earlier due to the extra warmth.

5 **Crevices** by steps or between rocks can create ideal spots for some plants, particularly alpines, that require excellent drainage. Alpines thrive in full sun, in thin soil in cracks in walls, or rock gardens— these mimic conditions in their natural habitat.

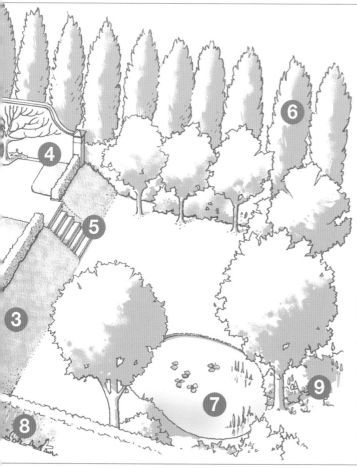

6 **Shelter belts** slow wind speed over some distance, creating a niche for large, leafy plants that can be made ragged or lose too much water in a more open location.

7 **Ponds** are ideal for submerged plants such as waterlilies, but consider also creating a boggy area to vastly extend the range of marginal and moisture-loving species you can grow and help attract more wildlife. Site them at the lowest point of the garden where they will look most natural.

8 **Hedges** can provide a plain backdrop for dramatic herbaceous plants. However, large, woody plants need plenty of water, and can often leave surrounding soil dry and impoverished. If they face north they can result in dry shade, which few plants can tolerate.

9 **Deep, damp shade** is ideal for lush, leafy plants that dislike high temperatures. Damp shade can either be sheltered and relatively frost-free or, if a barrier such as a hedge or fence is creating a frost pocket (*see p.56*), be cold and slow to thaw in winter.

Making the most of sunny sites

Sun-lovers tend to be among the most free-flowering of all garden plants. If you are lucky enough to have a sunny garden with reliably moist soil—from a natural water course, perhaps—you will be able to grow a wide range of plants. But more often, sun combines with little rain and you find that the soil dries out in summer. In a dry site, the trick is to select those plants that can cope with a lack of moisture and don't need constant watering, which is time-consuming and costly both to the environment and to your pocket.

Other needs

In addition to full sun, drought-adapted plants generally need some other things:
• Good drainage: few drought-tolerant plants will put up with a waterlogged soil in winter. As a general rule, it is cold combined with wet that kills plants, not cold alone.

Sun-loving *Verbena bonariensis* flowers from June until November, attracting bees, butterflies, and moths that bring color, sound, and movement to the garden.

• Low nutrient levels: overfertilizing encourages fast growth of soft, sappy foliage, which wilts in hot weather. Plants grown in poor soils also flower more profusely and for longer.
• Good air circulation: this helps reduce fungal diseases and rotting at the plant's "neck" (the point at which the plant emerges from the soil).

Often, a garden may have the right climatic conditions for these plants but unsuitably wet, heavy soil. In this case it is essential to improve the drainage so that plants are able to survive the winter months. Incorporate plenty of sandy grit in the topsoil—down to a depth of 10in (25cm) or so—or, alternatively, make raised beds using stone, brick, or wood. Build the retaining walls at least 16in (40cm) high, add a 4in (10cm) layer of ¾in (20mm) gravel in the bottom, and fill to planting level with gritty topsoil. Individual plants can be

Recognizing sun-loving plants

The best plants to use in a sunny garden with "average"-to-dry soil are those that would naturally be found in exposed positions with high light levels, low rainfall, and poor, fast-draining soils. Plants that can cope in such locations are, with a bit of practice, easy to identify because there are several characteristics to look for that have evolved for this reason. A sunny garden planted with suitable plants, such as rock roses and artemisias, will be much easier to establish and maintain than one with poorly chosen plants.

Rock rose
(*Helianthemum*)

Silver or gray leaves reflect heat and sunlight. Many silvery plants, particularly artemisias such as the *Artemisia alba* 'Canescens' shown here, are superb foliage plants.

A low-growing habit helps reduce the drying and damaging effects of wind in exposed places. This rose root (*Rhodiola rosea*) also conserves water with its fleshy leaves, silvery green foliage, and a thick, water-storing root.

Waxy leaves, like those on the pretty, white-flowered *Cistus salviifolius*, are coated with a thick waterproof layer to slow down moisture loss and reduce leaf scorch in extremely hot weather.

Small leaves, such as those of this rock rose, *Helianthemum nummularium*, reduce the surface area through which moisture can be lost. Some shrubs, such as Spanish broom (*Genista hispanica*), barely have leaves at all.

Individual plants can be planted onto raised mounds up to 12in (30cm) high and 3ft (1m) across. This is a very old technique and is especially effective for trees and shrubs.

Drought-tolerant, sun-loving plants are perfect for a variety of planting styles including sunny beds and borders, and they often thrive in containers on a patio, for example. Classic Mediterranean plants, including herbs like lavender and rosemary, are often used in formal knot gardens and parterres but they are, perhaps, at their best in informal, naturalistic styles. Gravel paths can draw the eye through the garden, winding among mounds of bright flowers and silvery foliage, interspersed with aromatic herbs and shrubs.

Top 20 plants for sunny sites

Allium 'Globemaster'
Artemisia arborescens
Calamagrostis
 brachytricha (a grass)
Cistus 'Greyswood
 Pink'
Cytisus 'Boskoop
 Ruby'
Elaeagnus 'Quicksilver'
Eremurus stenophyllus

Eschscholzia
 californica
Euphorbia characias
 'Lambrook Gold'
Kniphofia caulescens
Lavendula stoechas
Nepeta 'Six Hills Giant'
Nerine bowdenii
Nigella damascena
 (love-in-a-mist)

Ozothamnus
 rosmarinifolius 'Silver
 Jubilee'
Perovskia 'Blue Spire'
Phlomis italica
Stipa gigantea (a grass)
Tulipa saxatilis
Zauscheneria californica
 'Dublin'

A dry garden is an excellent choice for an exposed, windy site. The one shown here is on a hillside that evokes a rocky, Mediterranean slope by using silvery, spiky-leaved plants that weave in and out of large boulders. Despite its size, it contains plenty of inspiration for domestic gardeners.

Juicy peaches, nectarines, and apricots can be grown to perfection against a south-facing wall, where the maximum amount of sun and heat will make sure that they ripen, even farther north than their natural range.

Making the most of shade

You may consider a shady area to be gloomy, with far less potential than a sunny one, but in truth there are plenty of plants that thrive in shade. Moreover, shade is seldom at a constant level throughout the day and across the seasons, so observation is essential. In a north-facing garden you may find that close to the house, the shade cast is deep and constant, but that areas farther away are in sun at certain times of the day. Perhaps your garden is actually quite sunny, but a group of trees at one end, or in a neighboring garden, have created areas of shade. The amount of shade will vary according to how tall the trees are and whether they are deciduous or evergreen.

As always, plants that are adapted to the conditions will be the most successful; those that prefer shade are easily spotted (*see opposite*). Reliably moist soil in shade will open up opportunities for species that would naturally grow at the edges of streams and ponds, while very dry shade will require a different, more limited, range of plants.

Improving the soil

The main problem in a shady garden is usually the soil conditions. Trees growing in and around your garden require tremendous amounts of water and nutrients and can leave the surrounding soil dry and barren. That said, if you

Moist shade is enjoyed by a number of plants and they will do even better if you improve the soil and, perhaps, thin out some tree branches so the shade is less dense.

are lucky enough to garden on the edge of old woodland, your soil will have been enriched over centuries through a buildup of leaf litter. Shade cast by a building, depending on the exposure, can result in soil that is either dry and thin, or dank and structureless.

Soil pH (*see pp.38–39*) can be affected by trees—a large pine tree, for example, can sometimes acidify the soil around it as its needles fall and rot, and this will affect the variety

Ways to reduce the impact of a tree

Thinning, pollarding, coppicing, or "lifting the crown" of trees lets light down to the ground. This will help woodland flowers establish, especially if combined with improvement of 0

- **Pollarding:** all the main branches are regularly pruned back to the trunk or stem.
- **Coppicing:** trees or shrubs are cut down to ground level to promote multiple, vigorous, and decorative new shoots.
- **Thinning:** removes alternate branches.
- **Crown-lifting:** The lowest branches are removed to raise the height of the canopy.

Pollarding   Coppicing   Thinning   Crown-lifting

Living life in the shade

As with sun-loving plants, shade-tolerant species have adapted over millennia to the conditions in which they grow. You can recognize shade-lovers in the following ways:

Flowering in spring or fall makes the most of the relatively high light and high rainfall conditions when deciduous trees are leafless. Many bulbs—from winter snowdrops and spring daffodils to autumn cyclamen—use this strategy. They make the most of the short window of opportunity, flowering and replenishing their food stores, then spending the rest of the year dormant beneath ground.

Ability to move, either by running roots such as those of *Anemone hupehensis* or scrambling stems like honeysuckle, allows plants to grow toward areas with higher light levels. Some plants have flexible leaf stalks so that they can angle their leaves to catch the maximum light available.

Large leaves maximize the surface area through which light is absorbed. The leaves of this evergreen bergenia are also thick and leathery, helping reduce water loss.

Dark pigmentation in leaves allows plants to photosynthesize more effectively in low light conditions. Many ericaceous (acid-loving) woodland plants, including camellias, have very dark green, glossy leaves.

Densely packed leaves increase the light-collecting surface area. Some ferns, such as *Polystichum setiferum*, are also covered in hairs to trap moisture, so that they can establish and survive in comparatively dry soil.

of plants you can grow there. All of these problems can be overcome with a little know-how and effort.

Since most shade-tolerant plants originate from woodland environments, it makes sense to try to re-create similar conditions in your own garden by incorporating as much organic matter—composted bark, homemade leaf mold, and garden compost are most suitable (*see pp. 45–47*)—into the soil as possible. This can take time, especially under trees where roots prevent digging in compost to any depth. Here it is best to lay the compost on the surface as a mulch, and keep applying it every spring and fall so that it breaks down slowly into the soil or is drawn down by earthworms.

Letting in more light

Reducing very dense shade vastly increases the number of plants you can grow, and you can improve light levels in a number of simple ways. If the shade is cast by buildings, extra light can be reflected into the garden by using whitewash on walls. If dense tree canopies are to blame then thinning, pollarding, coppicing, or lifting the crown will increase light on the

Top 20 plants for shady sites

Actaea pachypoda	*Euphorbia amygdaloides* var. *robbiae*	*Matteuccia struthiopteris* (a fern)
Convallaria majalis	*Galanthus nivalis*	*Milleum effusum* 'Aureum' (a grass)
Daphne bholua 'Jaqueline Postill'	*Geranium phaeum*	*Rhododendron* 'Songbird'
Digitalis purpurea	*Helleborus foetidus*	*Sarcococca hookeriana* var. *digyna*
Dryopteris erythrosora (a fern)	*Hosta sieboldiana*	*Tiarella cordifolia*
Epimedium perralderianum	*Iris foetidissima*	*Trillium grandiflorum*
	Luzula nivea	
	Mahonia japonica	

ground (*see opposite*). Crown-lifting can create some lovely effects. By removing the bottom few branches and thinning out those above, a tree stops being a solid block and is given a see-through quality. Pollarding and coppicing give underplantings three or four years of enhanced light levels to help them get established. For some plants, like trillium, this kind of management is essential.

Painting a wall with a light-reflective paint—or even just a whitewash—will boost the amount of available light by "bouncing" it back into the garden.

Dealing with wet, sticky soils

Wet, sticky, clay soils can be among the hardest to work with: it is all too easy to destroy their structure and leave behind a gooey, unworkable mess. There is no need to be depressed about this, however, because clay can be the most rewarding of all soils if prepared well and planted with things that appreciate its moist, fertile nature.

Working wet soils is best attempted when the soil is at its driest, assuming it dries to some degree at some point in the year. This can entail cultivating at unusual times of the year, such as midsummer, and planting in early rather than late autumn when the soil is still warm and comparatively dry. It may even result in summer cultivation followed by spring planting. There are advantages to this approach since it ensures that, rather than sitting in wet soil through the winter, young plants can start actively growing and producing new roots as soon as they are put in the ground. How much cultivation is needed depends on how wet the soil is, and to what depth—this is easily determined by digging inspection pits at varying times of the year and in different locations (*see pp.36–37*). Armed with this knowledge you can then decide whether it is worth working with the prevailing conditions or better to try to manipulate them.

Top 20 plants for wet, sticky soil

Acorus gramineus	*Hosta* 'Wide Brim'	*Lythrum virgatum* 'Rosy
Alnus incana 'Aurea'	*Iris pseudacorus*	Gem'
Astilbes	*Juncus effusus* f. *spiralis*	*Primula bulleyana*
Caltha palustris	(a rush)	*Rheum palmatum*
Carex pendula (a sedge)	*Ligularia dentata*	*Rodgersia podophylla*
Darmera peltata	'Desdemona'	*Salix daphnoides*
Filipendula venusta	*Lysichiton*	*Smilacina racemosa*
'Rubra'	*camtschatcensis*	
Gunnera manicata	*Lysimachia ephemerum*	

Damp and drought

Soil that fluctuates from wet in the winter to dry in the summer can be improved by incorporating materials to improve drainage into about the top 12in (30cm) of soil. This helps water move through the soil and also creates air spaces so that roots can penetrate more easily. Grit, sand, and gravel are excellent long-term drainage improvers. Add loads of organic matter as well, to help the soil hold water through dry spells so that your moisture-loving plants don't suffer. Individual plants, especially trees and shrubs, can be planted on mounds of soil. This is an old technique to

Soil that is always moist can support many specialized plants that would be impossible to grow otherwise. If you have a large, wet area, then you could take your cue from nature and create a water meadow garden. This will not only make life easier but it is also a good way to attract wildlife.

A raised bed is a good option where conditions alternate between wet and dry, making cultivation especially difficult. It needs to be at least 16in (40cm) high and can be built from a variety of materials including wood, brick, and stone. Filled with topsoil improved with organic matter such as garden compost and, for clay soils, ample grit, it offers better-drained conditions.

prevent water from naturally settling where the soil has been disturbed—which often results in a newly planted specimen immediately drowning in a water-filled pit.

Reliably moist soil

If you are lucky enough to have a soil that always remains moist, the opportunity to grow huge, lush bog plants is just too good to pass up. Incorporating a little grit or light soil may aid structure to some degree, and the application of thick, dry mulch, such as chipped bark, is certainly worthwhile since it will help retain the moisture but also allow some pedestrian traffic—useful when it comes to weeding or replanting. In very damp gardens, consider constructing decks and raised boardwalks to provide seating areas and paths. You can then enjoy your garden all through the year without getting muddy feet or compacted soil.

How plants tolerate wet soil

Moisture-loving and marginal plants are suitable for reliably wet soils because they have adapted in various ways so they don't drown in wet, anerobic (airless) conditions. Moisture-loving plants thrive in the kind of moist soil found by ponds, streams, and rivers. Marginal plants are similar but prefer to grow in shallow water, or reliably wet soil that is regularly submerged.

Air channels that run from shoot to root allow oxygen to circulate around bog plants like arum lilies, whose roots would otherwise be starved of oxygen.

Shallow roots are typical because there is no need to search for water—bog buttercups, for example, spread across the soil surface.

Huge leaves are characteristic of wetland plants such as rodgersias; because there is no shortage of water it doesn't matter if they lose it rapidly.

Special equipment is used by some species. The swamp cypress is able to live in water because it develops breathing apparatus on its roots—the plant equivalent of a snorkel. Known as "cypress knees," they push up through the water surface and take in oxygen for the submerged roots to breathe.

Dealing with free-draining soils

By late summer, free-draining, sandy soils are often very short of water, and many plants just won't survive. Some plants, however, will thrive under these trying conditions (*see box, below*). Trees and shrubs, including conifers, are also good choices for these soils. Once established, their deep root systems make them pretty much drought-proof, although they will need watering for the first year or two until they have settled in. Nevertheless, even when you are growing well-adapted plants, it is still worth adding an organic soil improver to help soil structure and stability without restricting drainage. Composted bark, garden compost, and spent mushroom compost are all good choices.

Herb hedges are excellent running alongside garden paths and thrive on dry, well-drained soils. Rosemary (*left*) and lavender (*far left*), here *Lavandula* x *intermedia* Dutch Group, are both suitable for low hedges that smell wonderful as you brush past them.

Sandy soils

Light, sandy soils are easy to work, but water runs freely through them, washing out nutrients as it goes. Adding plenty of organic matter is important for nutrients and to help soak up and keep moisture. In addition, apply a general-purpose fertilizer in spring to top up nutrient levels. Rose fertilizer is a good choice because it tends to be rich in magnesium, an element often in short supply in sandy soils. Calcium is also easily washed out, and sandy soils are often acidic. You can easily check with a test kit (*see p.39*). In severe cases you may need to add lime every five years.

How plants tolerate drought

Plants that naturally grow in dry environments or on well-drained soils have several ways of coping with drought conditions. Nevertheless, a bit of extra care will work wonders. Water plants very thoroughly before and after planting and keep them just clear of the ground to leave room for a generous mulch (*see pp.44–45*), which will help retain soil moisture.

Thick, fleshy leaves have an large cells capable of holding moisture over a long period. *Agave americana* is a classic example, hailing from the dry deserts of the southwestern United States.

Hairy leaves work by trapping a layer of moist, still air close to the leaf surface so that it loses water less quickly. The pasque flower, *Pulsatilla vulgaris*, has softly hairy leaves and is available in many colors, such as the red 'Rubra'.

Long, thick tap roots, for example those of verbascums, yuccas, and this sea holly, reach deep into the soil in the quest for water, and store moisture and starch for lean periods.

Summer dormant plants retreat below ground to avoid heat. Many spring bulbs, including tulips, developed this strategy to avoid the heat of the Mediterranean summer. Some other types of plant, like *Geranium tuberosum*, do the same.

Many aromatic herbs come from the Mediterranean hillsides and enjoy dry, well-drained soils. They often have attractive foliage and pretty flowers, in addition to culinary uses.

Sandy soils are also prone to compaction. Just as breakfast cereals settle in their package on the way home from the supermarket, very sandy soils gradually settle and pack together. Again, plenty of organic matter is the answer; dig it in before planting whenever the soil is dry enough to work.

Lawns on sandy soil are especially liable to suffer from speedy drainage and compaction. Fall spiking, fertilizing, top-dressing with organic matter, and scarifying will be needed to keep them looking good (*see pp. 176–77*).

Chalky soils

Chalky or limestone soils are also very free-draining but are rich in calcium. Don't even think about trying acid-loving plants—camellias, for example—they will never really thrive, if they survive at all. Other plants, even those adapted to chalky soil, will greatly benefit from mulching, watering, and feeding. Organic matter, added frequently, is vital, although it should be used generously because it breaks down very quickly in lime-rich soils.

The best sod grasses prefer mildly acidic soil so lawns on chalky soil are seldom quite as good as on other types. Consider going for wildflower-rich mixes or eco-lawns, where clover in the lawn keeps it green in dry weather and adds nitrogen, which saves the need for fertilizing.

Top 20 plants for dry soils

Agave americana	*Genista lydia*	*Salvia nemorosa* (and its
Artemisia abrotanum	*Geranium* x *oxonianum*	cultivars)
Ceanothus 'Blue Mound'	'Wargrave Pink'	Sedums
Cytisus (broom)	*Kniphofia caulescens*	*Stipa barbata* (a grass)
Erodiums	*Lavandula angustifolia*	*Tamarix tetrandra*
Eryngium x *oliverianum*	(and its cultivars)	*Teucrium hircanicum*
Euphorbia amygdaloides	*Othonna cheirifolia*	*Tulbaghia violacea*
var. *robbiae*	*Phlomis fruticosa*	*Yucca filamentosa*

Dry shade is a tricky proposition: few plants can cope with the dual stress of dark and drought, but evergreen *Euphorbia amygdaloides* var. *robbiae* is one that can thrive.

Sandy soils in sun can get very dry, but *Tamarix tetrandra*, a small tree or shrub with feathery foliage and flowers, will grow well in such conditions, and in coastal climates.

Gardening on exposed sites

Like humans, plants are predominantly composed of water. This makes them prone to dehydration—a constant threat in an exposed garden, whether by the coast, inland, or at a high altitude. Wind can test plants to the limit, and only those species that are adapted to resist its drying effects, either by storing water in their leaves or roots, or by reducing the loss of water through their leaves, stand a chance.

On the positive side, exposed, open gardens usually have high light levels and excellent air circulation. This tends to reduce fungal disease and improve the flowering of plants such as roses, which hate being damp, especially when in bud. But strong sun can also fade subtle flower colors, and good air circulation can quickly turn to an eddying wind that damages plants.

Many exposure-tolerant plants originate in areas where the daylight hours are hot and dry and the nights are cold. Consequently, they share many of the same characteristics as plants that can cope with sun and drought (*see p.68*).

Coastal gardens suffer fewer frosts but must endure strong winds and salt spray. Low-growing species can cope especially well and will not interfere with stunning views.

Wind damage and stunting

Exposure causes slow, stunted growth—a tree in an exposed garden can be as little as half the size of one of the same age and species growing in a sheltered garden. Trees and shrubs can also be "pruned" by the prevailing wind. In an exposed inland garden, very cold winds are usually the main enemy. If you garden on a Pacific coast, you should benefit from a mainly frost-free climate because ocean temperatures rarely drop below freezing, and so keep the winds coming over them warm. On the down side, salt spray borne on the breeze can "fry" leaves and often kill plants as effectively as frost.

Wind-pruned trees and shrubs with weird and wonderful lopsided shapes can often be seen in the more open parts of the country.

Use plants to provide shelter

One way to counter the effects of wind on an exposed garden is to minimize it with a shelter belt of plants. Unlike solid walls and fences, which can cause wind to accelerate and eddy through a garden, plants slow it down gently (*see p.56*). Depending on how much room you have, a shelter belt can be anything from a hedge to a dense planting of trees and shrubs. One of the best hedging plants for seaside gardens is salt-tolerant *Griselinia littoralis*, while hornbeam (*Carpinus betulus*) makes a good, dense hedge for exposed inland gardens. In deeper plantings, use fast-growing trees and shrubs for rapid results, combined with slower-growing hardwood trees that can be "nursed" by the speedier species.

You can also use man-made windbreak materials. These usually take the form of a closely woven fabric mesh, which can be attached to regularly spaced posts, using tile or wood bars to prevent tearing. Use a single layer or double it up to give greater protection. A windbreak like this will slow the wind quite considerably over a short distance, making it the

Roses often thrive in exposed sites because the good air circulation helps prevent fungal diseases and general dampness. Choose varieties with strong flower-colors, such as 'Hertfordshire', that will resist fading in high light levels.

Top 20 plants for exposed sites

Inland	
Agrostemma githago	*Helichrysum italicum*
Artemisia ludoviciana	*Othonna cheirifolia*
'Valerie Finnis'	*Papaver rupifragum*
Bergenia 'Sunningdale'	*Potentilla megalantha*
Calamagrostis x *acutiflora*	*Teucrium hircanicum*
'Karl Foerster' (a grass)	
Ceanothus 'Blue	**Seaside or inland**
Mound'	*Crambe maritima*
Delosperma cooperi	*Eryngium* x *oliverianum*
Festuca glauca 'Elijah	*Euphorbia characias*
Blue' (a grass)	'Portuguese Velvet'
Geranium sanguineum	*Hippophae rhamnoides*
var. *striatum*	(also for shelter belts)
Glaucium flavum	*Phormium tenax*
	Sedum 'Herbstfreude'

perfect way to help establish shelter belt plants that might otherwise struggle to get going. The mesh can be removed as soon as the plants are settled—between three and five years. Individual plants can be cosseted in a similar way with a "cage" of mesh netting on posts, and trees or shrubs planted as small "whips" (usually one or two years old) can be given a head start if surrounded by a biodegradable plastic guard to create a warm and sheltered microclimate.

Success with exposure

Just because a garden is exposed doesn't mean that it can't be developed with style. Successful seaside gardens often take a cue from nature by using native plants that proliferate on the shoreline. These can then provide a backdrop for more exotic ornamentals. An alternative approach is to use shelter to grow plants that need more help to cope with the conditions. Thick wind-reducing plantings on the

boundaries of the garden, and a series of "garden rooms" surrounded by more hedges within, can create very sheltered places. In an area with a mild coastal climate, this will enable you to grow quite tender, exotic plants.

North America, however, has a huge range of regional climatic variation. In both the US and Canada, there are extremes of winter and summer temperatures throughout the continent; the land mass comprises everything from deserts and subtropical swamps to high mountains, plains, and prairies, Pacific, Atlantic, and Gulf Coast regions. What plants you choose to grow in these varied regions should reflect the prevailing climates within each area.

Shelter belts or hedges filter and slow wind very effectively to protect other plants in the garden. Choose plants of an appropriate size for your garden—pine trees (*Pinus*) will grow quite large, whereas roses (*Rosa*) are more compact.

Best shelter belt plants

Inland garden:	Seaside garden:
Acer campestre	*Griselinia littoralis*
Betula pendula	*Hippophae rhamnoides*
Carpinus betulus	*Pinus radiata*
Pinus sylvestris	*Quercus ilex*
Rosa rugosa	*Tamarix ramosissima*

Assessing your garden

Now you know a lot about your garden. You know the soil type and pH, you know whether it is sunny or shady, sheltered or exposed, and whether the soil is wet or dry. You even know the passage of the sun over your garden at various times of the day throughout the year—so important when deciding where to put a patio. You have already saved yourself a great deal of time, effort, and money, but there are still a few simple yet crucial questions you need to ask yourself:

• Who will use the garden? You may love spiky plants and ponds, but if you have a young family these will probably not be the best choice, or will at least need to be planned very carefully.

• What do you want to use the garden for? Gardens can be designed with entertaining in mind, as a fun space for children, or simply to show off a plant lover's collection. You might want to encourage wildlife, such as birds or butterflies, into your garden, which can be one of the most rewarding experiences, and in some

Flowers or fun? Children have a big impact on gardens, and if you have a young family you will probably want to include a lawn or play area. You will also need to think carefully about using thorny or poisonous plants, and features such as ponds.

cases can even help conservation efforts. You will need to consider how to balance your own needs with that of the wildlife you want to encourage. In many gardens, some or even all of these elements may be desirable.

• How much time can I spend taking care of it? Be realistic. Work out how much free time you have at the moment, without gardening, and then decide how much of that time you are willing to give up. On good soil, in a sheltered sunny site, few things are more pleasurable than puttering in the garden. But wintertime in a cold, exposed garden on clay soil can be very different indeed. The worst that can happen is that your garden defeats you and becomes a millstone rather than a pleasure, so this is an important question. Knowing how much time you want to spend will inform your plant choice, border sizes, even whether you have a lawn or not.

• What is the timescale for the garden? And what is your budget? It may be better to tackle a small area each year rather than embark on a grand and expensive plan. Start near the house with the area you see the most. This could involve laying a patio or redoing a border. Any hard landscaping should be part of an overall plan that can be carried out in sections as you can afford them. If there is a chance you will be moving, buying fast-growing plants might be a better idea than investing in long-term projects.

Entertaining outdoors is high on the list of many people's garden wants. If there is no room for a permanent grill, then consider a portable barbecue.

Which garden do you have?

Having thought about what you want from your garden and found out what you can reasonably expect to achieve, the next thing is to start to put it into practice. Your course of action will inevitably be affected by whether your garden is brand new, or you are working with an established or neglected garden. There are pros and cons to each scenario that will need careful thought.

New garden

In the case of a brand-new garden, the presence of builders' rubbish buried beneath something masquerading as soil is all but guaranteed. The most important aspects to consider are:

• **Your soil**. If it really is appaling, it may be tempting to buy topsoil. If so, make sure it is of good quality and from a local source. Good soil will be free from weeds and roots, with some natural aggregates and a nice, fresh smell. Reject soil that is dusty, stony, weedy, wet, or "blue." Soil turns blue when the air has been squeezed out; it is easy to spot—or rather to smell. Finally, and most importantly, check the pH to make sure it is as close as possible to your own garden's pH. Do this checking while the soil is still in the truck. A reputable supplier will not mind.

• **Planning**. Faced with a blank canvas it is all too easy to act without thinking ahead, and not get what you really want or need. Take a little time to go through the steps outlined in this chapter, observing not only your garden but also the wider landscape. Then you can begin to plan your own garden with confidence.

• **Establish your priorities**. Once your plan is complete, decide which elements should be established first and which ones can wait. While an ornamental pond and fountain may be top in the desirability stakes, it may be more practical to install a patio, garden shed, and a clothesline first.

Mature garden

If your garden is mature and established the task is, in a way, trickier. Here the considerations are quite different:

• **Do you like it?** Perhaps it is a beautiful cottage garden that is the envy of others, but you long for a minimalist approach? Reconstructing an established garden can be hard if others find nothing wrong with it, but putting your own personality on a place is all part of the experience of owning, developing, and enjoying a garden.

• **Choose what to keep**. There may be a number of features in the garden that are there for a very good reason. A mature tree might conceal a distant tower or overlooking windows, so consider all the existing features in your garden with care.

• **Assess the utilities and hard landscaping**. Gardens must be practical as well as beautiful and make good use of the space. It may be that previous owners saw the need for particular features through necessity and observation, so take time to be sure you are not removing something that you will have to put back. Conversely, the garden may be missing things you consider essential, like an outdoor faucet or space for a barbecue. Try to think practically to help avoid expensive errors.

Neglected garden

A neglected garden can be a real headache. Just where should you start? Before you do, think carefully about:

• **How to cope with the garden**. Beneath some neglected gardens are treasures waiting to be revealed, so it may well be worth a gentle examination first. This may guide your thinking on how to cope with renovating the garden as a whole.

• **Weeding**. Most neglected gardens have a good crop of weeds. On a small scale you can hand-weed; in a big garden, try tackling a section at a time. Using chemical weedkillers may be the only option if the problem is overwhelming. If you prefer not to use herbicides try clearing the area with a weed-eater, then cover it with light-excluding tarpaulin or old carpet, although this can take a few months to work.

• **A clean sweep**. If progressive renovation is out of the question, perhaps the best option is to think of the garden as "new" and consider the steps above.

Planning your garden 4

What do you need? • Planning color schemes • Design styles for beds and borders • How to draw up a planting plan

Design guidelines

The first step when planning your garden, whether you are faced with an overgrown jungle or an attractive yard that needs only minor adjustments, is to write down what you want from your space. Take time to visualize your dream garden. Does it include beds and borders packed with colorful plants, an activity area for the children, somewhere to entertain family and friends, or perhaps a combination of all three? Ask other members of your household to do the same and compare notes.

You also need to think about practicalities: Where will the trashcans go? Do you need a bike or tool shed? How much space is required for outdoor entertaining? Again, write down your answers to these questions so that you don't forget them when making your final plans.

A garden for everyone

If you have toddlers, place your borders toward the back of the plot and make a play area closer to the house where you can keep an eye on the children. Older children prefer to hide from nosy adults and will be happy at the far end of the garden. Remember, too, that boisterous youngsters and flower borders do not mix well, so consider erecting a screen, such as a pergola, trellis, or hedge, to demarcate their territory and prevent stray balls from damaging your plants.

Enthusiastic dogs that play on the lawn will not stop when confronted by a flower bed. In this case, it may be wise to place your plants in borders along the periphery of the plot or on a patio, rather than in beds in the middle.

Dogs love playing in gardens but few can be relied on to keep out of flower beds and borders. Protect your plants with low walls or hedges, and use heavy-based, stable containers.

Raised beds or sturdy wooden or stone edging also help prevent pets from using your flower garden as a playground.

In addition to making provisions for the family and pets, consider your own needs carefully. Establish where you are likely to sit in the main garden. Many houses have a patio or terrace by the house, but you may find a more suitable sheltered spot that catches the evening sunlight or provides the ideal place for lunch outside. Wrap beds and borders around your seating areas and fill them with scented and colorful plants that you can enjoy close up. These plants also attract insects and birds, providing a vibrant source of entertainment.

View from the sink

One of the most important views to note is from the kitchen window. Plan planting in this area to provide an enjoyable view as you stand at the sink. Or attract wildlife to watch by creating a small pool close to the

Screen play equipment from the rest of the garden with trees, shrubs, or other planting. In this way, you can create a semiprivate space for the children and a beautiful "grown-up" garden to enjoy.

window, but make sure it has sloping sides so that small animals, which might fall in, can easily scramble out again.

Also look at the view beyond your plot. If you look out over a lake, sea, or countryside, knit the landscape into your own designs by erecting a semitransparent or low border fence, or planting a hedge that blends into the background. On the other hand, if you are too close to neighboring houses, erect screens or covered pergolas that offer privacy.

Journeys of discovery

Design interesting walkways through your garden so that your visitors can see the features and planting from different perspectives. In small gardens, use diagonal lines to create longer paths that swing from one side of the plot to the other, making the garden feel larger. Meandering S-shaped paths have a similar effect.

For a large garden, use diagonals, S shapes, or more formal straight paths that dissect the space. Paths in the shape of a cross are effective in spacious gardens, and in small formal square plots, where neat parterre-style beds can be used to fill the gaps between the walkways.

Be sure that your paths end with a focal point to lead the visitor on, or to stop them in their tracks to admire the view.

Site patios and seating areas in warm, sheltered parts of the garden. Surround the area with shrubby plants to protect against chilly winds and provide shade from the midday sun.

Use intriguing focal points to draw visitors through the garden. Shapely urns, either filled with flowers or left empty, make beautiful eye-catching statements in gardens of all sizes.

Style and structure

Think about the style of garden you want. Do you like order and precision or are you drawn to more informal, naturalistic designs? Browse through home and garden magazines or visit friends' and neighbors' gardens for inspiration. As you wander around, take photographs and notes to remind you of what you liked when you get home.

The style you choose will affect the size, shape, and position of your beds and borders as well as the hard landscaping. Even if you do not want a neatly ordered or very formal garden, it is worth introducing a basic structure, so that your garden still looks interesting in the winter months. Consider planting a tree, and outline beds or borders with some form of edging, such as bricks, paving stones, clay tiles, or a low hedge to help define and structure the space. The harsh outlines will soon soften once the growing season starts and plants spill over the rough edges.

If you want to achieve an informal look, use flowing lines and oval- or kidney-shaped beds and borders; avoid wavy or

Formal gardens are created using straight lines, geometric shapes, and symmetrical patterns. Simple planting designs work well—don't be afraid to repeat plants.

wiggly lines, which can often look messy, especially when planting blurs the edges.

To create a neat, formal look, try geometric shapes such as squares, rectangles, and circles for lawns and patios. And establish a crisp design by setting carefully structured planting and hard landscaping in a symmetrical pattern.

Large swaths of colorful planting in broad, curved borders have a dynamic effect on designs. Find out when your chosen plants flower, and plan a succession of color all year.

All-season show

Take time to plan your planting, and you will be rewarded with nonstop color and interest throughout the year. Pay particular attention to displays that can be seen from the house, so that you can look out on a beautifully evolving scene, even in winter.

Evergreen trees and shrubs provide structure in winter (*see pp. 108–149*) and help block out unsightly views. Mix these with perennials that have attractive seedheads and retain their form rather than dying back down to the ground. Sedums, achilleas, and echinops are good examples of such sturdy perennials. Even though their winter display is not bright and may be snow covered, they create interesting shapes and prevent your borders from looking flat and lifeless. Perennials also provide a wonderful spectacle on frosty mornings, drawing birds into the garden to feast on the seeds and on insects hibernating inside empty pods.

Grasses offer invaluable interest in fall and winter gardens. The dried flower spikes of some, such as giant feather grass, moor grass, and Japanese silver grass, last well into fall, while miscanthus and calamagrostis remain upright until spring.

As the seasons progress, make frequent visits to gardens and garden centers to see what is in bloom. Again, make

Over winter, leave herbaceous plants to stand, rather than cutting back the dead growth. Their dried seedheads and stems will take on a magical quality when dusted with frost or snow.

notes and use your favorites in your garden plans, checking first that they suit your site and soil (*see pp. 32–51*). Also take note of their heights and spreads; this information will help you decide where to plant them (*see pp. 84–85*).

Working with an existing garden

If you have just moved and have an existing garden, take a year to see what comes up and how the plants perform. Dispose of any that you don't like or that do not thrive, and list the plants you wish to incorporate into your new plan.

Lift bulbs as soon as the foliage has started to turn brown, and lift and divide hardy perennials in fall or spring. Grasses are best left until spring before being moved.

Making a plan

Pull all your notes and ideas together and sketch an outline of your garden on a piece of paper. Either photocopy your sketch or lay tracing paper over it. Draw on trees, patios, paths, beds, and borders, and try a few variations until you are happy with one design. If you want just a rough idea of where to make new flower beds, your sketches don't need to be too accurate, but for a more detailed drawing, measure your garden and create a scale plan on graph paper. Use a scale of 1:100 for a medium to large plot, or 1:50 or 1:20 for a smaller spot. A scale plan is important if you are estimating the cost and buying hard landscaping materials, although a contractor or landscaper can also do this for you.

Focus on front gardens

Although front gardens may not be used as much as back gardens, you walk through them every day and they give a home that all-important "curb appeal." An interesting mix of flowers, scent, and foliage will send you off to work in a happy mood and provide a warm welcome home. Where winters are long and snow-filled, plant shrubs with colored bark, such as red osier, and trees with interesting outlines or bark, such as crabapples, pagoda dogwood, or Amur cherry. Herald the coming of spring with early crocuses and daffodils, such as *Narcissus* 'February Gold', create a blaze of color in summer with perennials and bedding plants, and put the sparkle into autumn with the fiery foliage of Japanese maples and cotinus.

Daffodils and English daisies add spring color to a tapestry of foliage plants, including boxwood, hostas, and other emerging perennials.

Themed gardens

If you are stuck for ideas for your yard, you could create a themed garden to give you a focus. For example, a Zen garden includes raked gravel areas, rocks, boulders, and planting designs to copy. Mediterranean gardens also have a well-defined look, with gravel beds filled with sun-loving plants and herbs.

Choosing color combinations

Flowers and plants offer an exceptional color palette that would make any artist envious. The subtlety in shades and hues, further enhanced by the different textures of the leaves and petals, creates a vast range of colors to play with. Remember that plants are not the only source of color in a garden, and it is also important to consider fences, walls, paving, and containers, all of which add to the final effect.

For some, the huge choice of color in the garden offers an exciting design opportunity, but for others, choosing color schemes can be nothing short of daunting. Many different color theories are used by garden designers, but if you are nervous that your garden may end up a frenzy of clashing hues or a poor palette of dull shades, the color wheel offers a helpful guide (*see below*).

Opposing colors

The color wheel is made up of primary colors (red, yellow, and blue), and secondary colors (orange, green, and purple), which are formed when the two primary colors on either side are mixed together. These primary and secondary colors provide the foundation for successful color schemes. You will see that each primary color sits opposite a secondary color. These "opposing colors" are complementary and work extremely well when used together in a garden context.

Using opposing colors guarantees an eye-catching display. This simple but effective combination of fiery orange cosmos and purple-blue morning glories works especially well.

Thus, red goes well with green, yellow with purple, and blue with orange.

Considering that most foliage is green, and that—on a good day—the sky is blue, it is difficult to be strict about this theory since almost all colors in the garden go well with blue and green. However, it is undeniable that blue and orange do combine very well, and that yellow and purple create a pleasing match.

Adjoining colors

Opposing colors are contrasting, and create visual excitement, but they can be a little overbearing. This is where "adjoining colors" come into play to tone down the overall effect. Adjoining colors sit side-by-side on the color wheel, and you can use them to create more subtle color combinations.

Adjoining colors were particularly favored by Gertrude Jekyll, the doyenne of herbaceous borders. Jekyll created many amazing gardens in the early 20th century, and her ideas still influence designers today. She divided the colors into two categories: cool colors, consisting of blues, purples, lilacs, and pinks, and hot colors, which include yellows, oranges, and reds.

Just as gray tones take out the harsh contrast between white and black, Jekyll saw that it was important to use the in-between shades to create subtle blends. So, instead of planting only yellows and reds, fuse the two with shades of orange and some plants with yellow and red in their foliage to carry the color theme throughout the year.

The color wheel

A color wheel is an at-a-glance guide to which colors work well together. It is easy to use and takes the guess work out of creating successful color combinations in the garden.

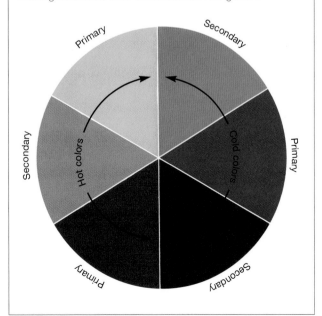

Monochrome planting

If you are disciplined enough you can restrict your palette to just one color. You could, for example, create a sunny yellow border, or a cool silvery-white one. It may seem straightforward to plant a monochrome garden using plants of the same color, but it is important to try to create variation and contrast within a plan, since without that it will appear bland and monotonous.

For example, when using white, do not restrict yourself to pure white flowers, but also allow cream, lime green, as well as pinkish and mauve-tinted whites. Likewise, choose the foliage of the plants carefully, and include pale to dark green, gray, silver, and blue. When opting for yellows or reds, go for the full tonal spectrum within those colors, and mirror your color choice in the accompanying foliage.

Green

This is the most dominant and important color in the garden, and there are myriad shades of green to choose from. For color that will outlast a flowering display, mix foliage in various shades of lime, apple, and blue-green.

Monochrome schemes can be monotonous unless you include interesting foliage colors. Here, cream and white flowers are mirrored by silver and yellow variegated hostas and grasses.

Seasonal color schemes

One of the most effective ways to use color is to allow the seasons to dictate the palette. In spring, nature seems so relieved that the dreary weather is over, it responds with a burst of sunny colors and every imaginable shade of green. As the season progresses into early summer the color palette calms down a little, concentrating on clean, fresh colors, such as the blues of delphiniums and geraniums, and white and pink roses and peonies. As summer heats up, so do the colors: warm yellows, burnt oranges, and velvety reds signal hot, sunny days. The fading light that heralds autumn is reflected in the subdued tones of asters. Winter's colors, while more subtle, are just as effective—white snowdrops never fail to cut through the gloom.

Spring sees an abundance of sunshine yellows and vibrant golds typified by narcissi.

Early summer has a rich palette. Here magenta gladioli, lilac alliums, and thalictrum shine in the sun.

Late summer flower colors heat up before autumn with amber heleniums and golden crocosmias.

Winter won't be dreary with ice-white snowdrops and cheery pink cyclamen.

Planning beds and borders

Strictly speaking, a border is a planting bed that runs along a property line, such as a fence, hedge, or wall, although traditionally borders were often used to enclose formal parterres or lawns. Beds, on the other hand, are free standing and frequently used as focal points in the center of a lawn or gravel garden. Formal gardens, such as parterres, use geometric-shaped beds, often edged with low, evergreen hedging and set out in a symmetrical pattern. Beds have always been used for growing vegetables, herbs, and flowers, and still offer a practical solution for vegetable gardens, with plants on all sides receiving sun throughout the day.

Traditional herbaceous borders

The true herbaceous border consists of only herbaceous perennials and is designed to perform from early spring into the autumn. The first herbaceous borders appeared in the 19th century, but their popularity did not truly blossom until the early 20th century, when Gertrude Jekyll brought them into the gardening limelight. In Jekyll's day herbaceous borders were often only expected to last for six to eight weeks in summer, while themed areas, such as iris gardens, peony beds, dahlia borders, and autumn gardens, took care of the other seasons. In our small, modern gardens, few can accommodate such themed garden sections, and we need our borders to perform for as long as possible.

Mixed beds and borders

Unlike a herbaceous border, a mixed one consists of different types of plants, as the name suggests. Although perennials still play a key role, they are assisted by shrubs and roses and may also include annual flowers to prolong the performance.

If the border is backed by a wall or trellis, the height of the flower display can be increased with a backdrop of climbers (*see pp. 134–39*). You can also create instant height within a border by adding a climbing frame, such as a tripod, for annual or perennial climbers to scramble over.

For the majority of gardeners, a mixed border is the answer to their needs, offering summer flowers and structure in the winter as well. This type of border does have its drawbacks, however, since woody plants have wide, spreading roots that take water and nutrients away from the perennials. As shrubs grow, they can also shade out smaller plants. One solution is to plant compact shrubs with smaller root systems among your herbaceous plants.

Plants billow over the path in these informal borders. A combination of grasses and herbaceous perennials provides a colorful display all summer, while background shrubs and trees offer year-round structure.

Lines of uniform planting confer an air of formality to this border. The boxwood trees have been pruned into balls and the foliage of berberis and salvia, rather than flowers, injects color.

Annual planting

Borders planted with annuals can be very labor intensive but will provide a great show throughout the summer. Since many flower over a long period, the overall effect can be much more impressive than an herbaceous border, where plants come and go as the season progresses.

The problem is that once the show is over in fall and everything has been cleared, the bed or border is empty for the next few months. The ground also has to be dug and prepared each spring before any seeds can be sown.

Shaping your borders

Although the majority of borders are formal rectangles that cling to the boundaries, the front edges can be curved to create an informal look. If you have a pair of facing borders, you could weave a path down the middle like a meandering stream, and simply let the borders to fill the spaces on either side. To allow easy access in summer when planting flows over the edges, be sure the path is at least 5ft (1.5m) wide.

An S-shaped pathway also creates planting spaces of varying depths. This is particularly useful in smaller gardens, providing you with a few wide areas for trees, large shrubs, and swaths of perennials.

Whatever your garden style, borders under 3ft (1m) wide can be very limiting; any less than this, and you will be continually battling against plants threatening to outgrow their boundaries, shade out lawns, or cover pathways.

Styles of beds

Beds can be informal or formal, depending on their shape and design. Those that are part of a formal layout or parterre are usually geometric in shape and neatly edged, while informal beds have curved outlines and less defined edges.

Formal beds are typified by neatness and symmetry. Planting is kept in its allotted space with walls of closely cropped boxwood (*above*), wood strips, steel bands, clay tiles, or even glass bottle bottoms.

Informal beds have softer outlines and can be positioned to lead the eye through your plot to a focal point. An easy way to define the shape of an informal bed is to lay down a hose on the ground, and follow the smooth, generous curves it creates.

Beds are ideal for growing vegetables since they allow you to tend your patch from all sides, eliminating the need to tread on the soil and damage its structure. Choose an open, sunny site for your beds.

Making a planting plan

Be generous when marking out the area for your bed or border. If you can afford the space, allow at least 10ft (3m) to provide a good planting width. You can then build up several layers of plants, one behind the other, and use shrubs and climbers to create height toward the back. If the choice is between two narrow borders and one deep one, you'll find the larger one more rewarding, regardless of how intimidating it may seem at first.

Key plants

Working from an accurate base plan makes designing a new bed or border much easier; it also helps you work out how many plants you will need to fill it (*see opposite*). When selecting the planting, think of your border as a stage performance and pick out the leading cast. This should include plants that have an important presence because of their handsome shape, decorative leaves, or long flowering season. Good candidates include colorful foliage shrubs, such as berberis and cotinus, as well as many grasses, sedums, and euphorbias. Repeating these every three feet (1m) or so brings rhythm into a design, which, in turn, makes it more soothing to look at.

Think of where you would like to see your stars: Sedums flower in fall and are good front-of-the-border plants, while

Key plants, such as tall wispy grasses, add focal points to borders and beds. Structural foliage plants are useful inclusions as their impact is more lasting than transient flowers.

the taller grasses, such as moor grass or feather reed grass, are better placed in the middle or background.

Mark the plants on your plan with a circle representing their final spread. Most of the larger perennials will spread to 18in (45cm), while smaller ones will reach 12in (30cm). Check plant labels for the spreads of shrubs and note that their size can be affected by your soil and garden conditions.

Planning in color

Once the key plants have been added to your plan, start moving in backup players that offer more subtle effects. Keep a note of their flowering times and colors, and, if in doubt, make an overlay with tracing paper, onto which you can mark the color of each plant using different markers or symbols. Do a few overlays for the different seasons to show when your chosen cast is in flower, where the gaps are, and at what time of year they need to be filled.

Contrasting flower shapes

Think of the contrasts in flower shape as well as the color, height, and season. Plants that produce spiky flowers, such as veronicas, delphiniums, foxgloves, and verbascums, or upright, linear foliage, such as irises or daylilies, are useful for introducing vertical accents. Those that produce round disklike flowerheads, such as sedums, yarrows, fennel, and all the cow-parsley relatives, create a horizontal plane. Mixing these two types of flowers paints an exciting picture. Distinctive spherical shapes, such as flowering onions and globe thistle, add to the structure. These help create some order among the flowers with less clearly defined outlines, such as gypsophila, lady's mantle, and catmint.

Measuring and planning a flower border

To create a plan for a rectangular or square border, measure the length and width and transfer your measurements to graph paper. For a curved border, take a few measurements at right angles from a fixed point, such as a fence, to the edge of the curve. Draw the property line on your graph paper and mark the measurements to build up a picture of the curve.

Now draw in your plants, positioning tall plants toward the back and shorter ones descending in height to the front. You can add interest by breaking this pattern with tall see-through plants, such as grasses, planted in the middle of the border to create an undulating effect.

Border size: approx 10ft x 5ft
(3m x 1.5m)

Example plant list

1. *Acanthus spinosus* x 1
2. *Geranium himalayense* x 3
3. *Rudbeckia laciniata* x 3
4. *Dryopteris filix-mas* x 3
5. *Macleaya microcarpa* 'Kelway's Coral Plume' x 2
6. *Carex pendula* x 1
7. *Leucanthemum* x *superbum* 'Wirral Supreme' x 3
8. *Campanula latiloba* x 3
9. *Aquilegia vulgaris* x 3
10. *Briza maxima* x 3

Acanthus spinosus Spiny leaves, and white flowers with purple bracts in summer. H 5ft (1.5m); S 24in (60cm).

Aquilegia vulgaris Blue, pink, or white late spring flowers appear above lobed leaves. H 36in (90cm); S 18in (45cm).

Briza maxima Tufty grass, with heart-shaped, dangling seedheads through summer. H 24in (60cm); S 12in (30cm).

Campanula latiloba Tall stems of lavender-blue flowers in mid- and late summer. H 36in (90cm); S 18in (45cm).

Carex pendula Evergreen leaves, and late spring catkinlike flowers on arching stems. H 4½ft (1.4m); S 5ft (1.5m).

Dryopteris filix-mas A clump-forming fern, its deciduous midgreen fronds unfurl in spring. H 3ft (1m); S 3ft (1m).

Geranium himalayense Decorative lobed leaves, and blue flowers in early summer. H 12in (30cm); S 24in (60cm).

Leucanthemum x superbum 'Wirral Supreme' Double daisylike summer flowers. H 36in (90cm); S 30in (75cm).

Flower beds and borders

5

Planning your display • Buying plants • How to sow and plant
Plants as design features • Making a gravel garden

Planning flower beds and borders

The planting of a border is like choreography: You need to choose and position the star plants as well as their supporting cast. You also need to take account of what plant flowers when, and decide which colors should be brought together and which kept apart (*see pp. 80–81*). Although this can take time, it is also a lot of fun. Even if you do not get it exactly right the first time, you can take comfort in the fact that you can change it next year.

Spring bulbs will fill the garden with color long before the new shoots of perennials emerge from the soil. In spring, plant your perennials. Then, in the fall, plant spring bulbs such as daffodils or tulips between them. If space is limited, use smaller bulbs, for example, anemones.

When you are caught up in the excitement of planting—usually in spring or fall—it is easy to forget to include plants that may look uninspiring at the time but will provide a good show in another season. Be sure to plan ahead carefully and create beds and borders that will perform well throughout the year.

Spacing and flowering times

Smaller flowering plants, such as aubrietas and doronicums, perform the spring show in the garden. Then, as the year progresses, larger flowering plants dominate. Many of the real giants, such as rudbeckias, do not come into their own

Mix and match plants with different flowering times, heights, and spreads when placing them in a summer border. You will then have some flowers opening throughout the season.

until late summer. You may be tempted to place all the small plants near the front and the taller ones toward the back of a border or center of a bed. However, the result can be rather dull, and it is also more difficult to get an even distribution of flowers across the display through the season. To avoid this, bring a few tall, airy plants, such as grasses or the slender-stemmed *Verbena bonariensis*, closer to the front. They will make the overall shape of the display more interesting, while still allowing you to see the plants behind.

When planning, allow enough space for each perennial plant to grow to its full height and spread. This may result in gaps between the plants in the first year, but don't worry: It is better than planting too closely and ending up with an overcrowded bed or border. You can also cover the bare soil, which will dry out quickly and give weeds a foothold, by growing a few hardy annuals in the first year (*see p.96*).

If space is limited, choose plants that perform at different times of year to cohabit in one area. Plant early-flowering primroses close to gypsophilas that bush out in midsummer when the primroses die back. You could also grow early-flowering oriental poppies with moor grass.

The style of your borders and beds is entirely up to you and will be influenced by the types of plants you prefer. If you opt for mixed planting, consider planting shrubs or small trees for year-round structure. Use stakes or a broom to mark their intended positions so you'll have an impression of how they will affect the rest of the garden.

Giving shape to beds

If you grow perennials in an open bed, rather than against a wall or hedge, they don't have to compete for moisture or light and rarely need staking (*see p.162*). Informal island beds have little architectural presence, so instead create structure through planting. Look for bold, architectural feature plants, such as Russian sage or *Euphorbia characias*. These have permanence, help draw the eye, and insert a note of calm into the flurry of flowering plants.

Leafy plants, such as ornamental grasses and hostas, offer structure with their long season of interest and help disguise the unsightly dying foliage of earlier-flowering specimens.

Bedding plants or annuals?

Traditionally, bedding plants are used in geometric, formal display beds and are stripped out and replaced at the start of each season. So, for winter and spring you could grow winter-flowering pansies, followed by English daisies, forget-me-nots, wallflowers, and spring bulbs, such as grape hyacinths and tulips. For the summer, try any of the many tender bedding plants, such as impatiens, heliotropes, lobelias, marigolds, geraniums, salvias, or petunias.

Although this system provides a great color display for many months of the year and allows you to experiment with different planting plans, it is labor-intensive. Twice a year, the bed has to be cleared, dug, and replanted. You also need to buy a large number of plants each time at considerable expense, or raise some of them in advance in a cold frame or greenhouse.

Easier and less expensive are hardy annuals. You can grow these from seed, which you can scatter on the spot where you want them to flower (*see pp.96–97*). The main drawback is that you may have to wait 10–16 weeks for the flowers to bloom. Success rates can also be unpredictable—numerous factors influence germination, such as the age of the seed, soil moisture, and temperature. Seedlings are also vulnerable to weather damage, and some pests and diseases.

This profusion of flowers can be achieved easily by either sowing seed indoors in spring or buying inexpensive plug plants—young plants that you have to pot on—from a garden center.

Ornamental edibles

If you have a small garden that lacks space for a proper herb bed or separate vegetable patch, why not grow a few herbs, fruit, and vegetables in the flower beds? Although you won't be able to grow enough crops to be self-sufficient, you can still enjoy the special satisfaction of harvesting your own produce. If you choose your crops carefully, you can also enjoy them as ornamental plants until they are harvested.

Red oak-leaf and 'Lollo Rosso' are examples of lettuces that look almost too good to eat. Swiss chard has large, handsome leaves and dramatic stems colored yellow, pink, or red, while the decorative beet 'Bull's Blood' has moody dark red leaves. Cabbages actually benefit from being grown with other plants, because cabbage white caterpillars are less likely to find and eat them. Try unusual ones, such as purple curly kale, or those bred for decorative purposes rather than taste.

Use attractive supports, such as obelisks or trellises, for purple-podded climbing French beans or the runner

Mix vegetables and flowers, such as cabbages, marigolds, and poppies, for a dazzling display. All can be raised from seed sown in the spring or fall.

Easy-care plants, such as rudbeckias and daylilies, have sturdy stems that don't need staking. Daylilies' strappy leaves also provide lush cover when early summer-flowering plants are dying back.

bean 'Painted Lady', which has abundant scarlet and white flowers.

If you have a sunny corner or wall, you could add one or two fruit crops. Espaliered fruit trees take a lot of care, but cane fruits trained up a trellis or tripod are not so difficult—try loganberries or tayberries. Alpine strawberries are another good choice: They grow easily from seed and make attractive ground cover.

Herbs are easy to use as part of a perennial planting. They nearly all have attractive foliage, some in shades of purple or silver, as well as pretty flowers, and they fill the garden with delicious scents. You can use shrubby herbs, such as rosemary and sage, in clumps or as dwarf hedging. The thyme 'Silver Posie' has variegated, dainty leaves, while lemon thyme has golden foliage and a lemony flavor. Also, try sowing basil, coriander, and dill every couple of weeks, in little patches, for a long harvest.

Easy-care flowering plants

If you choose your plants wisely, you can make life easier and reduce the time you spend maintaining them. Stick to sturdy herbaceous perennials and grasses, and avoid using annuals or bedding plants. Supplement the perennials with some small evergreens and groundcover shrubs, such as euonymus, heathers, or tiny-leaved creeping cotoneasters, in mixed beds and borders for year-round greenery.

Don't grow plants such as delphiniums and double peonies that need staking. Instead, look for easy-care alternatives. For example, monkshoods, like delphiniums, are great for punctuating a border with their tall flower spikes in shades of blue and purple. But unlike delphiniums, they are not eaten by slugs, and stay upright without staking.

Every garden has sites with different growing conditions, or microclimates (*see p.60*), so finding plants that perform well may involve some trial and error. Don't be afraid to move a plant if it fails in one spot; it may thrive elsewhere.

Once you have planted a bed or border, keep it free of weeds by mulching it regularly (*see pp.158–59*).

Seasonal easy-care plants

You can design your garden with low-maintenance plants and still enjoy color and interest throughout the year.

Spring bulbs, such as daffodils and alliums (*see left*), bloom for many years before you will need to lift and divide them. Alliums have sturdy stems that do not need staking and handsome, long-lasting seedheads.

Summer is the highlight of the flower-garden year. For a low-maintenance display, fill the borders with plants that reach for the skies. Siberian catmint has masses of flowers on tall, self-supporting stems (*see left*).

Fall flowers include chysanthemums and Michaelmas daisies. Also look for colorful berries or seedheads, such as these Chinese lanterns with their fiery orange seed capsules.

Winter blooms are precious commodities since few flowering plants brave the cold. Violas are among the most reliable, and perform best in a warm spot, such as on a patio. Hellebores also bloom in winter.

Choosing flowering plants

If you are confused by the choice of plants available, look for the tried-and-true star performers from each group of plants. These usually have shapely forms, plenty of flowers and buds, and good disease resistance—and will grow reliably in most gardens.

A plant bought from an established nursery is generally a better buy than a similar plant from a spring-only garden center. These latter plants often have trouble thriving, and the garden center may not be around later to answer questions. Look for green, not yellowing or wilted leaves—a sure sign that the plant needs nutrients and water. Check to see that the roots are not tangled and crammed in tightly; if it is pot-bound, your new plant will never grow properly.

Where to buy your plants

Your local garden center can be a good place to buy plants, since most have a wide range of well-grown stock, but you should be aware of possible pitfalls. Nurseries often tend to put plants in full flower on prominent display to entice gardeners into impulse buying. This is where research comes

A good plant is a healthy specimen that will grow quickly and strongly. Look for new stems or buds: A multistemmed clematis (*above left*) is a better buy than a single-stemmed one.

in handy. Stick to your list as much as possible and resist temptations—you may find you have no space or no suitable site or soil for a hastily purchased plant.

Many garden-center staff are not horticulturally trained, and so any advice they offer may not be authoritative. The expert staff are often on duty on weekends when the stores are busiest, so seek them out if you need advice. Finally, garden centers don't always grow their own plants, but may bring them in from a number of suppliers, so the quality can vary.

Specialty nurseries usually raise their plants on-site, and their staff can offer growing advice and help you identify the best cultivars for the conditions in your garden.

Many nurseries offer mail-order services, which enable you to get a wider range of plants. These centers ship plants to you, packaged so that they will not be damaged in transit. Always check with your local nursery for the correct heat and hardiness zones for any plants you buy. Buying a plant that will not grow in your area is a waste of money. Plants are also available over the Internet.

Guarantee

It's always worth asking whether the nursery offers a guarantee with its plants. If it does, keep the receipt so that if the plant dies within the specified time, despite your having followed the instructions on the care label, you should be offered a replacement plant or your money back.

Making your selection

Sometimes it is tempting to buy plants in flower because you can see exactly what the flowers look like, but root

At the garden center, take time choosing plants and stick to your shopping list. Always read the label to check that you have the correct plant and that it suits the soil and site in your garden.

growth ceases while plants are blooming, so they may take longer to establish. Tall plants often need staking, too.

If you are thinking of buying large plants for instant impact in your garden, remember that mature specimens are slower to recover from the shock of planting than smaller, younger ones. Large plants also have more leaves from which to lose water, and tend to dry out before their roots can establish and take up moisture. Young plants planted at the same time often overtake larger ones after a year or so.

Health checks

Most plants at garden centers and nurseries are container-grown. Make sure that you buy a healthy specimen with a balanced shape and multiple stems. Leaves should also be free from signs of pests or diseases, and there should be no algal growth on the soil mix. Check the root ball (see below): if there is a solid mat of roots, the plant is potbound.

Plants from friends

Gardeners are usually happy to pass on surplus plants obtained from dividing clumps of herbaceous plants or sowing a batch of seeds. Be careful to inspect your free plant thoroughly before planting, pulling away any weed growth. Perennial weeds such as bindweed often spread from garden to garden in this way and are almost impossible to eradicate.

When to plant

It is usually best to plant your purchases as soon as you have brought them home, but there are times when this is not possible because of the conditions (see p.94) or because you do not have time. In these cases, you need to care for the plants properly until it is possible to plant them. Container-grown plants can be kept safely in their pots for a few weeks before planting out, as long as you keep them well watered during dry periods.

If you buy tender bedding plants in early spring before the threat of frost has passed, keep them under cover (for example in a greenhouse, cool conservatory, or windowsill) until warmer weather arrives. Make sure you keep their soil moist and deadhead them regularly.

In a frost-free greenhouse, you can plant bedding in hanging baskets or larger containers and grow them on so they fill out before being set outside for the summer.

Containers in a greenhouse

Giving a plant a health check

You usually get what you pay for, so go to a well-run nursery or garden center for healthy, top-quality plants. However, even in the best establishments, it's still worth checking the plants over for yourself. The staff shouldn't object as long as you are careful, especially when you slip off pots to inspect the roots (see below), and always leave the plant as it was. Reject any plant that looks sickly or shows signs of disease or pest infestation – even if it's at a bargain price, you're just buying trouble.

Look under the pot – if there are no roots, or just a few, growing through the drainage holes the plant is probably not root-bound.

Gently knock off the pot to check that the roots are plump, pale in color, and not too congested, and the potting mix is moist.

Reject a weedy pot – weeds on the soil mix are a sign of neglect. They stress the plant as they compete for food and water.

How to plant

Most hardy herbaceous plants do best if planted in autumn, when the soil is still warm, in time for the late fall rains that help new roots grow. Tender types prefer spring planting.

There are times when you should avoid planting, such as summer or winter—new plants suffer in long spells of dry, very wet, or cold weather. Strong wind, fierce sun, and frost can all damage exposed roots. Also, avoid planting soon after heavy rain or a period of waterlogging, and don't dig or walk on clay soils when they're wet, since this can cause compaction, squeezing out oxygen needed by plant roots.

Preparing the planting site

Weeds abhor a vacuum, and any clear soil is likely to be colonized by them. If left to grow, they will dramatically reduce the amount of water, nutrients, and light that your new plants receive, just when they need it most. Take some time to clear weeds properly before planting. Use a fork to lever deep-rooted perennial weeds out of the soil; if you leave any roots, they may regrow.

Some ornamental plants, particularly those that form dense groundcover, such as geraniums, hog the border in much the same way as weeds. Make sure that you place new plants a decent distance away from them, or cut back the groundcover until the newcomers are established. Large hedges and trees may also compete with new plants for water and light. Avoid planting closer than about 18in (45cm) from walls, because the ground at the foot of a wall can be extremely dry—this area is called a rain shadow.

Staking perennials

Some tall-stemmed herbaceous plants, such as delphiniums, or those with large, top-heavy blooms, such as dahlias, may be blown or fall over when they are flowering (see p.162).

Prevent this from happening by inserting a single stake after planting. Bamboo canes are suitable for herbaceous plants, although a large dahlia may need a sturdier stake. Push the cane into the ground, just beyond the root ball, until it is firmly secured. Tie the plant stem loosely to the stake with soft garden twine, in stages as it grows.

Staking a delphinium

Planting a perennial

Prepare the soil of the planting area to get your plant off to a flying start (see pp.40–45). Add organic matter to improve the soil's structure and encourage new root growth—the farther the roots spread, the greater the area from which they can obtain water and nutrients. Water the plant well about an hour or two before planting, since a dry root ball is difficult to wet when planted.

1 Stand the plant in its pot in position within the border. Do a visual check—will it have enough room to spread to its mature height and width or will it be overwhelmed by neighboring plants?

2 Dig in plenty of organic matter, such as garden compost or well-rotted manure, over and beyond the planting area. Dig a planting hole about twice as wide and deep as the pot or root ball.

Support the root ball with one hand as you slip it out of its pot.

4 Stand the plant in the hole. Make sure that the top of the root ball is level with the soil surface; if needed, remove or add soil to get the level right.

3 Knock the plant out of its pot and gently tease some roots free from the root ball— this encourages them to spread into the surrounding soil, especially if the roots are congested. If you see any dead or damaged roots, trim them off with pruners.

5 Draw the soil around the root ball with your fingers to fill in the hole, making sure that the level of the plant doesn't change as you do so.

6 Use your heel to firm the soil gently around the plant. This removes any air pockets and ensures that the roots are in contact with the soil. Double-check that the plant hasn't become crooked.

7 Water thoroughly after planting to settle the soil around the roots and eliminate any air pockets. Apply a thick mulch to help keep in the moisture, and water your new plant in dry periods.

Sowing hardy annuals

You can achieve fantastic results quite quickly by sowing hardy annuals directly into the soil in spring, either to create an entire annual display or to fill gaps in beds and borders. It is usually less expensive than buying lots of summer bedding in trays. About three weeks before sowing, weed and fork over the sowing area. A week before sowing, use a hoe to clear off any weeds that have sprung up. This is worth the effort because it reduces the amount of weeding you need to do later, as well as eliminating competition for the water and nutrients that seedlings need to thrive.

Sowing for success

Annuals look more natural if sown in informal swaths, or drifts, that merge into one another. To obtain this effect in a bed or border, draw irregularly shaped areas, one for each annual, in the soil with a stake. Then mark out straight rows (*see opposite*) within the drifts and sow one type of seed in each. Sowing in rows will make it easier to distinguish the annual seedlings from weed seedlings. Then you can easily remove weeds by hoeing between the rows.

Once you have sown the seeds, don't forget to label them. In dry weather, water the seedlings using a watering can with a rose—a spout causes rivulets in the soil as well as puddling, which can wash seedlings out of the ground, and in some soils leaves a hard crust on the surface.

Hardy annuals provide an easy way to introduce a splash of color into your garden. Here, orange pot marigolds add zing to the soft blues and purples of love-in-a-mist and cornflowers.

Collecting seeds

Annuals produce seedheads in a variety of shapes, such as pods or papery capsules, and most are easy to collect for sowing early the following spring. It is not worth collecting seed from F1 hybrids, because the seedlings won't look like the parent plant. Choose a warm, dry day to gather seedheads. Remember to label your seeds, and store them in a cool, dry place out of bright light.

Ripe seeds are usually black, unripe ones are paler

Seeds fall easily from ripe seedheads

1 When seedheads (here, love-in-a-mist) turn brown, snip them off and lay on sheets of paper towel or newspaper to dry.

2 When the seedheads are completely dry, shake out the seeds onto a piece of paper. Pick out any chaff and store the seed in a labeled paper bag or envelope (plastic bags encourage mold).

How to sow annuals outside

Before sowing your annuals, prepare the soil well, removing all the weeds and forking it over. Most hardy annuals like free-draining soil, so if you have heavy clay, dig in some coarse sand or grit to open it up. Choose an open, sunny site, not too close to large trees or shrubs, which will reduce germination rates.

Always follow the recommendations on the seed packet for correct planting depths and spacing. Sow as thinly as possible, and once the seeds have germinated and the seedlings have produced a few leaves, thin them out by removing all but the strongest, leaving the correct space between the young plants.

1 Rake the soil to level it, and clear away large stones. Use the head of the rake to break down lumps and create a crumbly soil.

2 Make some straight seed drills with a bamboo cane by pressing it lightly into the soil, as shown.

3 Transfer a little seed to the palm of your hand, and gently tap it with your finger to trickle the seed gradually into the drill.

4 Cover the seeds by gently raking a fine layer of soil over the drills. Then firm the soil lightly with the head of your rake.

5 Water well, using a watering can with a fine rose. A sprinkling is less likely to disturb the seeds or cause a soil crust to form.

6 Protect seeds from being scratched up by birds and cats by covering the area with some twiggy sticks or a layer of netting.

Using ornamental grasses

For many centuries, grasses have been a key component in gardens, although until relatively recently these were limited to lawns or meadows. Since the latter part of the 20th century, ornamental grasses have been used more and more in our gardens. Even though they do not have the pretty, colorful flowers of most garden plants, they bring structure, height, fall color, winter silhouettes, and—most important of all—movement. Some, such as giant feather grass and moor grass, stand well into fall with their stems glowing golden orange, and grasses like miscanthus and calamagrostis remain attractive into the spring where they are hardy.

Choosing grasses

Grasses usually fall into one of two groups: clumpers or spreaders. Some naturally form perfectly behaved clumps, whereas others can take over your garden with their creeping rootstocks, so choose carefully.

There is now a large selection of grasses available that do not self-seed or spread wildly. If in doubt, check with your supplier, or have a close look at how the plant is growing. If it makes a neat, dense clump or tussock, it should not run; if you see shoots coming up all over the pot without forming a tight clump, beware. On light, sandy soils in particular, grasses, such as variegated gardener's garters, can become invasive and need to be regularly weeded out.

The winter garden will look much more interesting if it has some grasses, since they don't die down in fall like other herbaceous plants. The birds can also feast on the seedheads.

Placing grasses in the garden

You can plant grasses standing alone, scattered through other plants, or in larger drifts or swaths. How you do it depends on the type of grass you choose and the effect you wish to achieve. If you have never grown grasses, don't be timid. Be brave and think big. Try large drifts of the *Miscanthus sinensis* 'Kleine Silberspinne'—although not the tallest grass it is still impressive. *Calamagrostis* x *acutiflora* 'Karl Foerster' also looks good in a mass. You could use it to create a hedgelike screen, or add depth to a bed or border by scattering it through a planting of smaller flowering perennials.

Since many grasses last through fall, you can create a beautiful effect by siting them carefully. The slender flower spikes and orange stems of *Molinia caerulea* 'Windspiel' or 'Transparent' glow if they catch the late afternoon fall sun. As its name suggests, 'Transparent', like other moor

Sound and movement as grasses rustle in the slightest breeze add an extra dimension to a bed or border. Intersperse them among traditional flowering plants for contrasts of color and shape.

Keeping grasses looking good

Ornamental grasses need very little hands-on care to keep them growing well and looking good. As a rule of thumb, most evergreen grasses, including sedges and rushes, just need a light trim to remove damaged leaves and old flower stems. The best time to do this is in late winter, before any fresh spring growth emerges. Grasses that turn straw-colored in fall should be cut down to the ground in late winter, after you have enjoyed their frosted foliage. New growth will soon emerge.

Cut back old stems close to the ground, using pruners or shears. If the grass has sharp edges, wear eye protection and gloves.

Use loppers on thicker grasses, such as miscanthus, where the stems are more like canes. You may even need to use a saw.

Clear debris, such as old stems, using a spring-tined, or grass, rake. Work from the center of the clump and comb out any waste.

grasses, is almost translucent. If you position it at the front of a planting, it creates an intriguing, see-through screen, and the feathery plumes brush your face as you walk past. However, in the rain, this experience is less rewarding.

Naturalistic grass planting

In recent years garden designers have developed a way of planting perennials and grasses that mimics the plants' natural growth habits. Plants are chosen from a natural habitat with conditions similar to those in the garden. For example, if your garden is partly shaded, you should choose plants that originate from woodland margins, which will thrive in light shade with a few hours of sun each day.

Plants are placed in the way they would occur naturally. For example, grasses with creeping or spreading roots are planted in drifts and groups. Those that scatter themselves by means of seed are dotted about. Any bare soil is covered with groundcover plants or a mulch to keep weeds down. The result is a matrix, or community, of plants that are allowed to grow and evolve naturally. Taking care of such a design involves less maintenance than traditional gardening, since plants are not supported or deadheaded, but simply cleaned up when they are past their prime.

Caring for grasses

Most grasses grow naturally in poor soils and thrive on neglect—give them too much water, food, and fuss and you'll kill them. Large grasses, such as pampas, are an exception, and need an occasional feed to keep them vigorous: use a general-purpose balanced fertilizer. Grasses seldom need watering, except after planting and while they establish, but if their leaves roll up in a dry spell, it's a sign they need a drink. A mulch of shingle, gravel, shredded bark, smooth pebbles, or even pinecones conserves moisture and suppresses weeds.

Gravel is an attractive and effective mulch for grasses

Designing with bulbs

Regardless of the size of your garden, there is always space for bulbs. They discreetly die down when not in bloom, and their compact size means that they can easily be tucked in among other plants. When they do perform, they offer a high ratio of flower to foliage. If you plan ahead, you could have bulbs flowering in your garden nearly all year round.

Bulbs can be left to naturalize in lawns or to carpet shaded woodland areas in spring (*see right*). They also provide the early season's show in your borders, before herbaceous plants have stirred into growth, and make excellent companions for perennials and deciduous shrubs, filling the gaps between these plants.

Bulbs and their habitats

Bulbs have adapted to make the most of the conditions in their native habitats, and if you know where yours come from, it's easier to provide a good home for them in the garden. Woodland bulbs thrive in light, dappled shade, and some, like hardy cyclamens, grow well in dry shade. Some bulbs love hot, sunny sites, while others are delicate enough for a rock

Mass plantings of bulbs look better than single clumps, although over the years they will increase in number, so remember to lift and divide them regularly to keep them flowering well.

Naturalizing bulbs in the garden

When people talk about "naturalizing" bulbs, they mean creating a natural-looking planting. It could be in the lawn or under trees, with large drifts of bulbs that are left to multiply undisturbed from year to year. If you have been inspired by bluebells carpeting a woodland, you can create similar effects with daffodils, snowdrops, or crocuses (*right*).

garden. Spring and fall-flowering bulbs thrive under deciduous trees where they can flower before or after the trees are in full leaf. Early-flowering bulbs, like snowdrops, are more suited to a lawn; others thrive in open wildflower meadows; some, like daffodils, flourish around borders or on banks.

Many bulbs have learned to cope with extreme drought; they complete their growing cycle by the time spring is over and the summer heat bakes the ground. These bulbs, which include tulips, are perfectly happy to wait out the summer in very dry conditions; if necessary you can lift them out of the soil and store them to make way for summer-flowering plants (*see p.103*). The bulbs do not become active again until autumn, when the first rains come, or when you plant them out again.

Bulbs in borders

When planting spring bulbs in borders, you may be tempted to plant them close to the front because they flower early in the season. But since most other plants in the border won't be very visible, you can spread bulbs around in little clusters or drifts, from the front to the back. Then, as their foliage dies down, they will be hidden behind the emerging growth of shrubs or perennials. Later-flowering

What is a bulb?

It can be confusing when you discover that the word "bulb" is often used as a blanket term for any plant that has an underground food-storage organ. As well as true bulbs (as in snowdrops and lilies), there are three other forms: corms (gladioli), rhizomes (irises), and tubers (cyclamens). Each type of bulb has evolved to cope with distinct growing conditions.

True bulb Bulbs like this daffodil are made of leaves layered as in an onion, with a papery skin. Lily bulbs are looser in form and lack a papery skin.

Corm As in gladiolus, a corm is the thickened base of the stem and has 1–2 buds at its apex. Tiny cormlets may grow around the base.

Rhizome This is a swollen stem, which usually (as with irises) grows horizontally near the soil surface and has several buds along it.

Tuber Root tubers, like dahlias, have buds at the stem base. Stem tubers, like cyclamens, have surface buds.

bulbs are often better scattered in between other plants, which helps to disguise their unsightly dying foliage.

Seasons of bloom

The late winter and early spring show is dominated by bulbs with flowers in clear yellows and whites, such as trilliums, winter aconites, and snowdrops. These are soon followed by the first daffodils, like *Narcissus* 'February Gold'. It is worth studying the catalogs and picking a selection of daffodils for color through late spring. The pretty, scented pheasant's eye daffodils are among the last of the season to bloom. Early irises, hyacinths, grape hyacinths, and ipheions belong to the blue brigade that cheers spring gardens. Crocuses, meanwhile, come in purple, yellow, and white.

It is not until the tulips emerge that the color spectrum broadens. Tulips come in every color except blue, and range from the dainty (*Tulipa sylvestris*, great for naturalizing) to the seriously baroque. The parrot tulip 'Rococo' has fiery red, fringed petals with green streaks, reminiscent of the tulips depicted in old Flemish paintings.

As spring turns to summer, another important group of bulbs decorates our borders: alliums or ornamental onions. Their distinctive flowerheads, in globes or pendent clusters, range from the cheerful golden *Allium moly* and tall 'Purple Sensation' to the giant spheres of metallic, starry flowers of

Allium christophii—which are great for drying. More irises add dusky hues of blue, amber, rust, and purple.

Fewer bulbs perform at the height of summer, but they include some stunners. Lilies are elegant and stately, and many have delicious, strong perfumes. Gladioli add height. Eucomis, with its flowerheads of greenish or reddish starry flowers topped by a pineapple-like tuft, makes a wonderful architectural plant for late summer. Finally, color the autumn with crocuslike colchicums and vivid pink nerines.

A succession of flowers from bulbs can be enjoyed through much of the year, not just in spring. Try starting with snowdrops in late winter, followed by lilies in summer and nerines in autumn.

Planting and caring for bulbs

Bulbs are easier to grow than most people think, as long as you follow a few simple rules. In the wild, most bulbs grow in climates with hot, dry seasons, and they prefer light, free-draining soils in full sun. Bulbs from woodlands need rich, moist but free-draining soil, and dappled sun or part shade.

Buying and choosing bulbs

Most bulbs are available for purchase in their dormant state, so you need to buy spring-flowering bulbs in late summer or autumn and summer-flowering ones in spring. Don't delay buying until late in the season; if you buy bulbs soon after they come into stock, you'll get the pick of the healthiest and most vigorous.

Choose bulbs that are big, firm, and plump; plants from dried-up bulbs will not thrive. Reject any with blemishes—indications of pests or disease—or signs of rot or mold, as well as any which are missing their papery skins or have started sprouting. Look for bulbs that are labeled "from cultivated stock" or "nursery propagated" to avoid buying any that are collected from the wild.

Bulbs in pots should be planted at the same depth as in the open ground. Place the pot on feet to allow free drainage.

Planting tips

It is important to plant bulbs at the correct depth (*see below left*) because if they are too deep or too shallow, they may not flower (known as "blindness"). You should also space bulbs at distances equal to 2–3 times their width. Take care to plant corms and tubers with their growth buds facing up—the buds are not as distinct as on true bulbs.

Some bulbs are prone to rot in cold, wet, or poorly drained soils. If you have such soil, grow them in pots. You could also plant scaly bulbs, such as lilies, on their sides to stop them from accumulating moisture between their scales and rotting. If you have a very light, dry soil, fork in well-rotted organic matter to prevent the roots from drying out.

Planting "in the green"

Winter aconites, snowdrops, and anemones have tiny bulbs that dehydrate very quickly and often fail to produce decent plants. If you buy these bulbs, soak them overnight in water before planting to help kickstart them into life. It is best, though, to buy plants "in the green," which means they have been lifted directly after flowering while the foliage is still fresh. This gives them a chance to reestablish before becoming dormant. Although plants in the green are more expensive, they are also more reliable. If you have clumps in the garden, lift the bulbs as soon as they have flowered, tease them apart, and replant where you want them. Make sure that the pale bases of the leaves are below the soil.

Aftercare

While they are in growth, bulbs need feeding, watering, and deadheading. Tall-stemmed bulbs may also need staking (*see p.162*). After flowering, most bulb foliage dies back. Some gardeners bend the foliage over and tie it up to make it look neat, but this stops nutrients in the leaves from getting to the bulb and helping form flower buds for next year.

Planting depths

Most bulbs, like those of daffodils, should be planted at 2–3 times the depth of the bulb (*see far right*). For example, you will need to dig a 6in (15cm) hole for a bulb that is 2in (5cm) tall.

However, there are a few exceptions: Tulips need to be planted at 3–4 times their own depth. A few bulbs, such as nerines, prefer to sit with their growing tips at the surface. If your garden has sandy or light soil, or is in a very cold area, you should plant bulbs more deeply to protect them from drying out or freezing.

Depth for tulip   Depth for daffodil

Tulip: 1½in (4cm) bulb is best planted 6in (16cm) deep.

Daffodil: 2½in (6cm) bulb, planted 7in (18cm) deep.

Muscari: ½in (2cm) bulb is planted at a depth of 2½in (6cm).

Planting bulbs in a border

Most bulbs prefer free-draining soil because they like to be fairly dry when dormant, so it helps to fork some grit into the planting area on heavier soils. When planting, you can use a bulb planter which takes out a plug of soil for each bulb, but these can be time-consuming on stony soil or over large areas. Instead, dig out an entire planting area. For a natural effect, scatter bulbs on the soil and plant them, growing tips up, where they lie.

1 Dig a hole large enough to accommodate the number of bulbs you wish to plant – at the appropriate spacing and correct planting depth (*see opposite*). Add some general-purpose fertilizer and lightly fork over the soil in the bottom of the hole.

2 Position the bulbs in the hole with the pointed growing tips facing up. Discard any bulbs that show signs of disease or rotting.

3 Carefully fill in the hole with soil. Firm as you go with your fingers, making sure you do not damage the bulbs' growing tips.

4 Place chicken wire over the planted area to prevent animals from digging up the bulbs. Remove the wire when the first shoots appear.

Let the leaves die down naturally until they are dry and yellow, and then cut them off. Bulk up bulbs by giving them a dose of tomato fertilizer after flowering.

Left to their own devices, bulbs form large clumps, but they may flower less over time. To keep bulbs flowering well, divide them every 3–4 years. Using a fork, pry out a dormant clump, tease it apart, discard any diseased bulbs, and replant. Tulips tend to stop blooming after a few years where spring is fleeting. When soil warms quickly, tulips form many small bulbs rather than one large one. Deep planting (where soil stays cooler) helps delay this. After lifting, clean the bulbs, store them in paper bags or boxes in a cool, dry place, and then replant them in fall. Dahlias, gladioli, and tuberous begonias should be lifted and stored over winter (*see p.166*).

Planting bulbs in grass

Using a sharp knife or the edge of a spade's blade, make an H-shaped cut in the sod and fold back the flaps. If necessary, dig the soil to the recommended depth for the type of bulb. Either scatter bulbs over the area, then position each one,

growing point upward, where they fall, or place each one in a random pattern. Replace the soil and gently firm, taking care not to disturb the growing tips, then fold back the sod and firm.

Creating a gravel garden

Gravel gardens have gained popularity over recent years. If you want to grow a wide range of plants, a gravel garden offers the ideal habitat for those that originate from warm, drier climates and which may not be so happy in colder, damper weather conditions. These plants are often native to the Mediterranean and South Africa, and many, such as artemisias and lavenders, have gray and silver foliage and particularly like the free-draining, warmer conditions in a gravel garden.

Surrounding warm-climate plants with a "collar" of gravel helps them in several ways. Gravel reflects light, making optimum use of the available sun. It also improves drainage around the bases of plants, preventing delicate or young plants from rotting off. When it rains, the gravel stops mud from splashing onto foliage, which helps plants with hairy or woolly leaves survive the wet winter months—if they become too muddy, they are likely to rot.

Another reason that gravel gardens have become so popular is that they can significantly reduce the amount of time you spend maintaining your garden. Gravel provides a nonslip surface that needs little attention and looks neat and attractive all year. Lawns, on the other hand, require frequent mowing, as well as intensive care at different times of the year. If you have a very small front yard, you might consider installing a gravel garden there and dispensing with the chore of maintaining the grass, while gaining an interesting space to set off the front of your house.

Planning a gravel garden

Gravel gardens can look formal or naturalistic, depending on the way you use gravel with other hard-landscaping materials or structures, such as water features, and where you put it down. The gravel could simply fill in the spaces between the defined lines of formal flower beds or pathways, or, for a more informal look, you could use it to cover the entire garden, with planting inserted into it in irregular drifts. Alternatively, you could use several types of gravel or flat stones, such as slate, to create interesting patterns or contrasts of color and texture.

If you garden on a heavy soil and want to have a gravel garden, the first and most crucial step is to improve the drainage. Incorporating coarse sand and gravel into the soil will do this, but you need to add a substantial amount, not just a scattering. It is hard work, but worth it.

Lush planting is still possible in gravel gardens. Here, purple-flowered nepeta, or catmint, has been planted en masse to create a striking design (*above*).

Paving and gravel on this sheltered terrace (*left*) provide planting pockets for sun-loving thymes. These spread out to form a fragrant carpet, and combine with geraniums and lady's mantle in a low-maintenance planting.

Gravel garden plants

Choose drought-tolerant plants that will appreciate the free-draining conditions you have created in your gravel garden. These plants usually have foliage that is adapted to cut down on water loss—look for leaves that are silver in color, narrow and strappy, or covered in fine, downy hairs. Hummock-forming plants are also better at conserving water than those with a sprawling habit, while many spring- or autumn-flowering bulbs tolerate dry conditions by becoming dormant during summer.

***Achillea* 'Gold Plate'** is a clump-forming perennial with flat flower heads appearing from summer to fall.

Alchemilla mollis is a clump-forming perennial with soft, large, hairy leaves that wear raindrops like diamonds.

Artemisia, or wormwood, includes a range of annuals, perennials, and small shrubs with aromatic, silvery foliage.

***Dianthus* 'Little Jock'** is one of many pinks that bear long-lasting, often scented flowers all through summer.

Dierama is a summer-flowering plant that forms chains of corms each year. Once settled in, it's usually trouble-free.

Eryngium giganteum is short-lived, but this 3ft (90cm) perennial is worth growing for its persistent flowerheads.

Euphorbia characias is an evergreen, upright shrub that makes a great feature, flowering in spring and early summer.

Lavandula angustifolia is a compact shrub with gray-green leaves, and fragrant flowers in mid- to late summer.

Papaver orientale is a perennial poppy with huge flowers that appear from late spring to midsummer.

***Salvia officinalis* 'Tricolor'** is a handsome sage with aromatic leaves that are useful in the kitchen.

Sedum spectabile has large, persistent flower heads in late summer, attracting butterflies and bees.

***Sisyrinchium striatum* 'Aunt May'** is 20in (50cm) tall, with striped evergreen leaves. It blooms in early to midsummer.

Preparing the site for planting

If you invest some time in preparing the area for your gravel garden, you will need to spend only a few hours each season maintaining it. First, clear the proposed site of all weeds and vegetation, and then condition and level the soil (*see pp. 40–45*).

It is always wise to use a weed-suppressing geotextile or landscape fabric in a gravel garden. These are available from garden centers and are made either from a variety of materials woven into a fabric or from perforated plastic. The fabric forms a weed barrier over the soil, eliminating light needed for seeds beneath it to germinate and grow, but allowing rain to penetrate to ornamental plant roots. If weed seeds germinate on top of the membrane, they will not be able to root through it and are easy to pull out.

Before planting, lay your fabric over the soil. Make sure that it overlaps neatly, and peg it down with a few metal pins. You can buy these ready-made, or make them out of heavy wire—each should resemble a large hairpin. Arrange your plants in their pots on top of the fabric to judge the overall effect and check spacings. Avoid using plants that naturally spread by sending up shoots from the roots. When you are happy with your design, plant through the landscape fabric (*see right*), and spread a thick layer of gravel over the surface. Alternatives to gravel include crushed stone, slate chips, small pebbles, or cobblestones.

A layer of organic matter will eventually form between the fabric and gravel. A few weeds may root into it, but not if you weed deeply, so they will be easy to remove by hand-weeding the area a few times a year. Or you can use a flat hoe, sliding it between the fabric and gravel to dislodge the weeds' roots. On a dry day, the weeds will soon shrivel up.

Prepare the area by digging over the soil and removing any weeds. Dig in plenty of well-rotted garden compost or manure and, on heavy soil, add coarse sand or grit to improve drainage.

Planting a gravel garden

You could plant directly into the soil, if you wish, but you'll get better results if you lay a weed-suppressing fabric down first. Once you cover it with a thick layer of pea gravel or slate chips, you won't know it's there, but you will notice how it cuts down on weeding and watering. The fabric lets rain in, but like a superefficient mulch, helps stop it from evaporating.

1 Cut a piece of geotextile fabric to fit your bed or border. For larger areas, you may have to join several strips together. Leave a generous overlap along each edge and pin securely in place.

2 Position your plants on top of the landscape fabric (presoak container-grown plants in water for at least an hour). Make sure that you have left enough room for each plant to spread to its full width.

3 Using sharp scissors, cut a large cross in the fabric directly under each plant and fold back the flaps. Make it big enough to allow you to dig a good-sized planting hole.

4 Take each plant out of its pot and lower it into the hole—it should sit at the same level as it was in its pot. Fill in around the root ball with soil, then firm with your heel or hand.

5 Tuck the fabric flaps back around the plant stem. Pin the fabric in place if needed to close any gaps, taking care not to damage the root ball. Water thoroughly.

Tuck gravel around the plant stems to stop weeds from growing.

6 Spread a 2–3in (5–8cm) thick layer of gravel or gravel mulch over the geotextile fabric. Be generous, to prevent the fabric from showing through and breaking down, and level with a rake.

7 Water around the plants regularly until they are established, using a spray from a watering can or hose to avoid dislodging pockets of gravel. If any weeds get through, they should be easy to pull out.

Trees, shrubs, and climbers 6

Designing with woody plants • Buying woody plants • Planting and transplanting • Selecting plants for the site • All about hedges

Using woody plants

Just as a stage is set for a play, woody plants—hedges, trees, shrubs, and climbers—create an essential backdrop against which perennials and annuals perform. They provide structure, height, and screening as well as offering shelter and shade. Plan in your woody plants before the herbaceous flowers, and think carefully about where they will work best. As the largest plants in your garden, they will have the greatest impact. Look at where the sun falls through the day (*see p.58*) to make sure that trees and shrubs cast cool shade where it is needed, not over sun-loving perennials or seats.

Small, slender, upright trees will not restrict your choice of underplanting too much; here, shade-loving heucheras are mixed with bright euphorbias and artemisia to enhance a "dappled" effect.

Trees as focal points

Whether your plot is large or small, consider planting a tree or two. Trees offer many benefits, sending the focus up to a wide, open sky in a small garden, while creating intimate enclosures in larger spaces. They also make wonderful focal points, particularly if you select a striking specimen with a weeping habit, attractive stems, decorative foliage, or colorful blossoms and fruit. A handsome white-stemmed birch, multistemmed amelanchier, or fountain-shaped Japanese maple will draw the eye when planted at the end of a path, in the center of a lawn, or against a wall or a smooth evergreen hedge.

You can also use a tree to act like a curtain in your garden, partially masking the view beyond, creating intrigue and mystery, but then bringing the eye back to the foreground. This effect is particularly successful in deep, rectangular plots where a tree is planted half to three-quarters of the way down the garden.

What is a woody plant?

All woody plants have a permanent framework but they grow in different ways. The stems of climbers are flexible so they can twine around their support; shrubs produce lots of stems from the base; and taller trees have sturdy trunks to keep them upright.

Climbers produce long, flexible stems that they use to twine around, or hook themselves onto, their support. Others cling on with specially adapted suction pads or aerial roots.

Shrubs, such as this *Forsythia*, don't have a single trunk carrying them up to great heights but instead have several stems growing from the base at soil level.

Trees, such as these silver birches, usually have a single trunk (or occasionally more than one) that divides higher up to form a crown of smaller branches.

Softly drape the boundaries of your garden with foliage and color using a combination of climbers, small trees, and shrubs to create graduated layers of planting.

Fruit trees are well worth planting, too, even if you do not have the space for a real fruit garden. Quinces have an early show of flowers, followed by highly perfumed fruits in autumn. Medlar trees also flower beautifully in spring, and then bear brown fruits in late summer and early autumn, while mulberries are an incredible sight in late summer, dripping with juicy raspberry-like fruits that taste divine. Where space is very limited, think about training fruit trees as cordons or espaliers against a sunny, south-facing wall.

Structural shrubs

Ideal as background plants, shrubs provide solidity and structure, creating a sense of permanence in a planting plan. Avoid planting shrubs in a uniform line against a fence; instead, select plants of different heights and shapes and place them strategically in your beds and borders. Use large dark specimens behind light-colored flowers; small shrubs, such as dwarf boxwood, thyme, or euonymus to edge the front of a design; and those with dramatic foliage, such as Japanese fatsia, 'Sutherland Gold' elder, or a tree peony to provide focal points.

Remember that many shrubs have pretty flowers and berries, and their seasonal features should be considered carefully when making your planting plans. For example, while the white-flowered 'Aztec Pearl' Mexican orange will set off the oval blue flowerheads of 'Blue Mound' California lilac brilliantly, the orange blooms of a kerria matched with pale pink montana clematis 'Elizabeth' creates a sickly mix, yet both are very attractive paired with other partners.

Flowering shrubs provide seasonal color, as well as a solid backdrop of green when the blossoms are over. Many flowering shrubs produce berries later in the year, adding to their appeal.

Roses in the garden

Although traditional rose gardens have gone out of fashion, these beautiful plants offer a wide range of exquisite flowers and wonderful scents and should not be overlooked.

There are literally thousands of roses to choose from, with different habits and flower shapes that suit both traditional and modern garden settings. Bush and shrub roses look best when dotted around a border, where you can create effective color matches with hardy perennials such as geraniums and heucheras, grasses, or other low-growing flowering and foliage plants. In addition to setting off the roses, these herbaceous plants will also help disguise their often clumsy shape and leggy bare stems at the base.

Rambling roses are ideal for weaving through trees, and most are not as prone to disease as their shorter cousins, the climbers. Climbers tend not to reach up as high as ramblers and have larger flowers, often over a longer season; when draped over arches and pergolas, they create a romantic ambience both in formal and informal settings.

Create a traditional rose walkway by planting climbing roses either side of a pergola. Here, a white rambler is teamed with purple-flowered clematis and underplanted with lavender.

Clever use of climbers

In established gardens, you can make use of climbers, such as clematis or climbing hydrangea to brighten up shrubs or small trees when they are not in flower or fruiting. Or try parthenocissus, jasmine, or ivy to clothe screens, fences, or walls in less time than it would take for a shrub to hide them. Fast-growing climbers can quickly establish a sense of maturity in a new garden, as well as softening the look of doorways, arches, and pergolas. Trained along the back of narrow borders, climbers also come into their own, adding height, color, and interest, without intruding into valuable garden space. Whatever the site, soil, or climatic conditions in your garden, you will find a climber to suit.

Bamboo effects

Although not strictly woody plants—bamboos are actually perennials—their permanent woody canes allow you to use them like shrubs in the garden. The tall types, such as *Phyllostachys* or *Fargesia*, create elegant screens when planted in a row, and shorter bamboos, including *Sasa* and *Pleioblastus variegatus*, make good groundcover. Most bamboos, except very tall varieties, work well in containers, although many enjoy damp soil conditions and thus need frequent watering when grown in pots. Alternatively, use bamboos in geometric beds in contemporary gardens or to define and enhance Japanese or Oriental garden designs.

Bamboo screens lend a contemporary look to modern garden designs. Here, their crossed stems and feathery foliage are made more dramatic by the red background and uplighting.

Using hedges

Hedges make beautiful leafy garden boundaries, shielding your space from neighbors, buffering noise and traffic pollution, and providing a wonderful foil for herbaceous or mixed planting designs set out in front of them.

They can also be used as internal walls to create intimate spaces and define different sections of the garden, such as a play or seating area, or a vegetable, herb, or flower garden. These hedges do not need to be tall or obstruct the view: a clear defining line will send out the message.

A garden must hold surprises and offer areas to discover, and hedges enable you to create this sense of intrigue. Not being able to see all of your yard in one glance means that you and your visitors are encouraged to step out and wander around to explore its hidden secrets.

In addition to these decorative and structural qualities, hedges also serve as excellent windbreaks. Even the tangled stems of a deciduous hedge in winter will reduce the wind speed significantly, protecting tall or delicate garden plants on the leeward side. In an exposed garden, check the direction of the prevailing wind and erect hedges in its path for a warmer, more comfortable space.

Clipped purple beech makes a low screen with which to frame a feature, such as an urn or a seat. In the autumn the leaves turn brown but do not fall, generating year-round effect.

Environmental benefits

Trees are often called "the planet's lungs" because leaves take in carbon dioxide during photosynthesis and release the oxygen that we breathe (*see pp.18–21*). Carbon dioxide is one of the greenhouse gasses implicated in climate change, and the large size of trees allows them to remove it from the atmosphere on a larger scale than other plants.

Gardeners appreciate the shelter and privacy trees give, and their beauty. Native species in particular also provide food and homes for wildlife. Trees are very important and, being large and slow growing, are hard to replace once lost.

Trees and shrubs offer cover for birds to nest and roost.

Selecting woody plants

You can buy woody plants from a garden center or plant nursery in your area, or a nursery farther afield that offers a mail-order service. Garden centers are convenient, but many offer only a limited selection of popular plants in one or two sizes, which may be too restrictive if you have more unusual plants in mind, or if you plan a long hedge where lots of the same type of plant are needed.

Nurseries tend to have a wider range available, and can be more cost-effective if they sell bare-root or balled-and-burlapped plants that have been grown in the field; these can be less expensive than the container-grown plants sold by garden centers. Another advantage of going to a local grower is that the plants will have been raised in soil and climatic conditions similar to those in your garden. The drawback is that bare-root plants are available only during the autumn, winter, and early spring months when they are dormant, so you are restricted to planting during these times. Container-grown stock, on the other hand, can be planted at any time of the year, although your new plants must then be kept well watered throughout the growing season, from late spring to early autumn.

When you get home

Try to prepare the ground in advance of purchase so you can plant your trees, shrubs, and climbers as soon as possible. This is particularly important if you have bought bare-root trees, whose roots will dry out quickly. If you can't plant

these immediately, you will need to heel them in. To do this, dig a trench deep enough to accommodate the roots and some of the stem, roughly to where the soil mark indicates their original planting depth. Then place your trees at an angle so that the stem is supported, cover the roots and stem with soil, and water the ground well. Continue to water regularly until you can plant them out properly. Container-grown and balled-and-burlapped trees will survive unplanted for a few weeks provided that frost is not forecast, but again keep them well watered. In hot weather, "park" the plants in a shady spot to minimize drying out.

When to plant

Hardy woody plants are best planted from mid- to late autumn, when the soil is moist and still relatively warm. This allows the roots to establish before winter sets in, which will help the tree withstand any hot, dry weather the following summer. You can plant in midspring if you are committed to watering frequently as the weather warms up. Planting in midspring is also recommended, particularly for evergreens and conifers, if you live in a cold area, or are planting slightly tender trees and shrubs. Never plant if the ground is very dry, very wet, or frozen.

Bare-root plants should be planted immediately, but if the planting site isn't ready, dig a temporary trench, lay the plants in at about 45°, and cover the roots with soil. Water well.

Choosing a healthy plant

When at the garden center, look for healthy plants in clean, damp soil mix that show no sign of pests or diseases (*see below*). Leaves should not be discolored, pale, or wilting. Also, look for specimens with bright, new leaves or shoots, which shows that they are growing well. If you can, tap the root ball out of its pot and check that the roots have established themselves throughout the soil mix but are not going around in circles (pot-bound) or growing through the holes in the base and into the ground below. A healthy root system that is not pot-bound indicates that the plant should take off quickly once planted.

Container-grown plants are available all year. Don't choose a plant that seems much too top-heavy for its pot; its roots are likely to have become congested.

Balled-and-burlapped plants are grown in a nursery bed and dug up for sale. The roots are often trimmed first.

Growing tips should be healthy and leafy

Carefully untie the fabric once the plant is in its planting position

Signs of poor health

Reject any plant that looks in poor health since it may be carrying a disease that will affect your other plants. Don't be tempted by the "sales" corner.

You may think you are getting a bargain, but the plant is usually there because it has been standing around too long, has become pot-bound, and is unlikely to do well once planted.

Weeds on the soil surface show neglect

Reject any plants with diseased or wilted foliage

Tightly packed roots that create a solid mass in the pot will not grow well when planted.

Encrusted soil mix shows that a plant has been in the pot a long time

Weeds growing on the soil mix are a sign of neglect and will have deprived the plant of water and nutrients. They may also be carrying diseases that can affect the plant.

Dead leaves are a sign of neglect or disease, or both. If diseased plants and the surrounding soil mix are brought into the garden, the disease may spread to other plants.

Siting and planting trees

Trees provide permanent features in a garden. They will be there for a long time, and, once established, are difficult to move, so think carefully about what you want to plant and where. Note, also, the final height of the tree or, at least, its height after eight or ten years if it is a slow-maturing type.

In small city gardens there is rarely space to plant a large tree; it will not only plunge your own house and garden into darkness, but the neighbors may suffer too. Don't be tempted by melancholic weeping willows or blue Atlas cedars. By the time they are too large for the garden, you may need to apply for removal permission from the local authorities and pay an arborist to remove them without destroying anybody's property. Instead, think small (*see pp. 122–23*), or choose a tree that can be pruned regularly (*see p. 121*) to keep it within bounds.

Positioning trees

A tree in the garden is like a large piece of furniture in a house: its sheer volume limits its placing. Before committing to a final position, ask friends to help by holding up long sticks or brooms where you are planning to plant. Look at them from key points in the house, such as a kitchen or living room, and in the garden, perhaps from an entrance or seating area. Consider, too, the position of the sun in relation to the tree and the shade it will cast. Think of how and when you use particular areas. To create a brightly lit breakfast area, for example, plant your tree on the west side of the garden, or position a tree on the east or north side of your yard to catch the setting sun on a patio or terrace. A play area needs shade during the hottest part of the day, while vegetable beds need sun all day.

Key features

Having considered size and position, select a tree that will be happy growing in the soil and climatic conditions your garden has to offer. A local nursery that grows its own plants should be able to advise you as to what will perform best in your area. Besides these considerations, there are a host of decorative features that you should take into account.

A tree with colorful foliage (*left*), such as this pagoda dogwood (*Cornus alternifolia 'Argentea'*), creates a spectacular show in a border, providing height, design focus, and a shady area beneath for woodland plants.

The smooth, russet-colored, bark of this cherry, *Prunus serrula* (*above*), peels off to give visual and tactile interest all year. The tree is also covered with white spring blooms, and in the fall the foliage turns a lovely yellow.

Trees as focal points

Trees make beautiful, high-impact features in a garden room. Several of the dogwoods, such as the early summer-flowering *Cornus controversa* or *C. kousa*, and Japanese maples (*Acer palmatum*), with their cut foliage and autumn tints, make striking focal points in a lawn, courtyard area, gravel garden, or at the end of a vista. Or select a tree with multiple stems such as a silver birch, the white trunks and branches of which take on a leading role in dark winter months when the leaves have fallen.

Paired cherry trees (*above*) frame the archway at the end of this garden, directing the eye of the visitor along the grassy path to the area hidden from view.

The weeping silver-leaved pear, *Pyrus salicifolia* 'Pendula', (*left*) makes a handsome feature at the intersection of two gravel paths.

Because trees flower only for a comparatively short time, it may be best to regard blossoms as an added bonus rather than the main attraction. Fruits, berries, or interesting seedpods are, however, worth considering, often lasting longer than the flowers. But the most enduring feature of any tree is the color, texture, and shape of the foliage and stems. Feathery acacias and cut-leaf maples, for example, offer a light, soft touch, creating dappled shade. Or use the layered open habit of pagoda dogwood to introduce horizontal lines, or a cherry with an upright habit to add a vertical dimension.

While autumn color is a seasonal attraction, use trees with year-round yellow, red, or variegated foliage sparingly. The dark purple leaves of some varieties of cherry plums can add drama, but to prevent them from looking too monochromatic or gloomy, set them against lighter colors or where the sky forms a backdrop. Too much yellow can be overpowering, but trees such as golden fullmoon maple or the gold-edged form of tulip tree can brighten up dull areas. A touch of color to create contrast and variety is much more effective than a sea of bright hues competing against each other.

Matching trees to a modern setting can contribute to the clean, straight lines of a formal design, yet soften the effect with rustling leaves and richly textured and patterned bark.

Planting tips

Small trees establish themselves in a new spot more easily than large ones. The best pot size is one that you can carry home in a bag. Keep the roots of bare-root trees shaded and protected from wind, preferably covered by a sheet of plastic or plastic bag, or under a mound of mulch, to prevent them from drying out. Before planting, take a look at the tree's roots and remove any areas of damage.

Place a length of wood or a stake across the center of the hole to get the correct level for planting. Potgrown trees should sit at the same depth as they were in the container. When a bare-root tree is held at the correct level, the point where the roots start to flare out from the trunk should be slightly raised above the soil. Alternatively, plant to the mark of the original soil level on the trunk. If the hole is too deep, remove the tree and put some soil back into the hole.

It is not necessary to enrich the soil unless you have very sandy or poor soil. In fact, this hinders establishment, encouraging the tree's roots to remain within a nutrient-rich "comfort zone" at the planting site, rather than reaching out and down in search of resources.

Double staking will give a newly planted tree extra support in a wind-buffeted position.

Animal guards will need to be in place for several years to protect young trees from damage.

Stakes and animal guards

A single, low stake is generally agreed to be best for most young trees, allowing the stem to flex and strengthen in the wind without tugging at and dislodging the roots. However, for top-heavy and especially top-grafted trees, such as the weeping Kilmarnock willow, a taller stake is advisable, and in very windy sites, two stakes (*above*) can be used. You can use the stake to anchor netting guards in areas where small animals and deer are a nuisance.

Planting a container-grown tree

Prepare your site by clearing it of weeds and, if you have sandy or infertile soil, digging in organic matter over a wide area. Dig a hole, not too deep, but two to three times as wide as the root ball, and fork over and loosen the soil at the bottom. Avoid planting too deeply and in too narrow a hole—90 percent of all young tree deaths can be attributed to this problem.

1 Water the plant in its pot by plunging it into a bucket of water about an hour before planting. Then, remove it from its pot and tease out any compacted roots, and establish the correct depth with a stake.

2 Once the plant sits in the hole at the same depth as it was in its container, drive in the stake on the windward site of the rootball, and rotate the tree until the trunk sits comfortably parallel with the stake.

3 Fill in and firm around the roots and stake with soil. Add a buckle-and-spacer tree tie; this will need to be checked and loosened regularly as the tree grows. Water, and mulch as for a bare-root tree (*see opposite*).

Planting a bare-root tree

About four weeks before planting, prepare the ground. First, clear the site of weeds and grass: dig them out or use a herbicidal weedkiller. Dig in well-rotted manure or garden compost on infertile or sandy soils. Just before planting, remove any new weeds that have germinated. Water your bare-root tree by soaking in a bucket of water about an hour before planting.

1 Dig a circular hole as for container-grown trees (*see opposite*). Lay a stick across the hole and use it to check that the dark soil mark on the stem is just above it.

2 Hold the tree upright—or, better, get someone else to hold it—and backfill the hole with soil, a little at a time, firming it in and around the roots with your fingers.

3 Once the hole is filled, start firming with your heel from the edge to reduce the risk of the soil sinking and the planting level becoming too low.

4 Water in well, then check the level again and fork over to fill any dips. There is no need to fertilize. In fact, this is more likely to cause harm by burning the roots, which will then not be capable of taking up nutrients for at least the first year.

5 Pound a short stake into the ground at a 45° angle. Attach the trunk to the stake using a buckle-and-spacer tree tie that allows the stem to increase in girth without chafing. Check it at least twice during the growing season as the tree matures, and loosen if it is becoming too tight around the trunk.

6 Mulch around the tree with a fibrous, open-textured material, such as well-rotted compost. Spread it in a layer 2½–3in (5–6cm) deep, but keep it clear of the tree stem, where the dampness may cause rot.

Caring for trees after planting

Dehydration is the most common reason for the poor growth or death of young trees, so it is essential to keep your tree well watered during dry spells from spring to fall for the first two to three years after planting. Give each tree at least 11 gallons (50 liters) of water per week; this equates to about seven or eight full watering cans. A length of drainpipe sunk vertically into the soil at the edge of the planting hole can act as a useful watering aid, taking the water directly to lower soil levels, but it will tend to fill up with soil and mulch unless it protrudes above the ground so that it looks unsightly.

To reduce competition for water and nutrients from grass, other plants, and weeds, keep clear a circle of 1yd (1m) diameter around the tree and mulch it every autumn, keeping the mulch away from the trunk itself. Young trees also benefit from an annual application, in spring, of a general all-purpose fertilizer, such as blood-, fish-, and bonemeal. Before you mulch, or after you have pulled back an existing mulch, scatter the fertilizer around the base of the tree at a rate of 2oz per sq yd (70g per sq m), fork it into the soil, then water. Once the tree is well established, you can let the grass grow around the trunk, or plant some bulbs or shade-loving groundcover underneath, without slowing the tree's growth.

Water your tree well after planting, and then weekly during dry spells for the first two growing seasons, as trees are most vulnerable to dehydration when young.

Pest and disease problems on young trees may be treatable, but this becomes increasingly impractical as they grow large. Mature trees are usually quite adept at shrugging off problems in their own time, but if you suspect a serious ailment, you may need to ask for professional advice.

Removing unwanted growth

Try to make only those pruning cuts that are strictly necessary, although if a young tree is awkwardly shaped, it can be pruned lightly (*see pp.214–15*) to improve its appearance and avoid future problems, such as branches that cross and rest their weight on another, leading to splitting.

Suckers, if not removed promptly, gradually take over your plant. They grow from below the graft union on grafted plants and are shoots from the plant used as the rootstock—usually a more vigorous but less attractive plant. They appear low on the trunk below the bulge that is the graft union, or directly from the roots. Watersprouts, thin shoots that grow directly out of the trunk, often massed around pruning wounds, are unsightly and should also be removed as soon as you see them. When they are small, rub them off with your fingers, but use pruners once they become woody.

Removing watersprouts and suckers

Remove watersprouts and suckers as soon as you can, because they divert water and nutrients from the tree if left to grow. Suckers that grow from roots must be pulled off as close to the base as possible—pull back the soil to expose the area where it joins the root. If you cannot pull them off, use pruners to remove them.

Watersprouts that are growing through the bark or around a wound should be removed at their base; use pruners to avoid tears in the bark.

Suckers need to be cut off as close to the base of the shoot as possible. Rub off any regrowth with your fingers or foot as soon as it appears.

Special effects using trees

If you have a small garden and want to restrict the size of a tree, or you wish to encourage young colorful stems, or extrabold leaves, use the pruning methods shown here, known as pollarding and coppicing (*see pp.64–65*). Trees that respond well to this type of hard pruning include catalpa, eucalyptus, hazel, linden, paulonia, poplar, and willow (*see p.229*).

Pollarding

This restricts the size of a tree and encourages larger leaves (here a catalpa). When the trunk of a newly planted tree has reached 3–6ft (1–2m), prune back the branches to 1–2in (2.5–5cm) in late winter or early spring. Then, every year, prune back the young stems that have regrown, and thin out any congested stems.

Coppicing

In late winter or early spring, just before the leaf buds break, cut back all the stems down to the base to stimulate new shoots. Hazel and willow respond well to coppicing every year, but on poor soil it takes less out of the tree if you cut back half the stems one year, and the other half the following year.

Selecting trees

There is today a huge range of trees to choose from, large or small, slender or spreading, native or exotic. Generally speaking, the smaller your garden, the harder-working your tree needs to be in terms of its decorative features, so look for those with more than one season of interest. Where space is not a problem, trees with one breathtaking burst of beauty, such as the large magnolias, become feasible.

You should always keep in mind the potential height and spread of the tree, and never buy a tree without knowing this information. Trees may take many years, more often many decades, to reach anything like their mature heights, especially in a garden, but even so, you may be storing up trouble for future owners.

Trees for small gardens

Betula papyrifera The paper birch, slender and elegant. The new bark is copper-colored, then becomes white and peeling. H 70ft (20m); S 30ft (10m).

Cornus kousa 'China Girl' Starts to flower when very young, with lime green, petal-like bracts that cover the tree. H 22ft (7m); S 15ft (5m).

Trees for focal points

Ilex aquifolium Plain English holly makes an imposing tree, but there are many smaller cultivars, some with leaf variegation. H to 80ft (25m); S 25ft (8m).

Koelreuteria paniculata Graceful, spreading tree as wide as it is tall; the cultivar 'Fastigiata' is narrower and more upright. H 30ft (10m); S 30ft (10m).

Magnolia denudata Known as the lily tree, with spectacularly large, pure white flowers on bare branches in spring. Large, glossy leaves. Other magnolias may be trees or shrubs with pink, white, or yellow flowers, often scented. Some are evergreen and flower much later. H 30ft (10m); S 30ft (10m).

Trees for autumn interest

Acer palmatum 'Bloodgood' Leaves are dark red all year, becoming fiery red in autumn. Very slow-growing; not for alkaline soils. Japanese maples have leaves that may be almost entire or deeply dissected, but all varieties turn to yellow, orange, red, or bronze in fall. H 15ft (5m); S 15ft (5m).

Amelanchier lamarckii A broad, bushy tree, covered in clusters of white flowers in spring. Leaves color completely before falling. H 30ft (10m); S 40ft (12m).

Malus 'Butterball' One of the biggest, boldest fruit displays among the crab-apples. Pink-white blossom in spring. H 25ft (8m); S 25ft (8m).

Gleditsia triacanthos 'Sunburst' The golden-leaved honey locust, unlike the species, doesn't bear seedpods. Stems fiercely spiny. H 40ft (12m); S 30ft (10m).

Laburnum anagyroides 'Pendulum' A small, weeping laburnum, a favorite for town gardens. All parts toxic, especially the seeds. H 12ft (4m); S 8ft (2.5m).

Pyrus salicifolia 'Pendula' The weeping pear; narrow silvery leaves, profuse white blossoms followed by small, pearlike (but inedible) fruits. H 15ft (5m); S 12ft (4m).

Sorbus commixta Compact mountain ash from the Far East; white flower clusters in late spring, then berries. Good autumn color. H 30ft (10m); S 22ft (7m).

Prunus 'Okame' Very profusely flowering cherry in rose-pink. Leaves are narrow and dark green, turning orange and red in autumn. H 30ft (10m); S 25ft (8m).

Prunus serrula Lovely in every season, with glossy, peeling bark, white flowers, cherrylike fruits, and yellow autumn leaf color. H 30ft (10m); S 30ft (10m).

Robinia pseudoacacia 'Frisia' The golden-leaved false acacia, smaller than the plain species. White flowers; orange autumn color. H 50ft (15m); S 25ft (8m).

Trachycarpus fortunei For a very different look; the Chusan palm rarely reaches its full height in a garden setting. H to 70ft (20m); S 8ft (2.5m).

Nyssa sinensis The chinese tupelo; the slender leaves are bronze when young, then green, then many-hued in autumn. The native black gum (*N. sylvaticum*) also has brilliant fall color but may be invasive in warm climates. H 30ft (10m); S 30ft (10m).

Quercus ellipsoidalis An American oak, for acidic soil and a large garden. Smooth, gray bark and ellipse-shaped acorns. H 70ft (20m); S 50ft (15m).

Sorbus 'Joseph Rock' White flowers are followed by berries that by autumn are orange-red, among fiery foliage. Popular with birds. H 30ft (10m); S 22ft (7m).

Designing with shrubs

Shrubs are vital furnishings for the garden. They provide a permanent structure, adding seasonal interest. They can also be used to define areas of the garden, and to disguise trashcans, propane tanks, and compost piles, as well as neighboring gardens.

Shrubs are incredibly versatile and there is one to suit every design and location, whether your garden is large or small. They range from dwarf, ground-covering plants, suitable for the front of a border, to large architectural specimens that grow to several feet tall and wide, and make great screens or backdrops.

Planting styles

Shrubs can help define your garden style. For a modern or minimalist design, consider mass plantings of one plant, or two contrasting plants, such as the evergreen *Viburnum davidii* with its small white flowers followed by steely blue berries, teamed with clipped golden privet, *Ligustrum* 'Vicaryi'. In a more traditional setting, use a wider—but not too wide—range of plants for diversity and interest.

Some shrubs, for example the Maries doublefile Viburnum, with its wedding-cake tiers of horizontal branches, have such a striking appearance that they can be used to provide a focal point at the end of a vista, or a centerpiece in a lawn or gravel garden.

Year-round interest

To create an exciting shrub border, compile a list of plants that perform at different times of the year. If winter and early spring are your garden's weak points, choose plants that flower then; many have a wonderful perfume, such as witch hazel (*Hamamelis*), daphne, and winter boxwood (*Sarcococca confusa*). A useful front-of-border plant is the winter-flowering heather, *Erica carnea*, which, unlike other heathers, is tolerant of alkaline soil (*see pp.38–39*).

Stems also come into their own at this time of year. The corkscrew hazel (*Corylus avellana* 'Contorta') has wild, twisted stems, and dogwoods (*Cornus*) brighten up winter gardens with their colorful bark. Prune your dogwoods hard at the end of winter to encourage plenty of new colorful stems. Include a few evergreens with different leaf shapes and textures, as well as different shades of green to increase visual contrast. Glossy foliage, such as holly leaves or the dark green, narrow leaves of Otto Luyken cherry laurel, help reflect sunlight and sparkle in dull corners. Variegated leaves brighten things up, too. The ground-covering Emerald Gaiety wintercreeper and Quicksilver oleaster add a colorful note to the front of a planting design.

Spring and summer

The yellow flowers of forsythia and pink flowering currants (*Ribes sanguineum*) kickstart spring, together with the early magnolias. On acidic soils, try colorful rhododendrons and azaleas, pieris, and kalmia for a beautiful spring display.

Existing shrubs

If you have recently moved to a mature garden with established trees and shrubs, look critically at what you have. Consider each plant and decide whether you like it enough to warrant keeping it. If a shrub has become large and overgrown, you could prune it hard, thin it, or remove it altogether. If you decide to keep some plants, but replace others, pruning those that are retained will help to integrate new plants with old, as both will be of a similar size.

Maries doublefile Viburnum is a large shrub with horizontally layered branches laden with white flowers in spring. Its unusual shape makes it an eye-catching focal point in a border.

Flowering shrubs for late spring and early summer include barberry, lilac, and scented osmanthus and philadelphus, while smaller shrubs, including rock roses, potentillas, spiraea, hebes, and penstemons make colorful fillers for the front of the border or mixed in with perennials. For summer color, plant butterfly bush, hydrangeas, escallonias, fuchsias, and St. John's wort. The summer-flowering heathers also provide a show at this time of the year, provided that you have acidic soil to keep them happy. On a hot sunny site, try lavender, caryopteris, and Russian sage.

For year-round interest clipped evergreens are hard to beat. Plants such as santolinas (*here*) and box offer winter color and structure. Trimmed into low domes, either will work well with other mound-forming plants, such as lavender and catmints.

Autumn

This is the time to turn your attention from flowers to leaf color and fruits. The best foliage color is often seen when a long, warm summer is followed by a cold snap. The colors will also look brighter under sunny skies, so site your plants where they will receive as much fall sunlight as possible. Winning plants for this time of the year include Japanese maples, deciduous cotoneasters, and azaleas, dogwoods, and the interesting smokebush.

Birds soon devour their favorite fruits and berries in the fall, and in themselves add to the autumn display. To extend the season of interest, combine popular shrubs with a few whose fruit is less attractive to wildlife, such as some crab apples, yellow-berried cotoneasters, and roses, the hips of which often last throughout the winter.

Attracting wildlife

Shrubs provide food for small mammals, birds, and insects, supplying them with fruits, seeds, and nectar. They also provide cover and nesting areas for birds. Prickly, evergreen, and berried shrubs, including European *spindle tree*, barberry, elder, and cotoneaster will soon be found by the birds, while hebes, butterfly bush, lavender, and rosemary attract butterflies, bees, and other beneficial insects, such as hoverflies—the larvae of which eat aphids—into your garden.

Nectar-rich plants, such as the butterfly bush, *Buddleja davidii*, will attract butterflies and moths into your garden with its mauve, pink, red, or white summer flowers.

The red autumn berries of cotoneaster are a good meal for birds stocking up for winter. Site one near a window to watch them feeding. The white spring flowers also attract insects.

Elder (*Sambucus nigra*) has clusters of white spring flowers that attract insects, followed by beautiful glossy black fruits in autumn that are a treat for the birds.

Planting shrubs

Unlike herbaceous perennials, which create a good display from year one, shrubs are slower to establish and require a little patience. You have two options to fill your space quickly: either plant shrubs more densely than you should, then thin them out a few years later; or, give them enough space to allow each to mature into an attractive specimen, and for the first few years fill the gaps with annuals for immediate color, or tried-and-true perennials such as hardy geraniums. The perennials may, over time, be shaded out and disappear, or can be moved very easily to another location. Most gardening experts would advise the second option, as it is cheaper and easier in the long run, but dense planting can be useful if you want quick results and are prepared to move your shrubs (*see opposite*) before they get too big.

Site and soil

Before buying a shrub, be sure that it will suit the conditions in your garden: some plants thrive only on acidic soil, so remember to test your soil (*see pp.38–39*) before buying. Also, look at the aspect – will the plant be in shade or sun for most of the day? There is a wide range of shrubs that suit either, so whatever the aspect, there will be plenty of choice.

When to plant

Hardy deciduous shrubs, both bare-root and container-grown, are best planted between autumn and early spring. Fall planting usually helps the plants start off better the following year, but do not plant if the ground is very wet or frozen, and remember that the roots will not grow during cold spells. Plant slightly tender shrubs in spring, and all evergreens too if you live in a cold or exposed area, and keep well watered during dry spells. You can plant any containerized shrubs in summer, but they will need to be watered frequently.

Soil preparation

Dig out any perennial weeds, or apply a herbicidal weedkiller to the planting area a few weeks before you intend to plant. Dig over the soil and incorporate some well-rotted manure or garden compost to improve its drainage and water-retentiveness.

Planting a container-grown shrub

First, water your shrub well by plunging it, pot and all, in deep water for about an hour, then let it drain. To remove the root ball from the pot, turn the pot over and hold the shrub firmly with the fingers of one hand between the stems at soil level, then gently squeeze the sides of the pot, or tap the base, until it slides off. Gently tease out any roots that are curling around the root ball.

1 Dig a planting hole as deep and twice as wide as the the root ball of the shrub (here a viburnum). Place the plant into the hole and lay a stick across the top to be sure that it is at the same depth as it was in its original container. Adjust the hole's depth if necessary.

2 Set the shrub in the hole, backfill around the root ball with your hands and then firm in with your heel. As you firm in your shrub, create a slight saucer-shaped depression in the soil surrounding the plant to encourage water to collect naturally over the root area.

3 Prune lightly only if necessary: cut out any dead or damaged stems, and prune any that are growing toward the center of the plant back to a healthy, outward-facing bud or shoot. Water the plant well, and then apply a mulch, leaving a space around the stems.

Transplanting a shrub

If you decide a shrub is in the wrong place you can move it. The younger the shrub, the easier and more successful the move should be. The best time to transplant a deciduous shrub is in the autumn; move evergreens in the spring, just before the new growth emerges. Prune the shrub back by a third beforehand to compensate for root loss and make it easier to handle.

2 Dig a trench around the circle and use a fork to loosen the soil around the roots. With a spade, dig under the root ball so that it can be lifted out of the soil, cutting through woody roots if necessary.

1 Using a spade, mark out a circle around the outer edge of the roots. The roots of shrubs normally do not spread out farther than the extent of the stems before they were pruned.

3 Tilt the plant to one side and feed a piece of burlap or a tarpaulin under it. Then rock the shrub to the other side and pull the material through so that the plant is sitting on top of it.

4 With a large, heavy root ball like this one, you will need someone to help you carry the shrub to its new location in the garden.

5 In the new site, dig a hole twice as wide and the same depth as the root ball. Lower the shrub into the new hole as shown.

6 Fill in with soil around the roots, making sure there are no air gaps. Firm with your foot. Water the plant well and apply a mulch.

Selecting shrubs for year-round interest

Visit gardens and parks in all seasons to help you make your selection and take into account the existing plants in your garden, making a note of when and where an additional effect is needed. If you have a front and back garden, you may want to give them a different seasonal emphasis. Back gardens tend to be used most intensively during spring, summer, and early autumn, when the weather is milder and days are longer. The front garden, on the other hand, is used daily, and will benefit from some evergreens, as well as a few strongly scented winter and early spring-flowering shrubs, such as evergreen winter boxwood (*Sarcococca*), *Viburnum* x *bodnantense* 'Dawn', or a daphne to greet you and your visitors.

Winter stems and flowers

Cornus sanguinea 'Winter Beauty'
Unpruned, would grow to 10ft (3m), but cut back each year for winter stems (*see p.121*) makes H 3ft (1m); S 4ft (1.2m).

Corylus avellana 'Contorta' Commonly called the corkscrew hazel for its twisted stems. Can be coppiced (*see p.121*). H to 15ft (5m); S to 15ft (5m).

Hamamelis x intermedia 'Jelena'
Witch hazel with orange flowers on bare branches in midwinter. Good autumn leaf color, too. H 12ft (4m); S 20ft (6m).

Mahonia x media 'Charity' Upright and spiny-leaved evergreen, architectural, with large, spiky clusters of scented flowers. H to 10ft (3m); S to 6ft (2m).

Salix alba 'Britzensis' Excellent willow for pollarding or coppicing (*see p.121*), with bright young stems. Unpruned height to 80ft (25m).

Viburnum x bodnantense 'Dawn'
Deciduous shrub with powerfully scented flowers on bare stems from late autumn to spring. H 10ft (3m); S 6ft (2m).

Autumn color

Ceratostigma willmottianum Very striking blue late summer flowers; the leaves then turn bright red before they fall. H 3ft (1m); S 5ft (1.5m).

Cotinus 'Grace' A blaze of translucent color when backlit by autumn sunshine. Can make a small tree, but tolerates pruning. H 20ft (6m); S 15ft (5m).

Cotoneaster frigidus Large, deciduous shrub; profuse clusters of white flowers in spring. Fruits are yellow in 'Fructo Luteo'. H 30ft (10m); S 30ft (10m).

Euonymus europaeus 'Red Cascade' Spindle tree with an extraordinary mixture of scarlet-crimson leaves and fuchsia-pink fruits in autumn. H 10ft (3m); S 8ft (2.5m).

Camellia Many varieties with single (*here*), or double flowers, in early to mid-spring, and glossy, evergreen foliage. Usually around H 12ft (4m); S 6ft (2m).

Choisya 'Aztec Pearl' Compact evergreen; scented flowers in late spring, then again in late summer, especially if deadheaded. H 8ft (2.5m); S 8ft (2.5m).

Cistus x argenteus 'Peggy Sammons' Bushy, upright rock rose covered in a succession of large, pink flowers through the summer. H 3ft (1m); S 3ft (1m).

Kerria japonica 'Golden Guinea' Lovely, bright spring-flowering shrub with broad, hypericum-like golden-yellow flowers. H 6ft (2m); S 8ft (2.5m).

Hydrangea macrophylla 'Mariesii Perfecta' Lacecap, commonly sold as 'Blue Wave'; the blue color only reliable in acidic soils. H 6ft (2m); S 8ft (2.5m).

Perovskia 'Blue Spire' Hazy, atmospheric subshrub with silvery stems and leaves, and violet-blue flowers in late summer. H 4ft (1.2m); S 3ft (1m).

Rosmarinus officinalis Prostratus Group Low, spreading rosemary for a sunny bank. 'Capri' is a dwarf cultivar. H to 24in (60cm); S 4–6ft (1.2–2m).

Syringa vulgaris 'Katherine Havemeyer' Fragrant lilac with pinkish purple buds opening to lavender-blue flowers. H to 22ft (7m); S to 1.2ft (4m).

Fothergilla gardenii Small, dense, acidic-soil-loving shrub with white spring flowers and russet fall tones, good for a woodland garden. H 3ft (1m); S 3ft (1m).

Hamamelis vernalis The Ozark witch hazel, flowering on bare branches in late winter. Purple-leaved and weeping cultivars are available. H 15ft (5m); S 15ft (5m).

Leycesteria formosa A thicket-forming, deciduous shrub with green stems. Flowers followed by purple berries. H 6ft (2m); S 6ft (2m).

Viburnum opulus The guelder rose; native, deciduous shrub very popular with birds, with lacecap clusters of white flowers in spring. H 15ft (5m); S 12ft (4m).

Using roses

Guaranteed to bring a note of romance into your garden, the rose has, for many centuries, been one of the most sought-after garden flowers. With thousands of different types to choose from, think first about how you want to use yours. There are dwarf roses for patios and pots, large shrubs to fill gaps at the back of the border, and giant ramblers that will scramble over buildings and pergolas, or scale trees. You can opt for roses that flower once a year and usually bear fruits, or others that bloom throughout the summer.

Roses in small gardens

Traditionally, roses were grown in their own gardens, but few people today have the space to plant formal rose beds. You will also have a longer season of interest if you mix roses with other plants, and disguise the few prickly sticks left after annual pruning. Roses are also less likely to infect each other with blackspot or mildew when grown in a mixed environment, and surrounding flowers will attract beneficial insects that help to control aphids. A little blackspot or mildew will not kill the plant, but it is

Planting a rose

Use the same planting method as for a shrub (see p. 126). Before planting the rose, prune off any dead, damaged, or crossing stems and damaged roots. The location of the graft union (the bulge at the base of the stem) depends on your climate: above ground where winters are mild, well below where cold. Consult local growers for correct planting depth.

unsightly when it affects a whole bed of roses. This is less of an problem where other plants are used to mask the diseased foliage. It is better to disguise the problem than to apply pesticides that can harm the environment and wildlife. Look for disease-resistant varieties in catalogs.

Types of rose

Roses come in many shapes and forms, and because many are sold when dormant and pruned back, it is difficult to see what they will look like when mature. Before buying, familiarize yourself with the terms used for different roses so you get a plant that suits, and know its pruning needs (see pp.226–27). As well as the main types of roses shown here, the flower shape may also be described on the label—single, with the central boss of stamens visible; semidouble, with an extra ruff of petals; or double, with a rounded mass of over 30 petals.

Floribunda bush roses, such as 'The Queen Elizabeth' bear sprays of flowers. Like the hybrid teas, they flower best and most continuously if you cut off the dead flowers.

Shrub Some of the romantic old garden roses and the wilder species roses flower only once, others put on a longer show. Modern shrubs such as 'Sally Holmes' (above) all flower repeatedly.

Climbers Summer Wine, although unusual in its semi- rather than fully double flowers, is a typical modern climber in habit, with stiff, elongated stems that benefit from careful training.

Ramblers 'Seagull' is one of the most rampant of these vigorous climbers, with long, flexible stems that naturally scramble. Flowers are generally single, and borne in one great burst in summer.

Hybrid teas such as Fragrant Cloud bear flowers singly or in twos or threes. For the largest flowers, prune hard.

Training climbing and shrub roses

Roses flower more prolifically if their branches are trained horizontally, or near-horizontally, as all side-shoots then produce flower buds, rather than just leaf. A pergola (*see p.112*) is ideal for this, but even if your garden is small, you can grow larger shrub roses and climbers by carefully training them up a sunny wall. More compact shrub roses, such as 'Charles de Mills' or Gertrude Jekyll, can be pegged down, and this again produces more flowers by training the stems horizontally along the ground.

To train a climber on wall first attach a series of sturdy wires horizontally up the wall. Spread out the stems, and tie them to the wires with soft twine. Shorten sideshoots that stick out from the wall.

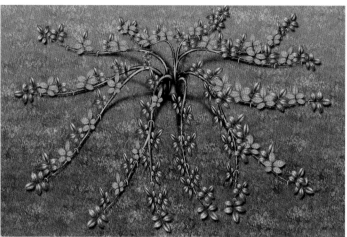

Peg down a shrub rose by anchoring the new growth in spring with wooden or metal pegs. Remove the stems that carried last season's flowers at their bases to encourage new growth to peg down next year.

Shape and foliage

Because many roses can be quite ungainly when not in flower, look for those with a good overall shape. Species roses, such as *Rosa xanthina* f. *hugonis*, are graceful, outwardly arching plants. 'Geranium' makes a handsome shrub, with its brick red single flowers, followed by bottle-shaped rosehips in late summer. Other shapely shrubs include 'Marguerite Hilling', with large, bright pink, single flowers throughout the summer, and 'Nevada', which produces creamy flowers.

Some roses also have interesting foliage, such as *Rosa glauca*, with blue-green leaves offset by dark red stems. A few roses have scented foliage, which can become quite powerful on warm summer evenings when the atmosphere is slightly humid. Try *Rosa primula*, the leaves of which smell of incense, or *Rosa rubiginosa* with its apple-scented foliage.

Rosehips

Single-flowered and species roses may only flower once, but the blooms are followed by colorful rosehips that light up autumn and winter gardens, and provide a useful food source for garden visitors, like birds and small mammals. Many of the rugosa roses, such as *Rosa rugosa* 'Alba', 'Charles Albanel', and 'Fru Dagmar Hastrup' bear chubby, round red hips, while others, such as the vigorous rambler *Rosa filipes* 'Kiftsgate', produce sprays of little red buttons.

Roses soften formal plantings; this central path is flanked with the delicate pink blooms of 'Felicia' and deep red 'Frensham', together with lavender and sisyrinchiums.

Finding the rose for you

With such a huge range of roses available, making a final choice can be daunting. When making your selection, think about how much time you want to commit to looking after your plants. As a rule, hybrid teas and floribunda roses, such as Freedom and The Times Rose respectively, tend to be the most demanding, requiring careful pruning and being intolerant of crowding by other plants, which is why they were traditionally grown on in separate rose beds.

If you have less time to spare, choose slightly tougher shrub roses. These include the old garden roses, such as albas and hybrid musks; English roses, including Redouté and Cordelia; rugosa roses, which are among the toughest, most undemanding roses available; all the species roses, like *Rosa pimpinellifolia*, *R. canina*, and *R. glauca*, as well as a large range of modern shrub and groundcover roses such as 'Marguerite Hilling', Bonica, and the Flower Carpet roses in their various colors.

The biggest problem for many small garden owners is the lack of sunlight. Roses are sun-lovers and will demand optimum growing conditions to perform well. It is especially important to plant those roses that flower more than once in the season in a sunny, south-facing position. If your garden receives sun for only part of the day, opt for once-only flowering types. The lovely alba roses come into this group and include beauties such as the creamy-white 'Alba Maxima' (*below*) and double-flowered, pale pink 'Great Maiden's Blush', both of which have the typically healthy, pale gray-green foliage that gives this group of old roses their distinctive character.

Choose easy-care shrub roses for a low-maintenance garden. 'Alba Maxima', for example, needs little pruning, tolerates some shade, and bears masses of creamy-white flowers.

Selecting roses

Roses are one of the groups of plants most commonly bought by mail order, simply because the specialty rose nurseries offer an extensive choice, compared to most garden centers. The only disadvantage of ordering by mail is that you cannot select the actual plant you want, although most of these firms have an excellent reputation and should respond immediately if you believe a rose has arrived in poor condition. Another option is to visit local botanical gardens, rose shows, and collections. Contact the American Rose Society at www.ars.org and the Canadian Rose Society at www.canadianrosesociety.org for plant information, a list of chapters, open gardens, and rose shows in your area.

Roses for patios

Little Bo-peep An excellent miniature rose for containers, very dense and bushy and covered with flowers all season. H 32in (80cm); S 3ft (1m).

Warm Welcome A miniature climber, good on a wigwam or obelisk-style support in a tub, flowering from top to bottom. H to 8ft (2.5m); S to 5ft (1.5m).

Cider Cup Miniature floribunda rose, with flowers in clusters, in warm orange-apricot-pink, with dark leaves and a fruity scent. H 30in (75cm); S 24in (60cm).

Pheasant Groundcover rose, actually a type of rambler that will spill over the sides of a large pot, or can be trained up a support. H to 11ft (3.5m); S 6ft (2m).

Roses for a pergola or arch

'Buff Beauty' Disease-resistant, with scented flowers over a long season. A lax shrub, ideal on a vertical support in a warm site. H 6ft (2m).

'Gloire de Dijon' Climbing tea rose, with "quartered" pompon blooms typical of old garden roses. Leggy, benefits from training (*see p.131*). H 15ft (5m).

Handel Modern climber, quite compact and lovely for an obelisk or an arch, making good new growth from the base each year. H 10ft (3m).

'Climbing Iceberg' Climbing version of the popular floribunda bush rose; very floriferous, sweet-scented, and not too thorny. H 12ft (4m).

Roses for a mixed bed

Baby Love A patio rose that makes an excellent front-of-border plant or a low hedge, very neat and well-clothed to the base. H 36in (90cm); S 30in (75cm).

Bonica A low shrub rose that makes excellent groundcover, with a long flowering season followed by bright red hips. H 3ft (1m); S 4ft (1.2m).

'Lovers' Meeting' Hybrid tea rose, a fabulous color for warm schemes or contrasted with dark blue salvias or catmint. H 3ft (1m); S 3ft (1m).

'Roseraie de l'Haÿ' Rugosa rose, with wrinkled leaves, making a large, dense shrub, flowers almost continuously until late autumn. H to 6ft (2m); S 6ft (2m).

Roses for scent

'Félicité Parmentier' Old garden rose in the alba group, with a single flush of beautiful and fragrant flowers. H 5ft (1.5m); S 3ft (1m).

Fragrant Cloud Large, vigorous hybrid tea, although the flowers, which fade to purple with age, are often borne in clusters. H 5ft (1.5m); S 3ft (1m).

Gertrude Jekyll An English rose, in the old garden style but repeat-flowering. Deadhead for a continuous show of flowers. H 4ft (1.2m); S 3ft (1m).

Valencia A hybrid tea, vigorous and usually healthy, with long sturdy stems that make it excellent for cutting. Very strongly sweet-scented. H 4ft (1.2m); S 3ft (1m).

Choosing and siting climbers

Climbers are real assets for small gardens, giving height without taking up too much ground space. Use their foliage and flowers to dress up trellises, walls, and other garden structures, or let them climb through trees and shrubs to prolong the interest of these natural supports.

Selecting climbers

While some climbers are quite small, reaching up to around head-height, others can extend to the top of large trees or over your house, so check the final heights of your chosen plants when making your plans. Also watch for mature specimens in other people's gardens or parks to see how they perform.

If you want to plant several climbers together so that they intermingle, make sure their pruning requirements are compatible. A late-blooming, large-flowered clematis, such as the dark purple 'Jackmanii Superba', makes a good match with one of the viticella types, such as the rich red 'Mme. Julia Correvon' or dark purple 'Etoile Violette', since both are pruned back to about 12in (30cm) in early spring (*see pp.224–25*). But neither makes a good match with early flowering types, such as *Clematis alpina*, which can be left or pruned after flowering, from mid- to late spring. When pruning the late-flowering variety, it will be all too easy to remove the wrong stems

Leafy climbers are the perfect plants to create a cool retreat. Here, ivy and climbing hydrangea scale the house walls, softening the brickwork. Both are self-clinging, and need no additional wires or supports to climb, but be aware that they can damage old masonry.

Annual climbers such as these black-eyed Susans (*Thunbergia alata*), and also morning glorys, sweet peas, and nasturtiums, are perfect for filling in gaps while a woody climber establishes, or for a wigwam support in a border.

and prune off the flowers of your spring performer as well. Likewise, it is best to plant together climbers with similar support requirements.

Siting climbers

In the wild, many climbers, including clematis, scramble up through trees and shrubs until they reach the light at the top. To imitate these conditions in a more open site in your garden, be sure the climber has its head in the sun, and use other plants around its base to help shade the roots.

You can also use an established tree as a coat hanger for one or two climbing plants. Trees with light canopies, such as old fruit trees or locusts, are suited to this because light filters through the branches and encourages the climber to work its way up through the canopy. Good candidates for this type of display include rambling roses, such as blousy pink 'Albertine' and creamy 'Bobby James', and summer-flowering, large-flowered clematis such as 'Perle d'Azur', which will start to bloom as the rose finishes.

How climbers climb

Different plants have developed different climbing techniques, and understanding how your plants climb will help you provide the best supports. Some popular "climbers," such as winter jasmine, plumbago, and potato vine (*Solanum*) are actually just spindly shrubs that cannot climb independently, and like any wall shrub, such as a firethorn, these need tying in as they grow.

Stem twiners such as honeysuckle and wisteria wind around their supports and can be trained along wires or up posts. Not recommended for growing through host plants as they may strangle them.

Stem roots These plants produce tiny aerial roots along the stems that cling to vertical supports, such as walls and fences. They can damage old walls. Ivies are the most widely grown.

Leaf stalk and tendril twiners such as clematis or passion flowers produce thin, flexible leaf stalks or tendrils that twine on contact with wires, trellises, or the stems of other plants.

Adhesive pads on the stems of plants such as Virginia creeper adhere to walls and posts, so they do not need wires, trellises, or stakes for support, and are useful for large surfaces.

Hookers Plants such as roses and brambles use the thorns along their stems to hoist themselves up over their support. Unless grown through a host plant, they often need to be tied in to direct their growth.

If you plan to use a conifer as a host, plant just outside the edge of the canopy, and use stakes to guide the stems up to the lowest branches. You can plant a little closer to the main trunk of deciduous trees. If possible, plant on the windward side of the tree, so that unsecured young shoots are blown toward, rather than away from, the stem.

When planting climbers against walls, remember that south-facing walls can be too hot for some. Sunlight and heat reflect off the walls during the day, and the bricks absorb heat which they then release at night. If you have a south-facing wall to cover, choose a sun-lover, such as a passion flower, wisteria, trachelospermum, or a grape vine (*Vitis*). The soil will also be dry next to a sunny wall, so plant about 18in (45cm) away from the structure, mulch generously in the spring, and water during dry weather.

Plant clematis and roses where they will receive the cooler morning or early evening sun, because both dislike the intense heat of a south wall, unless it is partially shaded.

Mixing annual with woody climbers

Like all woody plants, climbers can sometimes take a few years to establish. Before they reach their required height and spread, you can fill the space with annual climbers for instant results. Sweet peas, morning glories, and climbing nasturtiums are all good choices for sunny sites, although the latter also tolerates some shade.

To embellish a vegetable garden with a few climbers, opt for annuals because their root systems are less invasive than those of woody or perennial plants, and they will not interfere with crop production. Pole and scarlet runner beans work well, as do some varieties of cucumber, or even ornamental gourds.

Wisteria dripping with scented flowers is a stunning sight in spring, but remember that it is very vigorous, needs strong support, and must be pruned regularly (*see pp.224–25*).

Preparing for planting

When planting a climber against a wall or fence, attach any necessary supports first, before you prepare the soil, otherwise you will be trampling and compacting it while fixing up your wires or trellis. With freestanding supports such as arches and obelisks, if you can, it is worth digging over the whole general area before erecting the support, rather than trying to negotiate around the uprights afterwards. Be especially careful to work plenty of organic matter into the soil when planting next to walls and masonry pillars; the soil here may be full of building debris, and needs to be as water-retentive as possible to combat the "rain shadow" thrown by walls.

Attach wires to the support
You can screw vine eyes directly into drilled holes in wooden fence posts; for masonry, plastic anchors are recommended.

Using vine eyes

Vine eyes, available from all good garden centers and hardware stores, are invaluable for attaching wires to vertical surfaces, pillars, and posts. Not only can the wire be attached very securely, but it can be "tensioned," or pulled taut, by giving the vine eye a few more turns once the wire is in place. Use U-shaped metal staples as intermediate supports along long stretches of wire.

Dig in organic matter such as garden compost or well-rotted manure over a good-sized area around the climber's intended position. If the soil is very poor, for example in a newly developed site, scatter over and fork in some general fertilizer as well.

Planting against a wall or fence

Once you have prepared the soil and equipped the wall or fence with appropriate wire or trellis supports (*see left, and p.138*), it is worth planting conscientiously for the best chance of rapid establishment and quick coverage of the surface.

1 About an hour before planting, water the plant well several times, or submerge it in a bucket of water. Allow to drain.

2 Dig a hole about 18in (45cm) from the fence, not right up against it in the dry "rain shadow." Check the depth of the hole.

3 Use bamboo canes arranged in a fan-shape and leaning into the fence to form a temporary support on which to guide the climber's stems up to the permanent wires. The canes can be removed later.

4 Lean the plant (here, honeysuckle) against the canes; make sure it is still level with the oil (except for clematis, which should be about in (10cm) below the surface level). Backfill the ole with a trowel, then firm in with your fists.

5 Untie the plant from its original cane and remove this, then fan out the main stems and tie into the canes, using soft twine in a loose figure eight. Tying just above the cane's joints usually keeps the twine from slipping.

6 Fluff the soil up a little if you have been kneeling too close to the plant, then draw it up to form a circular ridge around the base of the climber, creating a saucer-shaped depression that will hold water.

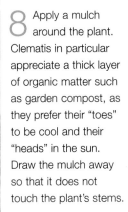

7 Give the plant a very thorough drenching with water. The hollow in the soil you have created will retain the excess water, allowing it to seep down into the root area. Water the new climber regularly in the months to come, especially if planting in spring.

8 Apply a mulch around the plant. Clematis in particular appreciate a thick layer of organic matter such as garden compost, as they prefer their "toes" to be cool and their "heads" in the sun. Draw the mulch away so that it does not touch the plant's stems.

9 Once the stems reach the wires, train the outermost ones horizontally along the lower wires, and the central ones up and along the upper ones, for good coverage.

Supports for climbers

The method by which your plant climbs (*see p.134*), as well as its vigor, should influence the type, strength, and size of the support you use for it. On walls, the least obtrusive support to add is galvanized wire; on the other hand, a fancy trellis can be used to add decorative appeal to workaday surfaces. Plastic and metal ties must be checked and loosened regularly, particularly on woody climbers. Twine or raffia, with some "give," are better.

Walls and fences For wall shrubs or roses, attach horizontal wires 18in (45cm) apart. For leaf or stem twiners, add vertical wires as well, or use large-mesh galvanized wire.

Pergolas and arches Attach vertical wires to run up and down opposite sides of the posts. Train and tie in your climber in a corkscrew fashion when the stems are young and flexible.

Free-standing supports The more vigorous and heavier the climber, the sturdier a wigwam, pyramid, or obelisk must be. Home-made bamboo cane tripods will do for annuals and most perennials.

Selecting climbers

Compared to other groups of plants, such as shrubs and perennials, there is quite a limited range of climbers available for frost-prone gardens—especially if you are looking for evergreens. However, as if in compensation, there are huge numbers of clematis, climbing roses (*see p.133*), and ivies to choose from. Other classic climbers are very hard to beat—including honeysuckle and jasmine for scent, or *Parthenocissus* for good coverage and an autumn blaze of color. You can, however, add more interest with more exotic-looking plants; for example, some passion flowers, are hardier than they look. Bold flowers can also be added by growing tender climbers as annuals, such as *Eccremocarpus* and the yellow canary creeper, *Tropaeolum peregrinum*.

Climbers for flowers

Clematis tangutica Unusual among clematis in having yellow flowers; late-blooming, with conspicuous fluffy gray seedheads. H to 20ft (6m).

Eccremocarpus scaber The Chilean glory vine, grows well as an annual in temperate climates, may overwinter in warm areas. H 10–15ft (3–5m).

Ipomoea purpurea Fast-growing annual, best in hot summers, morning glory flowers vary from blue to purple-pink, often striped. H 6–10ft (2–3m).

Passiflora caerulea Mostly hardy; shoul regrow if cut back by frost; these striking flowers are followed by large, egg-shapec orange-yellow fruits. H 30ft (10m) or more.

Climbers for north- or east-facing walls

Clematis 'Markham's Pink' Macropetala-type clematis with hanging flowers in spring followed by silvery seedheads. H 6–10ft (2–3m).

Hedera helix All are suitable for a cold wall; heights range from 12in (45cm) to 25ft (8m). This small ivy, 'Merion Beauty', is ideal for a basket, patio, or tub.

Jasminum nudiflorum Winter-flowering jasmine is a sprawling plant that must be tied in, and needs regular trimming to keep it flat. H 10ft (3m).

Pyracantha Shrubs that wall-train well; quite robust, so provide support to match. Small, white, spring flowers. Orange or yellow berries. H to 12ft (4m).

Climbers for scent

Clematis montana 'Elizabeth' A vigorous, fragrant clematis that is free-flowering for about a month in late spring and early summer. H 22ft (7m).

Jasminum officinale 'Argenteo-variegatum' Late summer-flowering, hardy, twining jasmine, with leaves edged in cream. H 40ft (12m).

Lonicera periclymenum Common honeysuckle, perhaps the most powerfully scented, the flowers and red berries are very popular with wildlife. H 22ft (7m).

Trachelospermum jasminoides The evergreen star jasmine needs a sunny, sheltered wall, flowers mid- to late summer. H 28ft (9m).

Climbers for foliage

Actinidia kolomikta Related to the kiwi, the pink- and white-splashed leaves are the main attraction, although on young plants leaves are green. H 15ft (5m).

Hedera helix Variegated ivies are good for lightening a gloomy wall, this is 'Eva', with small but dense foliage, heavily splashed with white. H 4ft (1.2m).

Parthenocissus tricuspidata Boston ivy and the similar Virginia creeper are vigorous woody climbers renowned for autumn color. H 70ft (20m).

Vitis coignetiae Ornamental relative of the grape vine with small, unpalatable fruits. Grown for its huge leaves and vibrant autumn color. H 50ft (15m).

Effects with bamboos

As relatives of the grasses, bamboos are not strictly woody plants, but from a gardening point of view, we tend to treat them as such because their tough woody canes live for many years. The absence of flowers, fruit, or other seasonal features is made up for by their graceful, swaying stems, and fine leaves that rustle in the breeze. The canes of some are unusually colored, ranging from gray-green and yellow to inky black. As a bonus, after a few years you can harvest your own bamboo canes to use as plant supports.

Siting bamboos

Bamboos range in height from 4–6in (10–15cm) to giants that will tower above a house. They vary in hardiness, too. The majority prefer moist soil, although *Pseudosasa japonica* tolerates shallow soil over alkaline soil, while most *Fargesia*, *Sasa*, and *Phyllostachys* tolerate shade. Some, such as *Pleioblastus*, tend to spread rampantly, but others, such as *Phyllostachys*, remain in a manageable clump. Ask for advice, and if choosing an invasive type, make sure you have sufficient space, or use a root barrier (*see right*). Bamboos often spread less in moist situations than in dry.

The majority of bamboos die after flowering, but don't let this put you off, since it may not happen in your lifetime. You can also avoid this by buying young plants, such as offspring of *Fargesia murielae,* which flowered in the 1990s.

Planting pointers

To prevent rampant bamboos from spreading throughout your garden, restrain the roots using a barrier at least 16in (40cm) deep, made of overlapping slates, steel, or nonperishable plastic. Bury the barrier vertically in the ground, with 3–4in (8–10cm) protruding above the surface, so that it encircles the bamboo. If you can, seal any joins so that no roots escape. Alternatively, dig down with a spade each year all around the clump, and slice off and dig out any roots outside the barrier.

A plastic barrier helps to prevent roots from spreading

Bamboos with attractive stems

Grown for their elegance and delicate foliage, some bamboos also have decorative stems. The lighter colored ones look great against a background of dark foliage, while darker stems are best set in a sunny site or against a colorful wall.

Phyllostachys aurea, the fishpole or golden bamboo, can grow huge in the wild but usually reaches about 12ft (4m) in the garden. Leaves are golden-green.

Phyllostachys vivax 'Aureocaulis' is a stout-stemmed, fast-growing bamboo with butter-yellow canes, sometimes green-striped. Can grow tall, to 18ft (6m).

Phyllostachys nigra has canes that become almost jet-black by their third year. A neat clump-former, it grows 10–15ft (3–5m) tall, and half that across.

Thamnocalamus crassinodus 'Kew Beauty' needs light shade for the best color display. Canes are slate blue when young, aging to pinkish-red. To 12ft (4m).

Show stoppers

Bamboos are a versatile group of garden plants. Architectural types, such as the elegant *Fargesia murielae* and *Fargesia nitida*, or the fuzzier-looking *Chusquea culeou,* look spectacular as a main focal point in a bed, or standing alone in a hard landscape setting, such as a gravel or courtyard garden.

Bamboos are particularly suited to modern designs, too. Try planting one species en masse in geometric-shaped beds to create a contemporary look, or use them in a row to make a dramatic screen, either as a border fence or to divide up the garden into rooms. For a screen or feature, consider bamboos with interesting stems, such as the black-caned *Phyllostachys nigra* (*see opposite*) or one of the yellow-stemmed types, such as *Phyllostachys bambusoides* 'Castilloni'.

Groundcover

Bamboos with a low, carpeting habit, such as *Pleioblastus pygmaeus*, which grows to a maximum height of about 36in (90cm), can be used as effective groundcover, since almost nothing will grow beneath them, and they need little attention. But, again, use them only where you can afford to let them run wild since they are hard to dig up.

A see-through bamboo screen creates a delicate divide between two areas of the garden, or two can be used to line a pathway, creating a tunnel-like feature painted with dappled light.

Using containers

It is possible to grow bamboos in containers, but you must use pots big enough for the roots, and never let the plants dry out. For smaller bamboos, pots should be at least 16in (40cm) in diameter; they need to be 36in (90cm) or more across for larger plants. Containers in contemporary designs and materials work very well with bamboos.

One of the best small bamboos for a container is the light, fernlike *Pleioblastus pygmaeus*, or, for something taller, try *Arundinaria gigantea* subsp. *tecta*, with its yellowish stems, which reaches about 6ft (1.8m) in height.

Feed the plants throughout the growing season (a slow-release fertilizer is ideal) and make sure they do not get too crowded by cutting out about one in three of the canes each year.

An elegant backdrop where space is tight, *Fargesia* forms an erect clump rather than spreading over and shading out any shrubs and plants in front of it.

Designing with hedges

Hedges have many uses within the garden. Most commonly planted as boundary screens, they can also serve as internal divisions or low edging for beds, borders, or paths. When close-clipped and uniform, hedges confer a neat formality; when mixed and billowy they are a garden in themselves.

Hedges have other practical uses, too. They make excellent windbreaks, and are more effective than solid walls and fences. Deciduous hedges in particular filter the blast and slow windspeeds, whereas solid barriers actually cause turbulence on the sheltered side, damaging plants and, more expensively, the fence. Evergreens help muffle the noise of traffic and offer year-round privacy, while dense, thorny hedges deter intruders—both the animal and human kind. For an impenetrable barrier choose prickly plants, such as barberry, firethorn, holly, or Japanese rose. These many benefits often inspire builders of new houses to plant hedges instead of putting up fences around gardens.

Hedges for wildlife

Hedges can enrich the garden by encouraging birds and other wildlife, providing shelter, nesting sites, and food in the form of berries and the insects they harbor. A wildlife hedge of mixed species, such as field maple (*Acer campestre*), hawthorn (*Crataegus monogyna*), holly (*Ilex aquifolium*), hazel (*Corylus avellana*), and spindle tree (*Euonymus europaeus*), will attract visitors all year. But don't clip it too hard if you want flowers and fruit. If space allows the occasional plant to grow into a small tree, so much the better. For extra flowers, plant viburnums and species roses, which also offer hips in autumn.

Closely clipped hedges provide beautiful natural backdrops to herbaceous borders, forming an unbeatable contrast for billowing, colorful plantings such as this.

Existing hedges

If you already have a hedge, you may consider it your pride and joy, or merely a chore. If your current hedge is not doing anything for you or your garden, you could dig it up and start again. This is not as drastic a step as you may think—hedges are indeed long-lasting, but they are also renewable and some grow faster than you might think. You could replace your old hedge with a low-maintenance version—beech (*Fagus sylvatica*), for example, needs just one trim per year—or, if space is limited, you could achieve a similar effect by training ivy through wire netting or a trellis to make a narrow divide.

Planning a hedge

All hedges take several years to establish and gain the required height but some, such as oval-leaved privet (*Ligustrum ovalifolium*), are relatively fast-growing (remember, though, that the faster they grow, the more frequently they will need clipping). While your hedge is maturing, you can erect a temporary screen of split bamboo or hurdles, or use a wire-netting fence as a boundary line. This netting can be left in place since it will be eventually be covered by the hedge.

If you can't wait, "instant hedges" (the plants are grown in containers) can be bought by the yard. They can be expensive, but your landscaper or contractor will probably prepare the ground and carry out the planting.

Evergreen or deciduous?

Evergreens give cover throughout the year, while deciduous hedges are see-through in winter, except for beech and hornbeam, which retain crisp brown leaves until spring. If you live in a cold, exposed place, choose a hardy, deciduous hedge that will withstand windy conditions, such as hawthorn (*Crataegus monogyna*) or hornbeam (*Carpinus betulus*). Plants for seaside gardens that are exposed to wind but are relatively frost-free include the hawthorn and hornbeam, and also the sea buckthorn (*Hippophae rhamnoides*), tamarix, and the evergreens broadleaf (*Grislenia*), holly (*Ilex*), and daisy bush (*Oleria*), all of which tolerate salty air.

For a smooth, formal evergreen hedge, look for small-leaved plants that tolerate regular close clipping. Two of the best choices for formal hedges are yew (*Taxus baccata*) and Lawson cypress (*Chamaecyparis lawsoniana*). Others include boxwood (*Buxus sempervirens*), fast-growing privet (*Ligustrum ovalifolium*), and shrubby honeysuckle (*Lonicera nitida*).

Mixed hedges

Informal hedges are often a mixture of flowering, berrying, evergreen, and deciduous shrubs planted close together. They are well suited to rural or semirural areas and informal garden settings, and need little or no pruning if they are to show off their beauty, so allow them a bit more space than a clipped hedge. You can achieve a more formal look by mixing plants of a similar growth rate and size but with different foliage colors, such as green and copper beech, or green and golden yew.

Dwarf boxwood and beech hedging have been combined to create an exciting textural contrast, while the spiky ferns offer yet more visual and tactile interest to this framework of foliage.

Use hedges as garden dividers where you want to split up your space into different rooms. Tall hedges here create a secret, sheltered enclosure, "furnished" with dwarf boxwood edging.

Consider the neighbors

Hedges may cause serious conflict between neighbors. First, keep in mind that they take up much more space than walls or fences, and many are unsuitable for the boundaries between very narrow gardens.

To stay on good terms with your neighbors, keep them informed of your boundary plans and do not allow your hedge to encroach on their garden. At planting time, be sure there is sufficient space for the hedge to spread, and, by mutual agreement, be prepared to cut it on both sides. Also, make sure that your hedge does not grow too high and shade your neighbor's property. Boundary hedges can be allowed to grow up to 6ft (1.8m). Internal hedges for screening parts of the garden can be taller, but think about how you will clip them before they get out of hand.

Plant with caution

Leyland cypress (x *Cupressocyparis leylandii*) has gained its bad reputation because, left untrimmed, it quickly grows to a great height. If it is then cut back hard, it looks unsightly. This vigorous grower also dries out the surrounding soil and depletes it of nutrients, and it should be discounted as a boundary for all but the largest of gardens.

Finally, never plant yew or rhododendrons between garden and grazing land since they are poisonous to livestock.

Buying and planting hedges

Success with a new hedge depends on preparing the soil thoroughly before your plants arrive and pampering them after planting and in the early years. Choose young plants rather than large specimens, since they will grow faster and soon overtake more mature plants, giving you a much better hedge for a fraction of the cost.

Buying hedging plants

Nurseries specializing in hedging offer a wide choice of young plants, and many also have a mail-order service. A good supplier will tell you how plants are packed for transit and offer planting and pruning advice. Suppliers advertise in gardening magazines and can be found on the Internet.

Plants supplied by specialists are offered in three forms: bare-root transplants, balled-and-burlapped, or in containers. Bare-root transplants are much cheaper than container-grown specimens; mixed native hedging is usually the most cost-effective option. Bare-root transplants are available from autumn to spring, but you can order them at any time of year and request a delivery date. Remember to ask for delivery in spring if you are buying evergreens or conifers and live in a cold, windy area, since this is the best planting time. Evergreens are also available balled-and-burlapped, where the plant is lifted from the field with its roots and some soil, and then wrapped to reduce root disturbance.

It's a good idea to buy a few more plants than you think you'll actually need in case some of your hedging dies. Plant

Preparing the ground

Few things are more frustrating than a hedge in which sporadic plants fail and die, so give them the best start possible with good soil preparation. Begin this at least six weeks before planting to allow the soil to settle. First clear the site of perennial weeds by digging them out, making sure that you remove the whole root system, or applying glyphosate weedkiller. Dig a strip the length of

Fork in organic matter

the hedge and 3–4ft (90–120cm) wide, forking plenty of bulky organic matter, such as compost or well-rotted manure, into the trench as you go. Plants grown close together need the soil to be as rich and moisture-retentive as possible.

the surplus in a quiet area of the garden or in containers that are large enough to allow the roots to grow. Keep these plants well watered until your hedge is established, and you are sure that none needs to be replaced.

When to plant

Bare-root and balled-and-burlapped hedging plants can be bought from fall to spring, but will not usually be lifted from the field in severe weather, so let availability be your guide. If plants are on mail-order, be sure you will be around to receive the delivery, and check it when it arrives. In cold areas, conifer and evergreen hedges will fare better if planted in spring rather than winter. Pot-grown plants can be planted when conditions allow but are best planted in mild, moist autumn or spring conditions. If you can't plant as soon as you receive your hedging, keep plants moist in their packing, and store in a cool shed.

Balled-and-burlapped plants are more expensive than bare-root plants but cheaper than those offered in containers.

Bare-root transplants should be carefully separated and planted out immediately to prevent the exposed roots from drying out.

How to plant a hedge

A single row of plants is sufficient for most hedging purposes, but for an extra-thick hedge—perhaps for wildlife or for extra protection in a very exposed site—a double row can be used, provided that you have enough space. In this example, a single row is being planted right up against a temporary hurdle fence.

Spacing along the row for most hedging plants, deciduous or evergreen, should be between 18–24in (45–60cm), but for smaller-leaved privet, boxwood, and *Lonicera nitida*, plant closer, at 12in (30cm). For dwarf edging hedges of boxwood or lavender, for example, plant 6in (15cm) apart.

1 Set out a line to mark the edge of the row or rows of plants. Dig a trench along it for bare-root plants; you can dig individual holes for containerized or balled-and-burlapped plants, after marking their positions.

2 Use stakes and a ruler or guide to mark out your planting intervals, either in a single row along one line, or in two staggered rows, laying two stakes 18–24in (45–60cm) apart as a guide.

3 Plant at the original planting depth—the top of the root ball, or to the soil mark on the stem of bare-root plants.

4 Return the soil and firm it well with your heels, creating a slight dip around plants.

5 Water in well. The slight dip around each plant will help direct water to the roots.

6 After watering, place a thick mulch of well-rotted manure, compost, or shredded bark around the plants, keeping it well clear of the stems. You can also lay landscape or geotextile fabric in strips on each side and cover with chipped bark.

Caring for your hedge

Once planted, your hedge will need to be looked after if it is to thrive. Most important, keep young plants watered for the first few years during dry spells until the hedge has become established. It should then not need additional watering except in dry periods in summer.

Feed all hedges in spring with a balanced fertilizer formulated for this purpose. At the same time, clear any weeds from the base of the hedge, and after rain, or when the soil is moist, top up any mulch.

Shaping young hedges

Young formal hedges may benefit from some pruning to shape and direct growth. Evergreens need only their sideshoots lightly trimmed into line for a few years after planting. Leave the main upright, or leading, shoot or shoots to grow to the final hedge height. Deciduous hedges that are to have a dense, formal shape require more early shaping. In general, cut back the main shoot and any strong sideshoots by one-third after planting and do this again in the following winter. Treat vigorous privet and hawthorn harder: when young, cut back to within 12in (30cm) of soil level in late spring. In late summer shorten sideshoots; then, in winter, cut the previous season's growth back by half.

Informal hedges need no shaping, although shortening any long, whippy shoots will encourage them to bush out.

Make a trim line by tying string to two stakes; insert them at each end of your hedge to make a clipping guide for formal hedges, such as boxwood.

Hedges with large, thick leaves, such as holly and laurel, should be trimmed with pruners; shears will cut the foliage, turning it brown.

Clipping mature hedges

Trim hedges in spring or summer, and leave informal hedges unpruned unless they are outgrowing their space or looking particularly messy. Snip off any overlong shoots and keep the height under control.

All formal hedges will need to be kept in shape with regular clipping. Regular trimming keeps growth dense and your hedge looking thick and lush from top to bottom. It also prevents it from expanding over the years. How often you clip depends on the plants and their rate of growth, but all hedges need at least one cut a year. For deciduous hedges and small-leaved evergreens, use garden shears or a powered hedge trimmer, keeping the blades parallel to the hedge at

Clipping hedges into shape

Prune formal hedges, such as beech and yew, from the time of planting so that the plants form a wedge or A-shape as they grow. These shapes allow light to reach all areas of the hedge, which will encourage even growth.

If you live in an area that has snow and ice, clip the top into a point or very narrow A-shape so that the snow cannot settle on the top where its weight may damage the hedge top. Be sure to trim the top hard once the hedge has reached the desired height to keep it from getting taller. For a hedge with a narrow profile, clip the sides regularly from the start. Trim it back each time to the last cut, for a smooth finish.

Beech with a pointed top to shed snow

"A-shaped" yew hedge with a flat top

all times for flat sides. For large-leaved evergreens, such as cherry laurel (*Prunus laurocerasus*) and tough-leaved holly, use pruners to cut back individual shoots.

Problem-solving

If a plant in a young hedge dies, dig it out and replace with a new one. It is worth removing some of the soil and replacing it with fresh soil from another part of the garden, enriching it with well-rotted compost or manure. In an established hedge, remove the dead plant and fill the gap with shoots of adjacent plants trained horizontally along strings or wires set between stakes.

Should your hedge develop gaps at the base it may be possible to layer low shoots (you may have to let them grow out first) in prepared pockets of soil (*see pp240–41*). In time they should root and grow to fill the spaces.

If a stem is forced out of position by snow or wind, but is undamaged, tie it back in place using soft twine or an old pair of panty hose. To lessen the risk of this happening in future, clip your hedge into an A-shape (*see opposite*).

Browning foliage, particularly on conifers, should be cut out as it will not green up. If it leaves a gap, tie adjacent branches together with soft twine or to a bamboo cane inserted within the plants. Keep an eye on the area in case more dead patches appear, which may indicate disease.

Renovating an overgrown hedge

Where an established hedge is neglected and overgrown, the first job is to clear it of weeds, such as ivy and brambles. Cut them back, and when new growth sprouts paint the leaves with glyphosate weedkiller—more than once if needed. Then remove any dead wood and cut the hedge itself back.

Fill gaps at the base of a hedge by layering a stem. Choose a low stem, and allow it to grow until it easily reaches the ground and can be pinned under the soil to root.

Conifers excepted (*see below*), it is best to spread this over two years—cut back the top and one side one year, and the other side the next.

Beech, hornbeam, and hawthorn can be cut back hard, by up to 50 percent, in late winter before new leaves appear. If regrowth is very poor in the first season, delay the second half of the job for another year (i.e. two years after the first cut). For an old forsythia hedge, cut out some of the oldest wood as soon as flowering is over. Among evergreens, yew, box, cherry laurel, privet, honeysuckle, holly, escallonia, evergreen barberry, and firethorn can cope with hard pruning, in mid- to late spring when growth is well under way.

For Leyland cypress and other conifers, reduce the height in early spring as growth is starting, by not more than one-third in any one year. Do not cut the sides hard as shoots that are bare of foliage will not sprout again. If this will not bring the hedge back to an acceptable size and appearance, it will have to be removed and replaced.

After pruning, fertilize and water well, and mulch with bulky organic matter, such as garden compost or manure. Continue to water generously during dry spells.

Top hedging plants

Your choice of hedging plant will be determined chiefly by the purpose the hedge is to serve, and the height to which you would like it to grow—remember that boundary hedges should not exceed 8ft (2m). For a formal hedge, some tried-and-true trees and shrubs are old favorites, but for an informal hedge, almost any shrub can be used. It's hard to judge what would make a good hedge when looking at young plants in a garden center; try visiting gardens open to the public to see a range of mature shrubs, and look for those that are well-clothed in foliage to ground level. Neatness of habit is not a prerequisite; some quite untidy shrubs, such as potentillas, forsythia, and even cistus, look very good when grown side-by-side as a hedge, taking on a more compact and floriferous appearance.

Evergreen hedges

Aucuba japonica Formal or informal. Glossy, large-leaved. Very tough, shade- and pollution-tolerant. Trim with pruners in late summer. H to 10ft (3m).

Berberis x stenophylla Informal. Small-leaves and very thorny arching stems. Good as a border hedge. Trim after flowering. H to 8ft (2.5m).

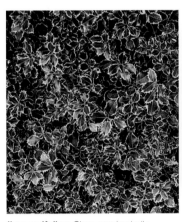

Ilex aquifolium Slow-growing holly. Grow informally, or trim with pruners in late summer for a formal barrier. Green and variegated cultivars. H to 30ft (9m).

Lavandula angustifolia 'Twickel Purple' Best as semiformal edging. Trim with shears in spring and after flowering to keep compact. H to 24in (60cm).

Ligustrum ovalifolium Formal. Fast-growing. May lose leaves in cold winters. Gold and variegated cultivars. Trim 3 or 4 times in growing season. H to 12ft (4m).

Lonicera nitida 'Baggesen's Gold' Best grown as a formal hedge but may burn in bright sun. Fast growing, needs several trims a year. H to 5ft (1.5m).

Deciduous hedges

Berberis thunbergii 'Rose Glow' Informal. Thorny stems. Attractive foliage makes a striking, dark, low barrier. Trim after flowering. H to 4ft (1.2m).

Carpinus betulus Formal. Hornbeam does better than beech in exposed sites, and holds its dead leaves in winter. Trim in mid- to late summer. H to 30ft (9m).

Fagus sylvatica Formal. Keeps its dead leaves in winter. Mix purple- or green-and-copper-leaved beech for a "tapestry" effect. Trim in late summer. H to 30ft (9m).

Forsythia x intermedia 'Lynwood' Informal. Glorious in flower in late winter/early spring, rather dull for the rest of the year. Trim after flowering. H to 10ft (3m).

Buxus sempervirens Informal or formal, boxwood grows to 15ft (5m). Use the dwarf cultivar 'Suffruticosa' for low hedge. Trim 2–3 times in growing season.

Chamaecyparis lawsoniana **'Pembury Blue'** Formal or semiformal. Quite fast-growing. Gold and green cultivars. Trim in spring and early autumn. H to 30ft (9m).

Elaeagnus **x** *ebbingei* Formal. Glossy leaves. Plain-leaved form makes a better hedge than the variegated types. Trim in spring or late summer. H to 10ft (3m).

Escallonia **'Donard Seedling'** Clip or grow informally. Most likely to thrive well in mild districts. Delay pruning until after summer flowering. H to 8ft (2.5m).

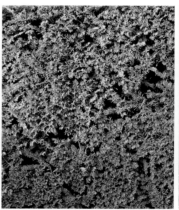

Prunus laurocerasus With aucuba, top choice for a large, glossy-leaved, semiformal hedge. Trim with pruners in late summer. H to 25ft (8m).

Pyracantha Informal (clipping removes flowers and berries). Spiny stems. Fruits are liked by birds. Red- and yellow-berried cultivars available. H to 10ft (3m).

Taxus baccata A formal and slow-growing yew. May need only one clip a year in summer or autumn. Golden cultivars available. H to 30ft (10m).

Thuja plicata Formal. The best cultivars of western red cedar are green 'Atrovirens' or gold 'Aurea' for garden hedges. Trim in spring and early autumn. H 6–10ft (2–3m).

Fuchsia magellanica Informal. Mature hedges are thinned, not clipped—cut out old stems to the base in early spring. Likes a seaside garden. H to 10ft (3m).

Potentilla Any *Potentilla fruticosa* cultivar makes a good low informal hedge, with a long flowering season. H 24in (60cm) to 5ft (1.5m), depending on the cultivar.

Rosa rugosa Informal. Best rose for a tall hedge. Grows vigorously and densely, very prickly stems. Large red hips in autumn. Popular with wildlife. H 3–8ft (1–2.5m).

Plant care 7

Tools and equipment • Watering • Mulching • Feeding and weeding
Providing support • Deadheading • Protecting plants over winter

Buying and caring for tools

All gardeners have a few favorite tools that they would not go without. When buying gardening tools and equipment, look for good-quality products, but don't feel you have to buy the most expensive. In most cases, tools in the mid-price range are fine, but beware of very cheap equipment that may not last long. Reputable companies normally offer a few years' guarantee, depending on the tool or equipment. You may also find that a household object or homemade tool does the job just as well. For example, the official tool used to make planting holes for seedlings or young plants is a dibber, but a blunt pencil is a good alternative.

Make sure the tools you buy are comfortable to grip and suit your size. If you're not very strong, you may be better off with a small spade or fork, since larger tools need more leverage to be used effectively.

Long-handled spade You may need to shop around to find tools like this, but they can help in avoiding aches and injuries.

Taller gardeners will almost certainly find digging more comfortable using spades or forks with shafts that are longer than the standard 28–29in (70–73cm). Shafts of up to 3ft (1m) are available.

Keeping order

Store your tools in a shed, preferably fitted with a lock. Always clean off soil from digging tools before putting them away, and clean and wipe over cutting blades with an oily rag. This will prolong the life of the tools. Invest in hooks, racks, and shelves, or make them yourself out of recycled timber, and get into the habit of hanging up your tools after use and coiling electrical wires neatly. Also clean and stack pots and bundle stakes together before storing. By keeping your shed neat, you will be able to fit more in, find what you need quickly, and avoid unnecessary hazards.

The basic tool kit

This basic tool kit, with the addition of a watering can, enables you to do most jobs in the garden. If you have a lawn, a spring-tined rake will be very useful, and a lawn mower is also a necessity (*see p.173*). Don't be seduced by the vast range of gadgets too soon. The more you garden, the more you will discover which tools will be helpful and which are gimmicks.

Hand fork and trowel
These are indispensable for weeding, planting young plants and bulbs, and small digging jobs. Hand forks are ideal for heavy clay soils. Small tools are easily mislaid in the garden; watch for those with brightly colored handles that can be spotted easily, or paint tools with wooden handles to make them more conspicuous.

Spade and fork These have shafts of different lengths and materials: Metal shafts are stronger than wood, and may be plastic-covered. Border spades and forks have slightly smaller heads, making them easy to handle and useful for light work.

Dutch hoe and rake A sharp hoe for weeding and a rake for leveling soil and clearing ground are both invaluable. Use a spring-tined rake on lawns to clear leaves and thatch.

Shears These are useful for trimming small to medium-sized hedges and long grass, and for cutting back herbaceous perennials when they die down. Some have a notched blade to hold thicker shoots for easy cutting. Before buying shears, check that they are light enough for you to use for a reasonable time.

Pruners and pruning saw Pruners are essential for many pruning jobs; choose a pair with a safety catch and cross-over blades. Try before you buy to make sure they feel right. Folding pruning saws are useful for cutting small branches, but one with a fixed blade is a better choice if you have lots of shrubs.

Caring for cultivation tools

Most digging tools are made from either carbon steel or stainless steel. To prevent carbon steel from rusting, clean and oil your tools regularly. Carbon steel hoes and spades will slide through soil more easily if you sharpen them occasionally. Some tools have a nonstick coating that may eventually wear off. Stainless steel tools are more expensive, but they are long-lasting, do not rust, and make digging easier because they cut through the soil cleanly and it does not stick to the blade.

All metal tools, including spades, forks, hand trowels, and rakes, need to be cleaned after use before you put them away. Brush off any soil, wash, and dry thoroughly.

Wooden shafts and handles of spades and forks need to be checked every so often. Sand off any roughness and wipe over with linseed oil to nourish and preserve the wood.

Carbon steel tools benefit from a wipe with an oily rag to prevent them from rusting, and blades will cut through the soil more easily if you sharpen them with a file.

Caring for cutting tools

Sharp blades make cleaner cuts when pruning and trimming. Pruners need frequent sharpening, since pruning soon blunts the blade. Good quality models are easy to take apart, which makes cleaning and sharpening easier, and allows a damaged blade to be replaced. Knives are often better than pruners for delicate jobs, and should be cleaned, oiled, and sharpened in the same way (*see below*). Keep a pocket-sized sharpening steel on hand to sharpen your blade as you work. Use a commercial tool or a metal file to sharpen shears. Sharpen only the beveled cutting edge, and tighten the screw holding the blades together.

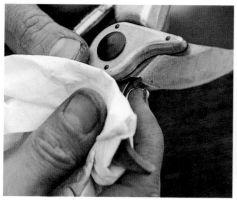

1 To clean the blades of pruners, spray on a little lubricant or household cleaner to remove any dirt and sap, and then wipe it off with a tissue. For dried-on sap, use a scourer or fine-grade steel wool and metal polish.

2 Smear some lubricant or light oil onto the beveled-edged blade and lightly rub it off with a nylon scourer or fine-grade steel wool. This helps prevent rusting and keeps the blade smooth between sharpenings.

3 Sharpen the blade with an oilstone or a diamond sharpening tool. Hold it at the same angle as the beveled edge and draw it across the edge. Gently rub the flat side of the blade to remove any burrs, then oil the blades.

Wise watering

Without adequate water plants will suffer and eventually die. For much of the year, from midautumn until spring, rainfall is usually sufficient, but there are times, particularly during late spring and summer, when there may not be enough rain. Supplies can run short as rapidly growing plants draw up the moisture from the soil, and at these times it is important to know what to water and how.

Prioritize your watering

Water is a precious natural resource and should not be wasted. You do not need to water everything in the garden, even during hot spells, because different plants have different requirements. It pays to learn about the needs of your plants and sort out your priorities.

Identify plants that really do need additional watering (*see box opposite*). Long-established trees, shrubs, roses, climbers, and hardy perennials that have formed extensive root systems can withstand periods of drought. Although it is important to water a new lawn, an established one can usually do without; even brown, parched grass will normally become green again when rain returns. Keeping a lawn lush during long spells of dry weather takes large amounts of water, and the extended use of sprinklers is wasteful and often not possible if there is a watering ban.

When planning or adding to plantings, choose plants that match your soil conditions. Drought-resistant plants, such as sedums and lavender, need little or no additional watering; others, such as conifers, will become scorched and remain unsightly forever if water is in short supply. Try to conserve soil moisture, so your plants do not run short (*see p. 156*).

After planting create a shallow, saucer-shaped depression around the plant to retain water over the root area until it has all soaked in. Then water well, using either a hose or a watering can.

Efficient watering

The best times to water are either early in the morning or in the evening, when cool conditions ensure that little moisture is lost through evaporation. Plants are also less able to take up water during the hotter periods of the day, and you risk scorching the leaves if water is left on them under a hot sun because it acts like a magnifying glass. Aim to water plants that are susceptible to slug and snail damage during the morning, as extra moisture in the evening encourages these nocturnal pests.

To avoid waste, only water plants that need it, and make sure the water goes onto the soil around the root area, rather than on the leaves or flowers. To encourage both rain and any water you apply to reach the roots of a new plant, make a saucer-shaped depression around it, edged with a berm of soil. Alternatively, sink a flower pot with holes in the bottom or a length of plastic pipe into the soil or container, close to the plant roots, and water through this.

When you water, a weekly soaking is better than a daily dribble. Light watering does not penetrate far and encourages the roots to grow up to the surface to reach it, where they are even more vulnerable to drought. Watering well guarantees that the moisture drains down to the lower levels of the soil, and the roots follow.

Lay a seep hose through borders or beds of thirsty plants. This is an efficient watering method; moisture seeps into the soil above the root zone.

Top watering priorities

These are the plants most vulnerable to drought. They will need additional watering during the growing season and in any long, dry spells. Water as soon as the top layers of soil around the plant feel dry, since a plant can sustain some damage by the time it starts to wilt. Remember, too, that you can minimize wastage, even when watering thirsty plants (*see pp.156–157*).

New plants still have small root systems, which have not had time to reach water held deep in the soil. Watering also helps settle the soil around the roots, which is why it is important to water after planting even if the soil does not seem dry.

Fruit and vegetable crops need water most when they are flowering and developing their fruits or other edible parts. If they run dry at these times cropping is badly affected. Many leafy vegetables wilt or go to seed in hot, dry conditions.

Wall-trained plants can be in a "rain shadow," sheltered from rain by the wall and house eaves. Consequently the soil around their roots is very dry. Remember to plant about 18in (45cm) away from a wall or fence; at this distance, the soil will hold more moisture. Mulch plants deeply in spring when the soil is moist, in order to keep it that way.

Newly germinated seeds and seedlings are small and vulnerable and will die if the roots dry out. Water seedlings in the garden with a can. Stand pots or trays in water so that they can take up moisture from below, and then remove them from the reservoir when the top of the soil is damp. This avoids water on the leaves, which increases a seedling's susceptibility to fungal diseases.

Conifers can suffer and may die in hot weather without enough water; if the foliage is badly scorched it may not regrow. Some, such as juniper and pine, are more tolerant of dry soil conditions and are good choices for warm, sunny gardens or sandy soil.

New lawns have to be watered until they are well established. Expensive new sod will literally curl up and die if subjected to drought. Established utility lawns containing ryegrass can do without water. They may turn brown but will become green again after rain.

Shallow-rooting rhododendrons fold down their leaves when short of water in hot, dry periods. Flower bud formation is affected, and plants will soon brown and die if not watered. These shrubs are not good choices for hot spots or sandy, free-draining soils.

Plants in containers need plenty of water because they are growing in a limited volume of soil mix, which rapidly dries out. In hot, dry, and windy weather check them daily, and twice a day in exceptionally hot summer weather or if the pots are small.

Conserving water

As with so many things in gardening, the key to conserving water lies in the soil. Well-structured soil that is high in organic matter retains more moisture than free-draining sandy types. Heavy clay holds moisture but plants cannot always extract from it the amounts they need. Whatever soil you have in your garden, you can improve its water-holding capacity by following these simple steps.

• In the vegetable patch, dig in bulky organic matter, such as garden compost or well-rotted manure, every spring on sandy soils and every autumn on heavy soils.

• Seal in the moisture with a mulch applied when the soil is moist after rainfall in spring (*see pp.158–59*). The best mulch for conserving moisture is bulky organic matter, but if you do not have large quantities of manure or compost available, use damp newspaper or landscape fabric (geotextile membrane) covered with bark chips or gravel. Plants in containers can be mulched with more decorative materials that may be too costly for large areas (*see p.197*).

Leafy perennial plants can act like a mulch. The leaves shade the soil, reducing evaporation, and create a cool, humid microclimate as they release moisture into the air around them.

Watering equipment

You may not need anything more complicated than a watering can and a hose to water your garden, but do consider other methods of irrigation that may be more efficient and save you time. When using a watering can, fit the rose on the spout, and use a spray adapter on a hose. A fast, solid stream from a spout or hose can easily wash soil from around the plants' roots and may destroy the soil structure. A gush of water is also likely to run off, rather than penetrate the ground.

Sprinklers should only be used on new lawns and other large newly planted areas. They are wasteful, and also water some areas more heavily than others. Avoid using them in windy weather, since the water will be blown off course, or in the heat of the day, when water will evaporate. Rotary types cover circular areas and oscillating designs cover rectangular areas; powerful pulse-jet sprinklers are only suitable for large gardens.

Leaky pipes or seep hoses are permeable and extremely efficient as little or no water is lost in run-off or evaporation. Lay them along the base of walls, between rows of vegetables and fruits, and through borders. They can be covered with a loose mulch, such as compost or bark chips. Most will not work with the low pressure of supplies from rain barrels.

Trickle- or drip-irrigation systems are useful for pots and in greenhouses. They have a main tube, which you attach to a garden hose, and a number of nozzles or spurs, depending on the area to be watered. The main tube runs from pot to pot, and water trickles out of nozzles or thin spur lines.

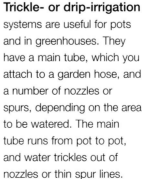

Automatic timers are a boon for vacations. They allow you to set the duration and timing of watering for maximum efficiency, and can be linked to control water to trickle irrigation systems, seep hoses, and lawn sprinklers. Test the timing before you go away.

- Avoid planting and any other digging during dry spells. This brings moist soil from the lower depths to the surface, where it will dry out, and sends dry soil from the surface to the lower depths, where the roots need water most.
- Keep weeds at bay, because they compete with plants for moisture. Pull them up, or hoe them off while they are young; dig out perennial weeds with the complete root system, or apply a glyphosate weedkiller (see p.161).
- Provide shelter to prevent wind from drying out the soil and increasing the rate at which plants lose water through their leaves (see pp.22–25). Erect a fence or plant a hedge to shield your garden from the prevailing wind. Newly planted trees or shrubs, especially conifers and evergreens, will establish better if they are protected by an artificial windbreak for their first year. Staple windbreak netting or burlap to posts driven into the soil on the windward side of the plant.
- Use water-retaining gel in containers and hanging baskets, particularly those on a sunny patio (see p.197). This could, in theory, be added to beds and borders, but the cost is generally prohibitive because very large quantities are required to make a real contribution to soil moisture. But it may be worth considering around vulnerable and precious new plants or recent transplants.
- While most plants will survive spells of drought once they are established, it makes sense to choose drought-resistant plants if you live in a particularly dry area or have a hot spot in your garden.

Collecting and recycling

With pressures on water supplies growing and the prospect of summers becoming increasingly dry, water conservation is important. Several water butts or rain barrels can be used to collect rainwater from downspouts. In larger gardens you can link butts together with an overflow pipe, and install butts next to sheds or greenhouses, as well as the house. Make sure the butt stands on a hard, stable surface and is high enough for you to get a can under the tap. Cover the top with a lid to keep out debris and mosquitoes. Aside from conservation issues, rainwater is best for plants; in some areas tap water contains high levels of lime and is described as "hard"; this is unsuitable for acid-loving plants such as rhododendrons.

Gray water, or waste household water, can also be used in the garden, especially when a watering ban is in force. Do not use any water that has passed through a water-softening unit or dishwasher, because it contains chemicals that will damage your plants. You can use dishwater that is not fatty or full of detergent, bath water with no bath oil in it, and water from rinsing clothes. Let the water cool and then use it as soon as possible to prevent bacteria from building up. Water onto the soil, not over the foliage. Do not add gray water to a water butt or use it in irrigation systems, and avoid using it on acid-loving plants, edible crops, seedlings or young plants, and lawns. If you want to recycle gray water regularly, you may have to call a plumber to add an extra outside tap and switching valve.

Plants for dry places

Look for small, narrow, succulent, or spiky leaves, since these are characteristics of plants that prefer hot, dry conditions. Silvery or gray surfaces reflect light to keep leaves cool, and a covering of fine hairs minimizes water loss in windy places.

Achillea
Armeria
Artemisia
Brachyglottis
Cistus
Cordyline australis
Cotton lavender (Santolina)
Eryngium
Globe thistle (Echinops, below)

Lavender (Lavandula)
Mullein (Verbascum, above)
Ornamental grasses
Phlomis
Phormium
Rock rose (Helianthemum)
Rosemary (Rosmarinus)
Salvia
Thyme (Thymus)

Water butts or rain barrels can be attached to the downspouts of your house and to outbuildings. The stored water is suitable for all garden plants except young plants and seedlings.

Mulching

Mulching means covering the soil between your plants with a layer of organic or inorganic material (*see opposite*). This has many benefits, but to reap the rewards, it is important to use the appropriate material at the right time and in sufficient quantity.

• Some organic mulches boost soil fertility as they break down, so less fertilizer is needed.

• Mulches suppress weeds, reducing the amount of weeding and competition for moisture and nutrients.

• A mulch provides a protective layer that minimizes loss of moisture from the soil, reducing the need to water plants during hot, dry weather, and also prevents the surface soil from being damaged or washed away by heavy rain.

• Bulky mulches help insulate plant roots from extreme temperatures, so that they don't get too hot or freeze.

• The more attractive mulches, particularly some gravels and pebbles, provide a decorative setting for your plants.

When to apply mulch

The ideal time to apply a mulch is mid- to late spring, when the soil is moist and has begun to warm up. Wait if the soil is frozen. Loose mulches insulate, and cold, frozen, or dry soil will remain that way for longer if mulched. First, clear all perennial weeds, such as dandelions, Bishop's weed,

Organic matter, such as well-rotted compost makes an excellent mulch for herbaceous perennials. As the growing season progresses, it will gradually rot down and enrich the soil.

and nettles, which will grow through mulching materials, apart from geotextile membranes and plastic sheeting. Then, after watering or a period of steady, penetrating rain, lay the mulch. If the ground under a mulch dries out, the best way to rewet it is to scrape the material to one side and lay a seep hose (*see p.156*), which will slowly water the soil. You can cover the seep hose with the mulch to disguise it.

Mulch new beds and borders thoroughly, covering the whole surface area, rather than just mulching around individual plants. You will then need only to replenish it once a year in spring. Some materials, like bark chips, last longer, depending on the depth that is laid.

Mulching depths

Lay organic mulches 4in (10cm) deep to control weeds and retain moisture. Leave a 4–6in (10–15cm) gap around the base of trees and shrubs to prevent their stems from rotting; you can mulch closer to herbaceous plants, but leave clear areas over the crowns of emerging plants, where the growth buds are situated. Lay gravel and similar inorganic materials 1–2in (2.5–5cm) deep, and apply large pebbles and cobbles in a single layer.

Be sure that you do not smother small plants, and keep an eye out for birds scattering mulching materials and covering young plants in their search for food in the soil beneath.

> ### Money-saving tip
>
> To economize on organic mulches, such as chipped bark, first lay cardboard over the soil surface to suppress weeds before covering with something more visually appealing. The cardboard will rot down in time. You could also use an inexpensive mulch, such as grass mowings, at the back of deep borders, and spread more attractive composted bark at the front.

Spread gravel around plants that need good drainage, such as sedums. When laid over a weed-suppressing membrane, it reduces maintenance to a minimum.

Organic mulches

Around your flowers and shrubs you can use bulky organic materials, such as chipped bark, garden compost, and well-rotted manure. These will gradually decompose, improving the soil structure and adding some nutrients. Where organic content and nutrients take precedence, they are the best choice, but if your garden style is formal, they can look a little messy.

Garden compost helps prevent weed seeds from germinating in the soil by excluding light, and breaks down moderately slowly, supplying important nutrients in variable amounts. It may contain weed seeds, but seedlings are easily removed. Use the yard waste compost produced by some local authorities or make your own (*see p.46*).

Leaf mold is ideal for woodland gardens or shrub borders and is easy to make (*see p.45*). It is quite low in nutrients, but a richer mulch can be made by mixing in grass clippings.

Farmyard or stable manure is an excellent mulching material but must be well rotted. It can be rather lumpy and

![Garden compost]

Garden compost

may include straw or bedding material. Stack fresh manure for 6–12 months before using. Manure breaks down fairly slowly, is a useful source of nutrients, and is particularly good for mulching roses and shrubs.

Composted bark is the most nutritious of the bark and wood mulches, and does not rob the soil of nitrogen as it breaks down. Use it around trees and shrubs, particularly rhododendrons and other acid-loving plants.

Chipped bark comes in grades from fine to coarse. The coarser grades are best used around shrubs and trees and in woodland areas. Chipped bark is low in nutrients and will deplete the soil of nitrogen at first. It is heavy and dense, excluding the light needed for weed

Leaf mold

seeds to germinate, and lasts for many years before it needs replenishing.

Wood chips are paler than chipped bark, and "raw" looking when fresh. They are slow to decompose and initially take nitrogen from the soil. Use for paths or at the back of shrub borders, not around young or herbaceous plants. Wood chips are often available in bulk from local nurseries.

Composted straw is a "utility" mulch. It is low in nutrients and may contain weed seeds, but it is fine at the back of a border where it cannot be seen. Buy bales of straw, water them, and leave to rot for a year. Use fresh straw under strawberries to keep fruits clean and dry.

Chipped bark

Composted straw

Cocoa shells are decorative, but have been shipped great distances and are costly. They decay fairly rapidly, and need topping up annually. Lay them 4in (10cm) deep, and water to bind them together. They may repel slugs but can attract dogs, who will get sick if they eat them.

Mushroom compost is a waste product from mushroom farms. It contains rotted animal manure, and thus will supply some nutrients and is relatively slow to decay. It is not recommended for use around acid-loving plants like rhododendrons, because it contains chalk.

Spent hops is a light-colored waste product from brewing. Low in nutrients and lightweight, it may blow around when dry and rots down fairly quickly. For best results lay a thick layer and water it.

Inorganic mulches

Use these mulches to discourage the growth of mosses and prevent soil from splashing onto flowers and leaves. They provide good surface drainage, and thus are useful around plants whose stems and leaves should be kept dry.

Gravel is decorative and ideal for areas devoted to drought-tolerant plants or around rock and alpine plants. Gravels are available in different colors and materials, including stone, glass, and metal. Depending on the type you choose, it can enhance traditional formal and modern gardens. Gravel mulches may help to deter slugs around susceptible plants like hostas.

Colored gravel

Coarse grit and stone chips are ideal for mulching small plants, such as alpines, succulents, or those with silvery or hairy leaves, in raised beds, troughs, or terracotta pots.

Cobbles and pebbles are attractive in both modern and naturalistic settings, especially around water features. Do not collect them from beaches, as this may be illegal. The stones available in bags from garden centers have been taken from rivers or lakes.

Geotextile membranes are permeable fabrics, widely used to suppress weeds. They are particularly useful around newly planted trees and shrubs, helping to retain moisture and suppress weeds. They are not attractive but are intended to be hidden under other mulches.

Black plastic sheeting can be laid over soil to warm it up in preparation for early planting or vegetable sowing, and to prevent light from reaching potatoes in place of mounding. It can also be laid around newly planted trees and shrubs with a camouflaging mulch on top, and is excellent for suppressing weeds.

Geotextile membrane

Feeding and weeding

Most garden plants survive happily with just an annual application of organic matter, such as a well-rotted manure or garden compost, which releases its goodness slowly over the growing season. It also improves soil water levels, which affect the nutrient content too, since nutrients are soluble and quickly washed away in free-draining soil.

That said, there are times when an additional fertilizer is beneficial, particularly if you are growing fruit and vegetables, or plants in containers. Fertilizers can also help to kick-start growth after planting, and reinvigorate plants that have been pruned hard.

What to fertilize and when

Before you buy or use fertilizer, read the instructions on the package to make sure it is what you want. Plants can only take up nutrients in a solution, so always water after feeding.
• Vegetables need a complete fertilizer applied before planting or sowing. The numbers on fertilizer packages indicate the percentage of that particular nutrient.
• Fruiting crops, such as tomatoes, appreciate a liquid feed of tomato fertilizer about once every two or three weeks.

• Permanent plants, especially fruit, benefit from a general fertilizer, such as blood, fish, and bone, in early spring after weeding and before mulching.
• Feed roses with a special rose fertilizer in spring after pruning.
• Temporary plantings in containers and hanging baskets soon use up the limited nutrients in the soil mix, so use a general-purpose liquid fertilizer every ten days in summer (*see p.200*). For permanent plantings in containers, such as shrubs, push controlled-release fertilizer tablets or pellets into the soil mix in spring (*see p.197*).
• Lawns need a fertilizer with a high nitrogen content in spring for lush leaf growth and one that encourages root development in autumn (*see p.176*).

Feed shrubs with a general-purpose fertilizer in spring. Sprinkle it around the plant, rake it in, and then water the soil

Important plant foods

The three major plant foods are nitrogen, phosphorus, and potassium, listed on fertilizer labels as N, P, and K. All plants need these to maintain good health. Other nutrients, such as calcium, magnesium, and sulfur, are required in smaller quantities, while tiny amounts of other nutrients are also vital but rarely deficient in garden soils. One exception is alkaline soil, which is unable to release manganese and iron, and causes yellow leaves on acid-loving plants. A general-purpose fertilizer has equal amounts of the major plant nutrients, together with other nutrients that are not always readily available in the soil.

Nitrogen (N) encourages lush leafy growth, and is the main ingredient in spring lawn fertilizers. It is highly soluble and quickly washes out of free-draining soils.

Potassium (K) promotes flowering and fruiting; it is sometimes listed as potash. Fertilizers for tomatoes and summer container plantings are rich in potassium.

Phosphorus (P) promotes healthy root growth, and is essential for young plants whose roots are developing. There is usually plenty in garden soil in the form of phosphates.

Regular applications of organic matter help promote healthy plants, although overfeeding may actually reduce the number of flowers produced by some annuals and perennials.

Correct fertilzing

When fertilizing resist the temptation to add a little extra for good measure; more plants are lost through overfeeding than underfeeding. Always follow recommended application rates and dilute liquid fertilizer accurately. If in doubt, err on the side of caution, since too much fertilizer promotes lush growth that is more vulnerable to pest and disease attack, and summer bedding tends to flower better if slightly underfed. Overfeeding can also cause "reverse osmosis," where plants lose, rather than absorb, nutrients.

Yellowing between the leaf veins is a common sign of malnutrition. It may indicate a lack of magnesium on acidic soils or crops given potassium–rich tomato feed; the leaves may also be tinted brown or red. Apply Epsom salts in autumn to replenish nutrients. Potassium deficiency causes yellowing, purple or brown tints, and poor flowering; a lack of flowers may indicate too much nitrogen.

Yellowing develops in acid-loving plants on alkaline soil, because they are unable to absorb manganese and iron from the soil. Test the soil pH (*see p.38*); if it is high, either grow more suitable plants, or use a fertilizer for acid-loving plants.

Weeding

There are several good reasons to keep your garden clear of weeds. They not only compete with flowers for light, nutrients, and water, but some, such as chickweed, also harbor diseases like cucumber mosaic virus, which may spread to surrounding plants. Weeds also look unsightly, and some of the more pernicious types, such as Bishop's weed and bindweed, can swamp a bed or border within one season if left unchecked.

Dandelion

• Weeding can be a time consuming job, but you can minimize the workload throughout the spring and summer if you start early and remove them before they flower and have a chance to spread their seeds around.

• Some stubborn perennial weeds, such as couchgrass and bindweed, spread by underground roots and stems. Others, such as dandelions, have a deep taproot. Try to dig out every bit of these weeds, because they can regrow and reproduce from even a tiny piece of root.

• A glyphosate weedkiller is effective for perennial weeds, spreading from the leaves to kill the roots but breaking down in the soil without harming other plants. It is available as a liquid for weeds that appear in borders. Cover surrounding plants when applying, to make sure the weedkiller does not touch them.

• Remember that digging the soil between plants can damage roots and will bring more weed seeds to the surface where they will germinate. Hoe as shallowly as possible, and remove weeds carefully by hand to minimize soil disturbance if they are close to the other plants, or when weeding in the summer.

• Weed seedlings need light to grow. When your soil is free of weeds, suppress any more by laying a mulch to exclude light (*see pp.158–59*).

When hoeing annual weeds, use the blade to slice the roots just under the surface. Hoe on a dry day and leave the weeds to wither on the soil surface, then compost them.

Supporting herbaceous plants

There is a general misconception that herbaceous plants must all be grown in sheltered areas and have to be staked. This is often not the case, and gardens full of movement are more dynamic and interesting; while woody plants will not bend much in the breeze, flowers and grasses will billow attractively. Many tall plants are self-supporting, including nicotianas, foxgloves (*Digitalis*), mulleins (*Verbascum*), and *Verbena bonariensis*. Choose carefully and you can grow a reasonable range of plants even in fairly windy sites. In such conditions, they often develop sturdier stems, more resistant to wind damage. Plants grown in a sheltered, protected spot or overfertilized soil are more likely to suffer in a sudden blast of wind than those that are exposed all season long.

You may want to grow some herbaceous plants that have delicate or weak stems, which almost inevitably splay out due to the weight of their flowerheads or are beaten down by strong winds or rain. In exposed gardens your choice of plants will inevitably be reduced without some support. In these cases, insert supports in spring, when leafy growth is just underway: however carefully you prop up the battered remains, plants that have flopped never recover their former glory. Although visible at first, the supports will soon be lost among the foliage as long as they are a little shorter than the eventual height of the plant, and some materials also have a charm of their own.

Metal grids fixed to vertical rods can be bought in dark colors, or made from wire held between stakes. These will be hidden as the plants grow up through them.

Invisible support for tall, thin-stemmed perennials and annuals can be made using stakes pushed into the soil around the clump, with dark plastic netting stretched between them. Use dark colored stakes if the clump is close to the front of your border.

Choosing suitable supports

A clump of bamboo thinned annually will yield a good supply of canes to be used as supports. If they are cut when young, the stems will be pliable enough to bend into hoops and semicircles. If you have space in your garden you could also grow a hazel or willow to cut back, or coppice, regularly for a supply of twiggy stems and thicker stakes for building rustic tripods.

Bamboo canes and twiggy sticks will do for many perennials (*see opposite*). You can also lift plants that have flopped with canes and string, but if you bunch the stems tightly they could look worse than before. For large-flowered, tall plants, such as dahlias, peonies, and chrysanthemums, supports that allow the stems to grow through them are more effective. Metal grids on long spikes can be raised as the plants grow. For very tall dahlias, delphiniums, and gladioli, tie each stem with garden string or raffia to a sturdy single stake.

Where a border flanks a path or lawn, hold plants back with metal or log edging, or make your own from freshly cut bamboo canes bent into arcs. Several of these can be used to form a low temporary fence or restrict bushy growth that may swamp lower plants.

Climbers planted in the border need sturdy supports. A bamboo tripod or curly metal poles will support annual sweet peas or morning glory, but a climbing rose or vigorous clematis will require something stronger, such as a wooden tripod or pillar (*see p.138*).

Eye protection

Cover the ends of bamboo canes; it is all too easy to miss them when you are working, and the ends can cause serious injury to eyes and face. You can buy cane tops, some of them very decorative, or improvise. Try lumps of modeling clay, small balls, or miniature plastic bottles, which you could paint bright colors.

How to prevent perennials from flopping

Not all perennials need support, of course, but it is advisable for tall plants with large flowerheads, thin stems, or both. There are many different ways of supporting your plants, and you may need to experiment with a few methods before finding the one that is best for your particular plants. Metal supports bought from the garden center are more expensive than bamboo canes, stakes, and string, but they can last for years if you remove them in the winter and are therefore a good investment.

The most basic supports are made from canes or stakes set in a circle around the stems and bound with garden twine. Use supports slightly shorter than the final height of the plant.

Birch or hazel sticks, also called pea sticks, offer natural-looking support poked into the soil around a clump, and can be bent into a cage. They may take root but are easily pulled out.

Long-lasting metal stakes come in various heights, and several can be linked together to encircle clumps of different sizes. Dark brown or black supports will be the least visible.

Making a support for climbers

You can make a large support with twiggy sticks for annual climbers, such as sweet peas (*Lathyrus*), thunbergia, and eccremocarpus. If you have a tree in your garden, cut young, flexible stems in midwinter and keep them somewhere cool and not too dry until you are ready to use them. Alternatively, find a local supplier of willow and use willow stems instead.

1 First make a basic framework by pushing sticks into the ground at regular intervals to form a circle. Bring the stems together at the top and either weave them to create a dome, or tie them together with twine. You can then trim off any unwanted shoots.

2 When you have the domelike frame of uprights in place, weave more stems around the support in horizontal bands about 18in (45cm) apart. Give extra strength to your structure by tying these to the vertical supports with twine where they cross.

Deadheading

Picking off the dead flowerheads not only tidies up a plant, but also channels its energy into producing new flowers and growth, rather than into seed production. As a result, deadheading will prolong the flowering display of some plants, for example roses, sweet peas (*Lathyrus*), and bedding plants, such as geraniums and verbenas, growing in containers and hanging baskets.

What to deadhead

Deadheading is not an exact science, but there are a few guidelines worth following.
• Large flowers, for example those of some geraniums, should be snapped off individually. The soft stems of most perennials and annuals are easily pinched through.
• If the tall flowering stems of delphiniums, lupins, and foxgloves (*Digitalis*) are cut off, new smaller heads will be encouraged to sprout lower down.
• Dainty plants with small flowers, like brachyscombe and lobelias, are best trimmed using scissors.
• Bulbs do not produce any more flowers if they are deadheaded, but they will channel their energies into producing bigger bulbs with increased flowering capacity for next year. So, it is worth deadheading daffodils (*Narcissus*), tulips, and lilies. Alliums also benefit, but you will have to forego their appealing seedheads.

Cosmos will bloom almost continuously throughout summer and up to the first frosts if you continue to deadhead it. Take the long flower stems back to the ferny foliage below.

• For repeat-flowering roses, in particular hybrid tea and floribunda types, pick or cut off blooms with pruners at the cluster point, one by one, if you wish, or just above a leaf. Shrub roses and out-of-reach climbers and ramblers are not worth the effort, and some roses, especially the species, will develop colorful hips if the flowers are left.

How flowers produce fruit

Plants produce flowers for just one purpose: to reproduce by seed. Once the female parts of a flower have been fertilized, the plant turns its energy into producing seed. Deadheading is most effective if the flower is removed as it is wilting, rather than when it is completely dead; this catches the plant before it starts to produce seed, diverting its energy back into new flowers. Taking off flowers at the stem tips also allows any dormant buds along the stem to produce more side shoots and more flowers.

Petals wither

Developing fruit swells

Fruit is ripe

Embryo fruit

1 The colors and sweet scents of flowers attract a range of pollinating insects. When the flower has been pollinated, the fruit containing the seeds begins to swell.

2 The flower has fulfilled its function as soon as successful pollination takes place, and its petals begin to wither and fall. The seeds start to develop within the fruit.

3 As seeds ripen, the fruit (here a rosehip) often changes color. Many fruits are eaten by birds and animals; the seeds are not digested but dispersed in their droppings.

• Shrubs and trees are usually difficult to deadhead, and many bear fruit; it would be a shame to spoil a late show of crab apples, or miss the berries on barberry, cotoneaster, or mountain ash (*Sorbus*). Rhododendrons and mountain laurel can be deadheaded by snapping off the flowerheads carefully with your fingers to avoid damaging the buds just below. Use

Daffodil flowers are removed by pinching through the stem just below the seed pod.

pruners to remove the flowers of lilac (*Syringa*) and to cut back broom (*Cytisus*) before the seedpods ripen; do not cut into the old wood. Stop deadheading in autumn to prevent new growth that will be vulnerable to frost damage.

Shearing back

An easy way of deadheading some plants is to trim them back with shears. Trim after flowering for more flowers, fresh foliage, or both. Try this with border campanulas, catmint (*Nepeta*), hardy geraniums, knapweeds (*Centaurea*), border salvias, and pulmonarias.

In early spring, shear back growth of winter-flowering heathers (*Erica carnea*), heath (*Calluna*), periwinkles (*Vinca*), St. John's wort (*Hypericum calycinum*), and ornamental grasses,

Hybrid tea roses and floribundas do not usually produce attractive hips. Cut back the stem to an outward-facing bud or a fully formed shoot to stimulate more flowers.

being careful not cut into the new shoots. Also shear off old leaves on barrenwort in late winter, before they flower.

When not to deadhead

Not everything in the garden needs deadheading. Some plants, such as annual poppies (*Papaver*), will not produce more flowers and usually develop seedheads if flowers are left in place. These can be very appealing, and the scattered seed is likely to result in a crop of seedlings the following year. Columbine, pot marigold, larkspur, and foxgloves also seed profusely. If too many germinate, weed out the excess; if none are wanted, deadhead the plants.

Shearing catmint back after it has flowered in summer will stimulate the plant into producing more fresh foliage and a second, smaller flush of blooms.

Leave to seed

Don't deadhead these plants, since they produce attractive seedheads that last, in some cases, for several months.

Achillea
Astilbe
Clematis like *C. tangutica* (*right*),
  C. orientalis, and their hybrids
Eryngium
Hydrangeas

Ornamental grasses
Poppies (*Papaver, left*)
Roses, especially species like
  R. glauca and *R. rugosa*
Sedum
Teasel (*Dipsacus*)

Protecting plants in winter

Some of your plants may not be completely hardy and will therefore be prone to winter weather damage in all but the mildest gardens. Others, such as summer bedding plants, are tender and need to be brought inside if they are to survive into the following year.

Protect plants at risk before the cold weather by storing tubers and bringing small tender plants into frost-free conditions. In milder regions, plants that are too large to dig up and store inside can be covered with a deep, insulating mulch, or wrapped up to protect them from the elements.

Young plants, such as geraniums and fuchsias, can be kept on windowsills indoors or in a frost-free porch but tend to grow spindly in the relatively low light and warm temperatures. To prevent this from happening, pinch out the growing tips of the plants and keep the soil mix barely moist over winter.

Lifting and storing

Except in very warm areas where frost is light or nonexistent, lift and store border chrysanthemums and tender bulbs and tubers over winter. Daisy-flowered border chrysanthemums are not totally hardy and should be lifted in mid- to late autumn. Cut down their stems to 6in (15cm) from the base, and store the roots, known as "stools," in labeled boxes or trays of old potting mix in cool but frost-free conditions.

Tender bulbs and tubers can be kept in any cool, frost-free shed, greenhouse, or conservatory, maintaining a minimum temperature of 40–45°F (4–7°C). Cut down the stems of begonias and lift the tubers just before the frosts start. Dry them off and dust with sulfur before packing them into trays of dry compost or bark. Lift gladioli in midautumn when the leaves are turning yellow. Snap off the stems and dry off the bulblike corms. You'll see a withered old corm under the new one; pull this off and discard it. You will also find baby corms, which you can grow on like seeds. Dust the new corms with sulfur and store them in shallow trays in a cool, dry, airy shed or a room indoors. Chocolate cosmos (*Cosmos atrosanguineus*)

Begonias are tender, and the tubers need to be lifted and stored before the first frosts of autumn.

should be lifted in autumn as a precaution in very cold areas. Dig up tubers before the frosts start, and store under cover in trays of barely moist soil. Check all stored bulbs and tubers regularly for signs of rot throughout the winter, and discard any that have succumbed.

Spring awakening

Border chrysanthemums will sprout new shoots in spring. These can be used as cuttings to produce new plants (*see p.244*); the old plants should be discarded. Dormant tubers and corms can be planted out in their flowering positions in midspring. Plant cannas just below the surface and dahlias 4–6in (10–15cm) deep. Remember to plant begonia tubers with the hollow side facing up.

Alternatively, if you have space, you can sprout tubers, rhizomes, and corms inside. In early spring, plant them in pots large enough to allow some root growth. If dahlias and cannas have formed large clumps, split them before potting, making sure that each section has one or more buds. Keep pots watered and in good light and a frost-free place, such as on a windowsill, or in a cool conservatory or heated greenhouse. Plant out when the danger of frost has passed. Plants started into growth indoors will flower earlier than those planted outside in midspring when dormant.

Tender bedding cuttings

If you prefer not to throw away your tender bedding plants in the fall, take cuttings in late summer or early autumn (*see p.245*). Overwinter the young plants in cool, frost-free conditions, keeping the soil only slightly moist. As temperatures rise in spring, the plants will grow sturdy and be on the point of flowering by the time you plant them out in late spring or early summer.

Protecting plants in the ground

Plants of borderline hardiness may survive outside over winter in mild gardens and sheltered areas, but it is still worth taking precautions against unpredictable frosts. Cover those that die down in winter, including chrysanthemums, dahlias, cannas, and chocolate cosmos, with a winter mulch of bulky organic matter, such as well-rotted manure, garden compost, leaf mold, straw, or composted bark. Scrape back the mulch in the spring to allow the new shoots to emerge. Single cloches can be placed over individual plants as an alternative to mulching. The cloches act like miniature greenhouses and keep off the rain.

Chrysanthemums and cannas, and other perennials that are not completely hardy can, in mild areas, be covered with an insulating layer of straw, pegged down with netting to prevent it from blowing away.

Penstemons, phygelius, some salvias, pittosporums, as well as hardy but young, newly planted evergreens can survive outside if wrapped loosely in a double layer of heavyweight horticultural fleece when severe weather is forecast. Remove the fleece when temperatures rise. You can also take cuttings from penstemons and shrubby salvias in case they don't survive outside; treat them as for tender bedding (*see above*).

Protecting bananas and tree ferns

Plants such as bananas and tree ferns are increasingly popular, but are not hardy at all in very cold areas. If you have a large specimen in the border, you will need to bring it inside or protect it from low temperatures and winter moisture, both of which can be fatal to these exotics. Tree ferns' hardiness increases with age, and young plants should be brought inside.

1 Cut off the leaves of bananas or tie them up in a column. Set canes around the clump and fix chicken wire to them, encircling the plant. Do this for the trunks of tree ferns in colder places but not mild areas.

2 Pack dry straw around and over the stems within the cage of chicken wire, so that the whole plant is covered. Pack the crowns of tree ferns with straw in the same way, folding the old fronds over the top.

3 Top all wrapped plants with a cover of clear plastic to keep out the rain. Finally, wrap the whole structure with fleece to prevent the wind from damaging the plant. Remove protection from bananas in late spring; unwrap tree ferns before growth starts.

Lawns and meadows 8

Looking after your lawn • Coping with weeds and other problems
Making a new lawn • Lawn alternatives • Meadow gardening

Lawn options

A lawn can have a magical effect on a garden. The open area of green it provides is soothing both to look at and to walk on. Lawns are very flexible since they can be cut to any shape from a rectangle to sinuous curves that provide open areas and link seamlessly to other parts of the garden by narrowing into paths. Formal or informal, traditional or avant-garde, a lawn can emphasize your chosen style according to how it is handled.

Most gardens, even small or new ones, are likely to have a lawn. To work well, a traditional lawn should be an even green with a crisp edge; otherwise it is unlikely to enhance the beauty of your garden. Look at your lawn closely: Does it pass muster, or is it scruffy around the edges and marked with brown patches? Is the grass fairly uniform, or are there assorted broad-leaved weeds, mossy or bare areas under trees, or coarse grasses sprouting in clumps here and there?

Whatever state it is in, a lawn can be improved by a program of regular maintenance and fertilizing (*see pp. 172–177*). Even if there are more weeds than grass, an acceptable everyday lawn can be achieved this way, as long as your standards are not unrealistically high. If you are more of a perfectionist, you should consider clearing the ground and starting over (*see pp. 182–184*). A new lawn from seed or sod will be of much better quality than one renovated from a very poor state. To do well, lawns need good light and good drainage. If your lawn suffers from shade or waterlogging, address these problems (*see p. 180*). In some

Grass facts

Lawns resemble the natural habitat of grass in many ways, which is why they work so well. In the vast grasslands around the world, grass is dominant; as a lawn it squeezes out weeds. The low growing point withstands grazing and trampling by animals in the wild better than broad-leaved plants; in lawns it escapes the mower's blades and quickly regrows after cutting to form a dense, wear-resistant mat.

Growing point is at the base of the plant

difficult areas, you may be better off considering other plants or different surfaces (*see p. 185*).

Shape and size

It is easier to mow and edge a simple shape. If your lawn has awkward corners, you could cut them out or broaden tight curves. For small gardens, a geometric shape works best—rectangular, round, or oval lawns are ideal. Small lawns invite close inspection, so neat edges are important and weeds are more noticeable than they would be in a large area. Tiny lawns, less than 4 sq yd (4 sq m), are hardly worth the effort and might be better replaced with paving or some alternative planting. Large lawns are easier to manage in many ways. Weeds are less noticeable, wear and tear makes less impact, and riding mowers can be used. In addition, gently curving shapes are easy to handle.

Steeply sloping banks can be mown with a weed-whacker, but a walled terrace or groundcover planting may look better and be easier to manage than grass. Gently undulating lawns are not a problem, but if your lawn has humps that are scalped by mower blades, leaving bare patches and hollows that fill with lush long grass, leveling the ground is advisable (*see p. 181*).

Grass paths are feasible where wear is light. Make them of mowable width, at least 36in (90cm); calculating the width in multiples of your mower blade will make mowing easier. Remember the edges: Are you prepared to trim them? Is there a hard edge? A hard edge of bricks, curbing, treated wood, or metal strip set below the level of the grass allows the mower to pass over the edge freely, saving much work.

An expanse of grass provides a quiet contrast to the busier planting in beds and borders, and there is nothing better to set off trees and shrubs.

What kind of lawn do you want?

An attractive lawn does not have to resemble a putting green, closely cut and evenly trimmed. This effect requires a great deal of work, and the fine grasses that give the smooth appearance will not tolerate heavy wear. If your lawn is well used, coarser grasses cut a little higher will suit your purposes much better. Grass does not have to be cut to a uniform height: You could leave an area to grow long and flower. This looks appealing and attracts wildlife, especially if planted with wildflowers and bulbs.

A neat patch of green for occasional summer use probably describes most lawns. An even, green lawn is worth achieving and it could add value to your house. It requires some attention, but a few weeds won't matter, and many people find daisies in the lawn charming.

For a playground use a coarser mix with rye grass, which is hard wearing. All lawns will suffer with heavy use, particularly in wet, very dry, or very cold weather. The grass should not be cut too short, and needs regular care (*see p.176*).

For a wildlife-friendly aspect allow the grass to grow long, and do not fertilize the lawn. Cut twice, first in late summer and again before winter, with a mower, trimmer, or shears. Over the years, wildflowers will move in, or you can plant them, including some bulbs, for a mini-meadow.

A perfect soft green lawn to set off your garden will need a high proportion of fine grasses. It must be watered in dry periods, especially in summer, and paths are essential. Be prepared to work hard, or hire a yardman or a lawn service to provide regular cutting, fertilizing, and care.

A path is similar to a playground, but if it is used all year round, consider laying stepping stones or replacing it with paving. If the lawn is narrow, consider widening it if possible, ideally to at least 6ft (2m), to spread the wear.

Looking after your lawn

To keep a lawn dense, green, and springy you need to fertilize and weed it, rake off debris and dead grass, and get air into the soil every so often after the wear and tear of summer. However, mowing is the most important job, and this must be done regularly while the grass is growing.

Mowing the lawn

Regular mowing encourages dense growth. Mow lightly but often, removing no more than a third of the grass blade at each cutting. If you let the grass grow long routinely and then cut it hard, the quality of the lawn will deteriorate.

Grass grows fastest in warm, moist conditions, whereas a fine lawn may need to be cut two or three times a week. For a regular lawn, a weekly cut is usually sufficient; remember that coarse-leaved grasses do not tolerate close mowing. In hot, dry weather, mow less frequently and allow the grass to grow longer than normal to conserve moisture. Don't waste the clippings: Mix them into the compost pile, except for the first two or three cuts after applying lawn weedkiller, which should be consigned to the trashcan.

Clean your mower after every use, removing any grass and wiping the blade with an oily rag. Instructions come with every machine, and these are worth reading. Regularly

Make mowing easier Plants spilling out of borders shade out grass and make mowing awkward. Cut back sprawling stems or lay a hard-paved edge to help keep edges neat (*see p.174*).

oil moving parts, and keep the blade sharp or it will tear the grass. It is easy to remove and sharpen the blades of a rotary mower, using an oilstone, diamond sharpener, or file. There are gadgets available to sharpen the blades of cylinder mowers, but these have varying degrees of success. Have the blades professionally reground if possible. On some models they can easily be replaced when they become worn or damaged.

Mowing guidelines and cutting heights

• Mow in spring, summer, and fall, and occasionally in winter in warm regions.

• Do not mow when the lawn is very wet, frozen, or during drought conditions in summer.

• Brush off any worm castings before mowing, or they will be flattened and smother the grass.

• Collect clippings unless you use a mulching mower (see opposite) to prevent a buildup of "thatch." The exception is in hot summers, when the clippings can be left as a mulch to conserve soil moisture.

• For a rectangular lawn, first mow a wide strip at each end, for turning the mower. Then mow up and down in straight strips, slightly overlapping the edges of each strip.

• For a curved or irregular shape, first mow a strip around the edge, then mow straight up the center. Mow each half as for a rectangular lawn.

• If a mower jams while in use, unplug it or remove the spark plug lead before investigating.

Cutting heights
Vary the cutting height with the season. If the grass has grown long, cut it back in stages, raising the blade to the highest point and gradually lowering it for subsequent cuts.

Top-quality lawn

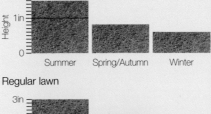

Regular lawn

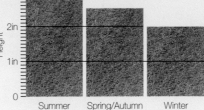

Seasonal adjustments It is simple to raise or lower the cutting blades on most mowers, and worth doing both for easier mowing and for a better-looking lawn.

Which mower?

Choose the right mower for your lawn size and type. Use a grass catcher to collect clippings, or use a mulching mower that chops them finely before feeding them back into the soil, where they are quickly broken down. Ideally choose a large mower with plenty of capacity, but before you buy make sure you can handle it and consider where it will be stored. If you have to lift it up steps, a smaller, lighter model may be better.

Electric mowers are light and useful for lawns near the house and electrical sockets. Always use a ground-fault circuit interrupter, secure the cable over your shoulder, and do not mow wet grass. Gasoline mowers are heavier but have no trailing cords, which makes them better for large lawns. Gas rotary models can cut damp grass. A good gas mower should last a lifetime, if serviced regularly and especially before being stored away for the winter.

Rotary mowers

These are excellent for regular lawns and long grass. Some have a mulching facility or a roller to leave stripes. Inspect blades frequently, filing out any nicks caused by hitting stones, and sharpen them regularly too, balancing them across the center line to avoid wear on the drive spindle.

Rotary blades slash through grass at high speed. Blunt blades tear rather than cut, causing grass tips to turn an unsightly brown.

Lightweight bag collects clippings

Rotary mower

Riding mowers

These are convenient for very large areas of lawn, over about ⅓ acre (0.1 hectare). You will also need a secure place to store the vehicle, with easy access to the lawn.

Replaceable metal cutting blade under housing

Large-volume box collects cuttings

Riding mower

Cylinder mowers

This is the type to use for small, closely mown lawns. For the best finish on fine-textured grasses, invest in a model with 6 or more blades. Hand mowers usually have 4 blades; they are ideal for small lawns, since they are lighter and smaller than powered models. All types perform best if they are serviced and the blades reground regularly.

Moving blades cut against a static blade like scissors. Blunt blades will tear the grass. The roller sets the height of the cut and makes stripes in the lawn.

Hand mower with grass box

Gas-powered cylinder mower

Trimmers or weed whackers

These are useful for long grass and where the lawn butts up against a wall. On some the head can be turned to trim edges vertically. Never use them near a tree, because the nylon line will damage the bark.

Flexible nylon line rotates 360° at high speed, slicing through grass

Nylon line trimmer

Hard mowing edge A course of bricks makes a practical edge to a lawn. If set at soil level, it makes mowing easier, and sprawling plants can soften the edge without shading out the grass.

Watering the lawn

Grass loses its springiness and starts to discolor when it is low on water, which is mainly in summer. New lawns and high-quality lawns must be watered, unless there is a watering ban. Water as soon as you notice that the grass does not spring back after being walked on. Most other lawns can be left unwatered; the tougher grasses in these lawns will turn brown as they become dormant, but when it rains again they will recover and soon become green again. If at all possible, it is easier and less wasteful to wait for rain. Don't water lightly and often; soak the lawn at weekly or longer intervals.

Lawn sprinklers are the usual method of watering but are wasteful. To maximize their effectiveness and reduce evaporation, run them in the cool of morning or evening, or during the night. Seep hoses or perforated hoses can be used, but need to be moved across the lawn by about 8in (20cm) every half hour. For large high-quality lawns, consider installing pop-up sprinklers or a robotic watering device that moves automatically after an area is soaked.

Trimming the edges

Keeping the edges neat improves the look of any lawn. The edges can be cut sharp where the lawn meets the soil of a bed or border, or it can butt up to a hard surface. In the latter case mowing is much easier if the hard surface is at soil level, so the mower can run smoothly over the edges. Even where a lawn runs up to a border, it is a good idea to lay a mowing edge of bricks to keep a sharp divide and allow plants to spill over but not onto the grass.

If your lawn has a hard edge, you should clean up the grass at the edge occasionally using shears, preferably long-handled edging shears, or a trimmer. Without a hard edge, you will need to cut the edges of the lawn fairly frequently, using a spade in conjunction with shears or a trimmer, or preferably a half-moon edging tool, which has a flat blade. Powered edging machines are available for large lawns.

How much water?

If you have to water your lawn, do it thoroughly, so the soil is moistened to a depth of 4–6in (10–15cm). Shallow watering results in a lawn that is more vulnerable to drought. Lawns need about 1in (2.5cm) of water per week, including rainfall. Check the amount you apply with several straight-sided jars marked at this depth, scattered across the lawn.

Make a neat edge

Recutting the edge is easiest when the soil is moist but not wet. Lay a plank on the lawn to stand on and cut against, or use a taut length of string as a guide. Sever the grass roots where they are spreading into the bed or border (*right*). When you have finished working in one direction, work back in the other, pressing the spade or edger against the cut surface to make it firm and shiny. Put the trimmings on the compost pile. After every other mowing, trim with shears or edging shears (*far right*) or a trimmer with an adjustable head for edging.

How to repair a broken edge

If not repaired, damaged edges will continue to deteriorate, and like any bare patch, they also provide an open invitation for weeds to establish. Reseeding a damaged edge is rarely effective, so try tackling the problem using this simple technique.

Stand on a board and cut against it to get a straight edge.

1 Check the lawn regularly. Damaged edges look unsightly, and create opportunities for weeds that will affect the lawn's overall quality.

2 Cut out a rectangle of sod around the damaged area. Cut a generous area, or the sod will fall apart as you lift it out.

3 Undercut the rectangle with a spade. Try to cut the sod to as even a thickness as possible, with at least 1in (2.5cm) of soil.

5 Re-lay the piece of turf, turning it around so that the broken edge faces inward, and the cut edge aligns with the edge of the lawn. Check the fit and level, and make any adjustments. Butt up the edges, and press down the refitted section firmly.

4 Lightly fork over the newly exposed soil to break up the surface and to encourage re-rooting. Add soil if necessary and firm well.

6 Fill the hole with top-dressing (see p.176) and work it into the joints to help them knit together. You can reseed the hole if it is large, using an appropriate grass seed. Water, and keep an eye on the repair until the grass has started to regrow, weeding and watering if required.

Lawn care through the year

Task	Spring	Summer	Autumn	Winter
Mowing	Weekly	1–3 times a week	1–2 times a week	Occasionally if grass is growing
Fertilizing	Spring/summer lawn fertilizer (high nitrogen)	Spring/summer lawn fertilizer in early summer, if not given in spring	Autumn lawn fertilizer (high potassium) in early autumn	
Watering new lawns	In dry periods if needed	Weekly in dry periods	In dry periods if needed	
Scratching or scarifying			Where moss is not present	
Aerating			Every 2–3 years after scarifying	
Top-dressing			Immediately after aerating	
Raking	To remove surface debris	To remove surface debris	To remove fallen leaves	To remove fallen leaves
Moss control	Apply moss killer		Apply moss killer. Scarify when the moss is dead. Improve drainage by aerating. Add 1 part pinhead charcoal to the top-dressing ingredients (below).	Use a soil testing kit to check soil pH (see p.39). If it is acidic, apply ground chalk or ground limestone at 1½oz per sq yd (50g per sq m).
Weed control	Apply lawn weedkiller if necessary, or a weed-and-feed formulation	Apply lawn weedkiller if necessary and not done in spring	Apply more lawn weedkiller if necessary in early autumn	Adjusting soil pH as for winter moss control will also help to control weeds
Repairs	Humps, hollows, and bare patches		Humps, hollows, and bare patches	Humps, hollows, and bare patches

Feeding your lawn

A starved lawn will turn a pale yellowish green. To avoid this, feed your lawn at least once a year with the lawn fertilizer appropriate to the time. Check the product to make sure you are buying what you need and always follow the manufacturer's instructions.

• Spring and summer fertilizers are high in nitrogen to encourage rapid, lush growth and good color. Apply them in spring or early summer.

• Autumn fertilizers are high in potassium to toughen up the grass for winter. Apply them in early fall.

To scatter feed evenly and accurately, use sticks to divide the lawn into 1yd (1m) squares.

Hand-feeding lawns Weigh the amount of fertilizer for 1 sq yd (1 sq m), which is given in the package, into a plastic cup. Mark the level and use this as your measure.

Lawn fertilizers come in granular and liquid formulations. Liquid fertilizers are watered on. They are quick acting and suitable for small lawns. The granular forms have a longer-lasting effect but need to be watered in if there is no rain within two or three days. They must be spread evenly, so invest in a wheeled spreader if your lawn is large; this will need to be adjusted so that the fertilizer is applied at the correct rate.

Autumn rejuvenation

If your lawn feels hard, it has become compacted. Regular use compresses air spaces in the soil, and you need to alleviate the situation by aerating every two or three years when the soil is moist, so the grass roots can breathe again. Hollow-tining gives the best results, especially on heavy soils; you can rent a powered tiner for large lawns. Spiking with a garden fork is suitable for small lawns on light soil. A spiked roller makes the job easier, but the penetration is not as deep. For large lawns you can use a powered slitter, but the blades only make shallow cuts that penetrate and aerate thatch. After aerating, brush in a gritty top-dressing to improve drainage and add nutrients.

Making top-dressing

Estimate the area of your lawn: You will need 4lb/sq yd (2kg/sq m) of top-dressing. Buy the ingredients in bulk and mix up on a large plastic sheet, using a bucket to measure one part.

3 parts sandy loam or good-quality topsoil
6 parts horticultural sand
1 part peat substitute, such as composted bark or coir

Autumn lawn care

The droughts and wear of summer can leave lawns hard and patchy. Improve them by scratching out dead grass "thatch" and opening up compacted soil to let the roots breathe and rain and nutrients penetrate. This helps grass to grow deeper and survive drought. Rake up leaves and brush off worm castings; when grass is covered for any time, it turns yellow and may die.

Thatch found on the lawn surface is caused by a build-up of dead grass and debris.

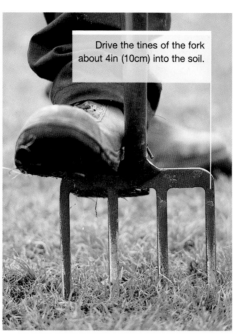

Drive the tines of the fork about 4in (10cm) into the soil.

1 Use a spring-tined rake to vigorously scratch out or "scarify" thatch. Treat moss and make sure it is dead before scarifying; raking live moss spreads the problem around.

2 Aerate the lawn every 2–3 years. This is easiest when the soil is moist. Drive in a fork (on heavy soils use a hollow-tiner) to remove cores of soil, every 4in (10cm).

3 Apply top-dressing (*see opposite*) directly after aerating, spreading the mixture evenly over the surface—one bucketful will cover approximately 6 sq yd (5 sq m).

4 Work the top-dressing well into the grass and the air holes using the back of a rake or a stiff broom. To make the job easier, allow the mixture to dry slightly before brushing it in.

5 Finally, apply an autumn lawn feed at the rate recommended on the package. For an even spread, scatter half the fertilizer in one direction and the other half at right angles to it.

6 If the lawn looks sparse, sprinkle over some seed. Choose a seed type to match the rest of the lawn, and use about half the amount recommended for sowing a new lawn.

Lawn problems

Rare is the lawn without a weed—weed seeds are constantly being blown into your garden or brought in by birds. A good lawn-care routine will deal with many weeds: Regular mowing exhausts them, and healthy, strong-growing grass will simply crowd them out. Mowing the lawn too short, letting it grow too long, or failing to feed it can all provide an opening.

Spot weed treatments are useful for spraying, painting, or smearing onto individual broad-leaved weeds, but these treatments do not work efficiently on grasslike weeds.

Weeds will move into bare patches where the grass has been worn away or weeds have been dug out by hand. Prevent this by re-seeding. If you can match the seed mix to the existing lawn, so much the better, but it will soon blend in either way.

Rake the lawn before mowing to lift up weed stems into the path of the blade, and always use a grass bag to prevent weeds from spreading. For very weedy lawns or difficult weeds, use a suitable lawn weedkiller, or apply a weed-and-feed formulation in spring.

Moss in a lawn is a sign of bad growing conditions, such as low fertility, compacted or poorly drained soil, and shade; it is more troublesome on acidic soils (*see pp. 38–39*). Autumn lawn care and spring feeding will help (*see p. 176*). Test the soil, and if the pH is low, apply lime in winter at the rate of 1½oz per sq yd (50g per sq m).

Isolated weeds can be dug out with an old kitchen knife or a special tool called a weed grubber. Cutting around the plant will allow you to remove the entire taproot of weeds such as dandelions. Reseed any bare patches left after weeding.

The usual suspects

Typical lawn weeds fall into two types: Some are low-growing wildflowers, while others are undesirable coarse grasses or grasslike plants. What they all share is an ability to survive regular mowing. Once they have germinated, they spread through the lawn by creeping stems, runners, or through seed in grass clippings, and early action is advisable to contain the problem. Dandelions have deep taproots and if their tops are cut off, more small plants grow again from any part of the root left in the soil. Creeping buttercups creep to form mats. Daisies do the same, but to many they are a delight and not a weed; similar views are held about clover. Some weeds can safely be encouraged, especially in wildlife-friendly long grass; others will smother lawn grasses and need to be controlled.

White clover (*Trifolium repens*)
Mat-forming weed indicating poor, slightly alkaline soil. Its roots contribute nitrogen. Use a lawn weedkiller.

Annual meadow grass (*Poa annua*)
This is a tufted grass that spreads by seeding. Dig out plants by hand before they flower.

Creeping buttercup (*Ranunculus repens*) The creeping stems form mats. Weedkiller is not reliable; you may have to dig this out by hand, so catch it early.

Moss This indicates poor conditions, especially on acidic soils. Use moss killer in spring or autumn, but it may to return underlying cause is unresolved (*see left*).

Self-heal (*Prunella vulgaris*)
A mat-forming weed, which is best dealt with by use of a lawn weedkiller. This could be left in meadow grass.

Slender speedwell (*Veronica filiformis*) Control the mats of tiny leaves by feeding the lawn to encourage growth, and scarifying in autumn.

Dandelion (*Taraxacum officinale*)
Use a spot weedkiller or dig out the tap-root. Deal with dandelions before they have the chance to seed.

Yorkshire fog (*Holcus lanatus*)
A coarse-leaved, creeping grass. Slash repeatedly with a knife to weaken bad patches, or dig out and reseed.

Lesser yellow trefoil (*Trifolium dubium*) An annual weed that is often quickly spread by mowing without a grass box. Control with lawn weedkiller.

Field woodrush (*Luzula campestris*)
A clump-forming, grasslike plant which prefers acidic soil. Dig out by hand; apply ground-up lime in winter.

Broad-leaved plantain (*Plantago major*) A solitary plant with a taproot, which spreads by seed. Dig out the roots by hand or use a spot weedkiller.

Pearlwort (*Sagina procumbens*)
This is a creeping weed that forms low mats of grassy leaves. It can be controlled with a lawn weedkiller.

Daisy (*Bellis perennis*) Leave the rosettes in place if you like the look of a daisy-spangled lawn. If not, dig out the roots by hand.

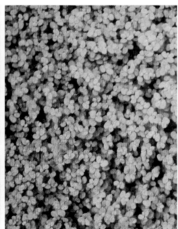

Baby's tears (*Soleirolia soleirolii*)
Forms mats of tiny leaves, thriving in damp sites. Lawn weedkillers are ineffective; rake it out.

Yarrow (*Achillea millefolium*) The mats of ferny leaves thrive in dry soil; they also stay green in dry weather. Dig it out by hand or use lawn weedkiller.

Using weedkillers

- Always keep original packages, following the instructions exactly, and do not store diluted weedkiller.
- Always use a separate, labeled watering can for liquid weedkillers.
- Do not use on windy days; the weedkiller will drift into borders.
- Apply 2 or 3 days after mowing, when the weeds have grown new leaves to absorb the chemicals.
- Do not mow for a few days after treatment to allow the weedkiller to reach the roots.
- Do not add clippings from the next few mowings to the compost pile.
- Some weeds will need 2 or even 3 treatments at 4- to 6-week intervals.

Lawns and shade

Grass growing in light or dappled shade can thrive, but the deep shade from trees is often too much to allow growth. The grass becomes thin, and moss is likely to develop.

You may be able to open up the tree canopy by judicious pruning to let more light penetrate. Shade-tolerant seed mixes are available, but they are fine grasses that do not cope well with heavy wear or close cutting. Consider using alternative groundcovers in shady areas, such as moss, shade-loving plants, or a bark mulch (*see p. 185*).

Waterlogged lawns

Poorly drained lawns are beset with problems since grass roots die through lack of oxygen. If water sits on your lawn after rain, it can point to a high water table or to poor drainage.

An impervious layer of compacted soil or "hardpan" below the surface can result in poor drainage. It is possible to relieve compaction and penetrate the hardpan by spiking if it is not too far below the surface (*see p. 117*); smeared layers of hardpan near the surface are common.

If the problem lies deeper, more drastic and expensive action will be required. Curing the problem may involve digging drainage trenches or laying a system of drainage pipes. It could be easier to abandon all thoughts of a lawn in these circumstances, and instead grow plants that thrive in moist conditions (*see p. 66*).

Lawns on a clay soil can be especially problematic, as winter moisture leads to dead patches and moss growth, while in summer the roots of the grass may fail to reach moisture deep in the soil. One way of overcoming this is to follow the method used to make golf greens, and lay the lawn on a layer of coarse sand. First, improve the soil with generous additions of organic matter and careful cultivation. Then spread a layer of horticultural sand 2–3in (5–8cm) deep over the surface and place the sod on top. The grass will root through the sand into the fertile clay below and make good growth. In summer the roots will be able to extract moisture from the moist soil below the sand, and in winter excess water will drain through the sand, and result in a lawn surface that is far less wet.

What's wrong with my lawn?

All lawns inevitably develop discolored patches or problems from time to time, often caused by adverse weather conditions. Keep an eye out for the first signs of trouble, because prompt treatment will usually prevent permanent damage to your lawn. If the same problems keep reappearing time and again, look at the underlying conditions in your garden; tackling the causes will be far more effective in the long run than repeatedly treating the problems they create.

Earthworms

Scorch/yellow patches May be due to fertilizer that was unevenly distributed or not watered in, or to dog urine. If you see a dog urinating on the lawn, water the area thoroughly immediately.

Snow mold This fungus is most common in late winter. It is a sign of poor aeration and too much nitrogen. Scarify and aerate the lawn. More common when grass is long, so close-mow in fall.

Drought Yellowish, strawlike patches; the whole lawn may be affected. Let the grass grow longer and leave clippings on the lawn to reduce evaporation. Water or wait for rain.

Worm castings Earthworms leave small, muddy mounds on the lawn in spring or autumn. These are unpleasant, but not damaging, and are nutrient-rich. Brush them off into borders before mowing.

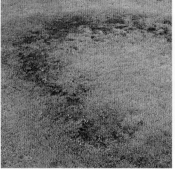

Fairy rings Fungi living on matter like old tree roots make rings of lush grass. The grass dies out between them and toadstools appear. Fungicides do not kill them. Feed, aerate, and water the lawn.

Mole hill Moles may pass through a garden or come to stay. Ultrasonic devices or smoke in the tunnels may drive them away, but trapping and releasing them elsewhere is more reliable.

Leveling humps and hollows

Hollows can fill with long grass, while humps may be scalped by your mower, damaging the blades and leaving bare areas for weeds to invade (*see p.178*). Don't try to roll the lawn flat, as this will only compact the soil. If humps and hollows are affecting mowing, lift the sod in the problem area and adjust the soil level. This is best done between autumn and spring.

> Check depth of hollow. Shallow dips can be filled with a top-dressing mix (*see p.176*) in spring. Level the top-dressing with the back of a rake and cover the area with netting to protect it until the grass grows through.

1 Assess the depth and extent of the hollow by laying a plank across it. Using a half-moon edger or a sharpened spade and the plank as a guide, cut a double "H" (HH) shape. Starting at the center of the cross (where the H shapes intersect), insert a spade horizontally under the sod to make a flap that you can lift up.

> Keep the flap as thin and even as possible—about 1in (2.5cm) thick.

2 Peel back the four segments along the legs of the H shapes. You can level off the soil on the undersides of the flaps once you have peeled them back; this will help to give you a smooth finish.

3 With all four segments peeled back, fork over the exposed soil to break up compaction. Add or remove soil as required, adding sand for drainage if necessary, then rake level, removing stones or debris.

4 Shuffle across the ground to firm it lightly, then rake it over again to break up the surface. This ensures that the grass roots will make good contact with the soil when the sod is replaced.

5 Roll the flaps of sod back into place, and lightly firm. Double check that the area is now level with the rest of the lawn. Make any necessary adjustments to the soil level before you finally replace the sod.

6 Knit edges of turf together as when laying a lawn, and tamp down all over, beating it down with the ball of your hand or the head of a rake. Top-dress the seams with a mixture of sand and soil, and brush in. Water thoroughly.

Making a new lawn

If you want a new lawn, you have the choice of laying sod or sowing seed. Whichever method you choose, the site must be well drained, level, and cleared of weeds. This means preparing the soil thoroughly, at least five weeks and ideally several months in advance, to give it time to settle.

• Kill or clear all perennial weeds, plus the old grass if you are replacing a badly neglected lawn. The easiest way is to use a glyphosate weedkiller, although more than one application may be required.

• Next, cultivate the soil, first skimming off any existing sod. If you prefer not to use a weedkiller, you can dig out weeds by hand during cultivation.

• A good lawn requires 8–12in (20–30cm) of well-drained topsoil; the subsoil should also drain well. With these conditions the grass will root deeply, reducing the need for watering. Where the depth of topsoil is irregular, the lawn will dry out more quickly in shallow areas and develop brown patches. If your topsoil is shallow, it is worth buying enough to achieve an even depth across the site.

Sod or seed?

• Laying sod gives you an instant lawn, usable in about eight weeks, when the sod has taken root. However, good-quality sod, like good-quality carpet, can be expensive.

• Seed costs less than sod, and the wide choice of grasses means you can satisfy your requirements more exactly, but it will be up to a year before the lawn can take heavy use.

Buying sod

Buy sod from a reputable specialist. Sod from good suppliers is grown in fields and lifted to order. If possible, you should inspect the sod to check the quality. Usually there is a choice between high-quality ornamental sod, containing only fine grasses, and utility grade, which has a proportion of hardwearing rye grasses. Some suppliers will grow special sod to order, but this is even more expensive and takes about 18 months.

Preparing the site

Dig over the area, plus an extra 6in (15cm) all around, thoroughly and methodically, removing weeds and incorporating soil improvers (see pp.40–41). On heavy clay or wet soils, mix plenty of sand into the topsoil to improve drainage. On light, sandy soil add a 3–4in (8–10cm) layer of bulky organic matter during digging; this will help to retain moisture and nutrients.

Accurate leveling

For this you need wooden pegs, a hammer, a straight edge or plank, and a level. On each peg, paint a line in a noticeable color at the same distance from the top. Insert a peg where the surface level is right with the mark at soil level. Knock in the other pegs at about 3ft (1m) intervals to create a grid across the site, using a level to check that the tops are all aligned. Once the grid is in place, add or remove soil as necessary across the site until the surface is level with the line on all the pegs.

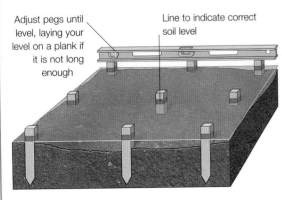

Adjust pegs until level, laying your level on a plank if it is not long enough

Line to indicate correct soil level

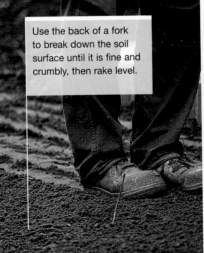

Use the back of a fork to break down the soil surface until it is fine and crumbly, then rake level.

After raking, leave for at least 5 weeks to allow soil to settle, then lightly hoe off any weed seedlings.

1 After digging and leveling, while soil is moist but not wet, tread over the site with the weight on your heels to eliminate soft spots that might later sink, giving an uneven surface. Repeat at right angles.

2 Rake off stones and debris; if soil is stony, rake again at right angles. A few days before laying sod or sowing, lightly rake in a balanced organic or compound granular fertilizer at the recommended rate.

Laying a sod lawn

The best time to lay sod is early autumn or early spring. Sod should not be left lying around, so agree on a delivery day and time when you can set to work immediately. If this proves impossible, unroll each one and lay it flat, grass side up, on paving or plastic and water if necessary. It will keep for a few days like this; grass left in rolls will soon yellow and may die.

1 Sod should be laid on soil that is moist, but not wet. Lay the first row of sod rolls along one edge of the site, tamping down each piece with the back of a garden rake. This will eliminate air pockets and bring the sod into close contact with the soil, encouraging it to root.

2 Make a tight seam with the adjacent piece of sod. To do this, raise the edges slightly, push them together so they are almost overlapping, and press down firmly with your thumbs. Tamp down once more along the seams to prevent the edges from lifting.

Lay the sod rolls so that the joints in adjoining rows are staggered, like bricks in a wall.

3 Continue to lay the sod in rows. Protect the sod that has already been laid by working on a plank to lay the next row. Continue until the site is covered, firming as you go by tamping down with the back of a rake. Do not use small pieces of sod at the edges; they will quickly dry out. Use a full-size sod at the edge, and put the smaller piece in the gap behind it.

4 Scatter fine sandy soil, or good topsoil mixed with horticultural sand, over the surface. Brush it well into the joints to fill any gaps and encourage the sod to knit together.

To create curved edges, lay a hose or rope to the required shape. Hold it in place with bent wire pegs and cut against it with a sharp spade or edger.

Edging the lawn Always cut to a guide; a hose is ideal for curves. For a straight edge, push in pegs at the corners and stretch string taut between them. Stand on the lawn side, on a plank aligned with the string, and cut against it.

Immediate aftercare

Keep newly laid sod well watered, because if the pieces dry out they will shrink and curl, and gaps will appear between them. Give a newly laid lawn a good soak, and if the weather is dry, continue to water it regularly, up to twice a week at first. It is not enough to wet the surface: To encourage rooting, water thoroughly, so that the underlying soil is moistened (*see p.174*). Pay particular attention to the edges and corners, which are most likely to dry out.

Take care not to disturb the sod before it has rooted; it is best to keep off it for at least three weeks. To check rooting, try peeling back one corner of a few newly laid pieces of sod; if they do not lift easily, the grass has rooted. Once this has happened, you can mow the lawn as necessary, but set the blade high, to about 2in (5cm). Avoid all but the lightest use until the lawn has been down for eight weeks.

Seeding a lawn

The best time to sow a lawn is in early autumn when the soil is warm and moist. The next best time is spring, but the soil may be cold after winter, which will delay germination. Scatter seed by hand; a seed distributor may be useful to cover large areas. Sow the seed over a slightly greater area and cut a clean edge a year after sowing when the lawn is established (*see above*).

1 Prepare the ground (*see p.182*). If hand sowing, divide the site into 3ft (1m) squares with string or stakes. Stir the seed to mix evenly. Weigh out seed for 1 sq yd (sq m), following the directions on the pack. Pour into a plastic cup, mark the level, and use it as your measure. As a guide, 1oz (30g) is roughly a handful.

2 For even distribution, scatter half the seed over the square in one direction, and half at right angles to it. Use the same criss-cross method if sowing by machine. Repeat for each square. When all the seed is sown, remove the strings or stakes.

Lightly rake, aiming to cover most of the seeds. Protect from birds with netting if possible.

Do not apply lawn weedkiller for at least 6 months after germination. Weed by hand instead, carefully firming any grass that is loosened.

3 Seedlings should appear within 14 days. Water regularly. Make the first cut, on a high setting, when seedlings have reached 3in (7.5cm). For autumn-sown lawns maintain this height until growth slows. The following spring you can gradually lower the blade height.

Alternatives to grass

If you decide your lawn is too small, too rough and weedy, too steep, or too much trouble, there are a number of practical, low-maintenance alternatives. Choose soft play bark for a children's play space, pave it for an all-weather entertaining area with raised beds, or create a sunny gravel garden. If moss is a problem in your lawn, you could just give in and enjoy it; alternatively try filling spaces in shade or under trees with a tapestry of groundcover plants.

Paving with thyme Leave out a slab here and there in paving to make room for a small tree or low shrub. Plant small ferns or creeping Jenny in moist, shady cracks, and creeping mints and thymes in sunny crevices and gaps, where they will release scent when stepped on.

Gravel garden In a sunny, well-drained garden, gravel or pea gravel spread 1in (2.5cm) deep over a geotextile fabric will suppress weeds and create a seaside mood. Plant with gauzy grasses, spiky phormiums and yuccas, shrubby potentillas, lavenders, sprawling rock roses, thymes, and other plants that enjoy good drainage.

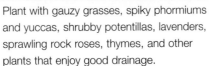

Shade-loving groundcover Plants such as cyclamen (*above*), hellebores, or *Vinca minor* grow well under trees. Some, such as lilyturf (*Liriope*) and ajuga, even put up with dry soil. Once they have settled they will look after themselves, especially if you lay a mulch to suppress weeds and retain soil moisture. Moss often grows naturally in damp shade where grass struggles (*right*). Let it spread, don't walk on it too often, and plant early-flowering bulbs like snowdrops (*Galanthus*) or lily of the valley (*Convallaria majalis*).

Meadow gardening

A meadow is an area where grasses and flowering annuals, bulbs, and perennials are allowed to intermingle and seed themselves. It looks natural and artless, but in reality getting the balance right can be quite difficult, especially in a traditional meadow of native species of grasses and flowers. Keep in mind, however, that you don't have to use native plants. The term "meadow gardening" includes a variety of naturalistic planting styles and you may find that it is easier to create a meadow with a range of annual species or a mixture of more exotic perennial cultivars and grasses.

In addition to being beautiful, an established meadow is also a wildlife haven, providing shelter, nectar, and seeds to sustain a varied colony of local fauna. Even a small meadow encourages biodiversity by providing a "green corridor" that enables the wildlife to travel across the landscape.

By creating a meadow, you will be establishing a balanced plant community that should develop with little interference on your part, so planning is crucial. You need to assess the soil type (*see pp.36–39*) and growing conditions (*see pp.54–61*)

A traditional wildflower meadow consists largely of wild species, which have smaller, more delicate flowers than the cultivated varieties found in garden borders.

Plants for meadows

Annuals

Agrostemma githago (Corn cockle)
Borago officinalis (Borage)
Calendula officinalis (English or pot marigold)
Centaurea cyanus (Cornflower)
Eschscholzia californica (California poppy)

Lagurus ovatus (Hare's tail)
Nigella damascena (Love-in-a-mist)
Papaver rhoeas (Corn or field poppy)
Papaver somniferum (Opium poppy)
Salvia viridis (Annual clary)

Border perennials
Achillea (Yarrow)
Aster

Calamagrostis x *acutiflora* 'Karl Foerster' (Reed grass)
Festuca glauca (Blue fescue)
Foeniculum vulgare (Fennel)
Geranium
Hemerocallis (Daylily)
Iris sibirica
Sanguisorba officinalis (Greater burnet)

of the meadow site. Then you should choose a mixture of plants that is appropriate for your plot. If you don't, not all the plants in the meadow will thrive equally, causing weaker species to disappear and thugs to take over.

The most popular kind of meadow occurs on free-draining, sunny chalk downs, which are ideal for ox-eye daisies (*Leucanthemum vulgare*) and field scabious (*Knautia arvensis*). But you can also have a meadow on damp ground, a good site for meadowsweet (*Filipendula ulmaria*), or in shade under trees, where the woodland dog's tooth violet (*Erythronium*

For an exuberant late-summer to autumn meadow, try mixing grasses with exotic perennial daisies from the border in hot hues, such as asters or rudbeckias (*above*).

An annual meadow, with its glorious show of flowers (*left*), depends on annuals that like freshly cultivated soil and are prolific self-seeders, since the meadow is dug over each year. Here, scarlet poppies, blue cornflowers, and white ox-eye daisies predominate.

dens-canis) will thrive. Meadow-seed specialists offer a range of mixes to suit different soil types and conditions.

Traditional wildflower meadows

The key to success with wildflower meadows is low soil fertility. If the soil is relatively fertile, the wildflowers will not be able to compete with vigorous grasses and after a couple of years, very few flowering plants will remain. So choose an area that hasn't been cultivated recently, or take steps to reduce the soil's fertility (*see p.188*).

There are two ways of creating a traditional meadow. You can sow seeds onto a bare patch of ground, or you can plant wildflowers in an established grass patch. Details of how to do either of these are given overleaf.

Annual meadows

When left to its own devices after the soil has been disturbed, any plot of land very quickly turns green as the seeds in the soil germinate. First come annuals like poppies and cornflowers, and then the perennial grasses and flowers that take over in the following years—a phenomenon often seen on shoulders following roadwork. If you dig over or plow up a meadow every year, you will prevent the perennials from establishing, giving the annuals space to spring up anew each year from self-sown seeds. If you like, this type of meadow can be composed predominantly of flowering plants with little or no grass.

To sow the annual meadow, you can use a prepared mix, or buy your own choice of annual seeds and mix them for a natural, random effect. Sow in autumn, if your mix consists of hardy annuals, or in spring, as shown overleaf. Turn the ground over in autumn after the plants have shed their seed, and the display will be reproduced the following year.

Exotic meadows

Meadows of native wildflowers have a subtle beauty because of the delicacy of their flowers. If you want a bolder display with an extended flowering season, include non-native perennials and their cultivars, which generally have larger, more brightly colored blooms. You can also add bulbs such as crocuses, daffodils, tulips, and snowdrops. However, keep in mind that this will complicate your mowing regime.

Preparing to sow a meadow

It is possible to reduce fertility slightly in a lawn in the year or two before you sow a meadow, by mowing repeatedly and removing the cuttings to prevent the nutrients from returning to the soil. Stripping off the topsoil, the most fertile layer of soil, also helps, but it is hard work and you'll need to find a new home for it. (You might even be able to sell it; good-quality topsoil is always in demand.) It also depends on your soil type: If you have a deep, rich topsoil, it may not be possible to remove it all.

You can prepare the soil immediately before sowing (*see right*) or preferably do it a few weeks beforehand. This allows any annual weed seeds in the soil to germinate so that you can hoe off the seedlings before sowing.

Caring for a newly sown meadow

In the first year, most of the flowers will be produced by the annuals. Don't be tempted to leave them until autumn: You must mow the meadow in early summer, as soon as the first flush of annuals has set seed, and remove the thatch. This will allow light to get to the foliage of the young perennials so that they can grow into vigorous plants that will begin to flower in the second year. Mow again in autumn. It will take a few years for the meadow to develop to its full potential, so do not be disheartened if not all the plants flower in the first few seasons; more will follow.

Enriching existing meadows

If you already have a meadow that does not have enough wildflowers to create an impact, you could make it prettier by introducing more flowering plants. One way of doing this is by seed: Clear the vegetation from small areas about the meadow, then level and rake the soil before sowing wildflower seeds in each area. If you would rather plant into the meadow, you can cut costs by buying plug plants, where available, from specialty nurseries. Better still, grow them yourself. Plug plants are young plants that have been sown into small cells of soil mix, so that each is supplied with a miniature root ball. If planted in autumn or early spring, plug plants soon establish and thrive in a meadow.

Another easy way of enriching a meadow is by altering the mowing routine. You may find that if you mow a few weeks later than usual, more plants will ripen and shed seed. You can also alter the flowering season of a meadow by mowing. Many people leave a meadow to flower in spring, then cut it in late spring or early summer once the spring bulbs die down and the seeds are shed. Try cutting the meadow a few times in spring, then leaving it to grow up for a summer display instead. You could even divide your meadow into separate areas that flower in different seasons.

Sowing a wildflower meadow

The best time to sow a wildflower meadow is during autumn. This is because some of the dormant seeds won't germinate unless they experience a period of cold first (*see p.31*). The soil warming up signals that winter is over and spring is on its way, thus prompting the seeds to germinate. Even so, some seeds may not germinate in the first year, but will do so in the following year.

1 Following the instructions on the package, weigh out the total amount of seed required to cover the site. You will find that you need only a little, usually about ½oz (15g) of seed to to 1 sq yd (1 sq m of soil). Pour the seed into a measuring cup to judge its volume.

2 Add a bulking agent, such as dry sand or bran, at a ratio of 1 part seed to 5 parts sand. The sand is easy to see, which will help you sow evenly over the plot.

3 Mix the sand and seed well. Divide the resulting volume by the number of sq ft (sq m) of your plot, so you know how much you'll need to sow in each 9 sq ft (sq m).

4 Dig out any perennial weeds, such as Bishop's weed or bindweed, from the plot, being careful to get their roots. They will be harder to eradicate after sowing.

5 You may want to remove some topsoil to reduce soil fertility (and clear weed seeds). How much depends on your soil type, but about 6in (15cm), including sod if any, will help.

Divide the plot into 3 x 3ft (1 x 1m) squares with stakes or string to make it easier to judge each sowing area.

6 Dig, fork over, or rototill the area to make sure that it is not compacted. Then level it with a rake, removing large stones, and tread over the site to firm it, as for a lawn (see p.182). Rake it again, lightly, to form a crumbly surface (fine tilth). Divide the plot into squares, and scatter the seed lightly over it, sowing one square at a time to provide even coverage.

7 After sowing, remove the stakes or string and use a spring-tined grass rake to cover the seed just barely with soil. Take care not to bury the seed too deeply or gouge into the soil.

8 Gently firm the area by tamping down with a rake, or lightly treading or rolling the plot. This ensures that the seed is in contact with the moist soil, which is vital for germination.

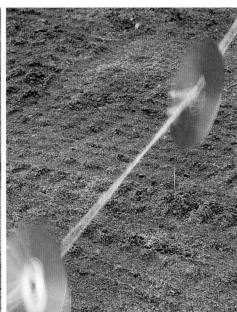

9 Protect the area from birds by stringing up CDs. Cover the ground with twiggy sticks to prevent cats from rolling or digging in the soil; remove the sticks once there is a haze of green.

Containers 9

Choosing a container • Planting containers and hanging baskets
Looking after plants in pots • Good ideas for container plants

Growing plants in containers

Plants in containers add color and interest to your garden, as well as broadening the range of plants you can grow. Containers inject drama into areas where planting in open ground is not possible: well-chosen plants enhance paved areas, softening hard brick and concrete surfaces, and bringing color to dark corners with bright flowers or foliage. Suitably planted containers can reinforce the style of a garden. An olive tree, yucca, or palm in an urn may lend a Mediterranean feel to your garden; an Oriental ginger jar with a bamboo or maple is ideal in a Japanese-style setting.

Containers also allow you to grow plants that dislike your garden conditions. For example, if you have alkaline soil but would like shrubs that need acidic soil, such as azaleas and pieris, they will thrive in pots of acidic soil mix. Or if your soil is dry, you can keep astilbes and hostas moist. Tender plants, such as agaves, which prefer dry, well-drained sites and are not reliably hardy in most areas, can be grown in pots even in gardens with wet or waterlogged soil, and moved under cover in winter. And plants with different soil needs can be grouped together in individual pots to create combinations that would be impossible in the open ground.

Plants in containers are easy to maintain and control. Feeding and watering can be regulated and monitored, while deadheading and pruning are simple, as plants are movable. When a plant's season of interest has passed, you can simply replace it. Plants that grow too vigorously in open ground, such as certain bamboos, are restrained by pots, while slower-growing species that are easily swamped in a border can be pampered. Pests and diseases are easy to treat, and slugs and snails are less of a problem because plants are lifted above soil level. However, plants in pots do depend more on you for water, food, and general care than those in the open garden. If their needs are not met, they will deteriorate quickly.

Containers are useful for people who are living in a place for only a short time because the plants are portable rather than fixtures in the garden. Almost any plant will adapt to life in a container, although some are best viewed as short-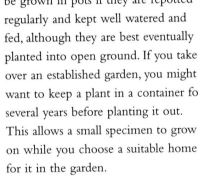term subjects. Even young trees can be grown in pots if they are repotted regularly and kept well watered and fed, although they are best eventually planted into open ground. If you take over an established garden, you might want to keep a plant in a container for several years before planting it out. This allows a small specimen to grow on while you choose a suitable home for it in the garden.

Places for pots

Container plants can be positioned anywhere, but patios and terraces are prime locations, as they perform best in a sheltered spot. In exposed sites, pots dry out quickly and may blow

Group your containers to help maximize impact. It also makes watering easier, and the plants benefit from extra shelter and higher levels of humidity. A color theme can add continuity to a group with mixed foliage textures and plant forms. Treat the group as one huge container when arranging the plantings.

Use plants with strong shapes, like cordylines, to create an instant focal point. Grown in containers, they offer a quick and easy way to change the emphasis.

over; few plants survive this for long. As a result, containers may have to be moved to a warmer position, particularly in winter. Just as in the open ground, it is important to put container plants in the right place, and to group those that like similar conditions together in a suitable spot to achieve healthy displays for positions in both sun and shade.

It is simple to create and change a display. Large and impressive single pots can be used as focal points. Pairs of identical pots with matched plantings are ideal either side of steps or paths, and if placed to each side of a doorway can emphasize architectural features. Conversely, containers can hide eyesores, such as inspection covers, drains, or gas cylinders. Massed containers can also help keep sunny areas cooler by reducing the surface area reflecting sunlight.

Containers are useful in other, less obvious ways, too. Plants such as lilies or tulips, which bloom spectacularly but only for a limited period, can be plunged into the border still in their pots to fill seasonal gaps. Once their flowers fade, the pots can then simply be lifted and replaced. A group of containers holding ferns, hostas, and other shade-tolerant plants can also prove an effective solution in the difficult conditions found under established trees, where the ground is typically dry, poor, filled with roots, and difficult to cultivate.

Gardening without a garden

Many homes have outdoor spaces that are largely paved or concreted. Containers are the ideal solution to gardening in this environment. Some houses have hard surfaces next to house walls, which prevents climbers and wall shrubs from being grown in the ground. With care this may be overcome using containers; some climbers, including jasmine and certain clematis, grow well in pots.

Even with no garden at all, you can still grow plants in containers. If your home has wide window ledges, it is easy to position windowboxes, as long as the windows do not open outward; otherwise, hang them from the wall on brackets. Hanging baskets also require no ground space: hang them in a sheltered spot where they are easily accessible for maintenance and watering. Wall-mounted pots can brighten a bare wall, although they only hold a small amount of soil, so plants require copious watering in summer. For all these containers, sturdy hardware is vital. Windowboxes are heavy when planted and watered, and must be securely fastened in position. Even if the base rests on the window ledge, attach it with hardware at the sides. Hanging baskets, in particular, require strong supports to take the weight of saturated soil.

Windowboxes allow those without much space outside to grow beautiful plants. Avoid placing them in exposed positions, and make sure they are secure and can be watered easily.

Choosing containers

When choosing a pot, there are several factors to consider. Most importantly, the container must suit the plant. The plant should look good in the pot, but you must also consider how fast it will grow. Squeezing a large plant into a small pot makes watering difficult, and the top-heavy display will be prone to blowing over.

The container should also complement rather than upstage the plant. A plain, unfussy design is generally best, but the bolder the contents, the more ornate the pot can be. A tall container shows off plants with pendent growth, such as fuchsias, while small, low-growing plants, like sedums, look better in flat pans.

The style of the pot should complement its surroundings. Stone, wood, or lead suit traditional settings, while galvanized, plastic, glazed, concrete, or even glass pots are appropriate in a modern garden. With careful positioning and planting you can mix a range of shapes and styles. When grouping pots, put the most attractive on the outside and hide basic plastic ones in the center.

From a practical point of view, plants that will be brought inside for winter (*see pp.206–207*) are easier to move in light containers, and those that need plenty of water are best in containers that are not porous. Stone or concrete pots are generally less likely to blow over, and plastic is less prone to damage than terracotta.

Terracotta and clay

These are versatile materials, with pots available in a wide range of shapes and styles: urns, vases, bell pots, pans, bowls, and jars. But be aware that plants grown in jars will be tricky to repot if the root ball is wider than the neck of the pot.

Herb planter
Pots with planting holes in the sides as well as at the top are often used for herbs and strawberry plants. This crowding entails extra watering, especially in a porous pot.

Terracotta urn
Plants and pot are perfectly balanced; a tall central abutilon provides structure, while verbenas and tumbling petunias soften the edges of the planting.

Glazed clay pots can be very gaudy; here bright red petunias counter the high-gloss finish, making sure that attention remains with the plants rather than the pot.

Pottery profile

Advantages
- Porous terracotta pots allow root ball to breathe and reduce chances of waterlogging in winter
- Long-lasting and attractive, with a huge range of shapes, sizes, and glazed colors
- Machine-made pots are inexpensive
- Glazed pots come in a wide range of colors

Disadvantages
- Porous nature of terracotta pots means plants need frequent watering, especially in summer
- Easily broken if they are toppled over when wind catches taller plants
- Some may be damaged by cold weather
- Hand-made pots are expensive

Uses
- Glazed pots are good for specimen plants, especially in oriental-style gardens
- Terracotta is ideal for citrus plants

Synthetic materials

Plastic, fiberglass, and resin containers are affordable and widely available. The best imitations of terracotta and lead are convincing, and they are lightweight, frost-proof, and almost unbreakable. They may disintegrate after a few years where sunlight is intense.

Large synthetic pots are easily moved about. This makes them ideal for tender plants, such as cannas (*right*), which must be moved indoors to survive winter, and decorative foliage plants, like hostas (*left*), which can be shifted around to mask flowers that are past their prime.

Synthetic profile

Advantages
- Good moisture-holding properties, frost-proof, lightweight, and most are inexpensive
- Available in a wide range of colors and styles
- The more expensive ones are very durable and will not crack or fade as quickly

Disadvantages
- Poor insulation, and are easily blown over
- Inexpensive types can be short-lived and ugly

Uses
- For plants that are regularly moved around
- Use inexpensive types as liners for heavy pots

Metal

Thanks to modern techniques, a wide range of shapes, colors, and styles of metal containers are now available, many of which are well suited to contemporary settings. Metal may be galvanized, painted, or coated to help protect against rust, although some finishes will gradually tarnish.

Stainless steel
The flared top of this stainless steel pot is exaggerated by the spreading habit of the plants. Clean lines and a shiny surface make this perfect for a minimalist setting.

Lead containers are most at home in a traditional setting; some are old water troughs or rain water cisterns.

Galvanized metal will not rust, although the surface will lose its shine and dull with age.

Metal profile

Advantages
- Wide range of styles to suit contemporary or traditional gardens
- Robust and long-lasting
- Attractive

Disadvantages
- Good-quality pieces are expensive
- Lead containers are heavy
- Shiny finishes show up any mud splashes, and will eventually dull
- Gets very hot in sun; poor insulation qualities, although using a liner will help to protect roots

Uses
- Good for permanent plantings

Stone

Among the most desirable and long-lasting containers. Stone urns look splendid in a traditional setting, especially once aged, making them ideal as a focal point or architectural feature in a period garden. Contemporary designs are also available. Reconstituted stone has all the advantages of stone, but it is inexpensive and widely available.

Reconstituted stone can be molded into traditional shapes or given a modern twist. A mound of flowers balances this urn's shape, while ivy softens the edges.

Modern stone This chunky terrazzo pot has an air of stability that complements the subtlety and texture offered by the grass, flowers, and foliage it contains.

Stone profile

Advantages
- Durable and long lasting, and stone ages well
- Weighty and stable
- Good insulation properties
- Good-quality stone containers are features in their own right
- Wide range of shapes and styles available

Disadvantages
- Heavy
- Stone is expensive
- Concrete and reconstituted stone can look stark, especially when new

Uses
- For permanent plantings and in exposed spots

Wood

Natural wood planters are unobtrusive and provide a perfect foil for plants. Wood is light and easy to handle, but it must be treated if it is to last.

Half barrels make excellent large containers. They are often used to grow big specimens, but are just as suitable for bedding.

Versailles tubs and wooden planters may simply be wooden frames into which a liner pot is placed. Many woods will start to break down when it comes into direct contact with wet soil, so using a liner pot inside these tubs prolongs their life.

Wood profile

Advantages
- Not easily broken, and long-lasting if treated
- Lightweight
- Good insulation properties
- Available as large containers

Disadvantages
- Susceptible to rotting, so need regular emptying and treatment with preservative
- May not suit all locations

Uses
- Versailles tubs are traditionally planted with topiary, standard bay trees, or citrus
- Seasonal displays of bedding allow maintenance

Preparing to plant

Once you know what you want to grow and what you want to grow it in, the next step is to choose the soil mix. This is a vital decision: this small volume of material must support the plant, hold food and enough water to supply the root ball and sustain the plant, and drain well enough to prevent roots from rotting over winter. The pH of the soil is also important, and determines the plants you can grow.

Ordinary garden soil is unsuitable for several reasons. It does not contain the balance of nutrients that plants grown in containers need, and it is also prone to losing structure when repeatedly watered in a restricted space. Garden soil may also contain weed seeds and harbor pests and diseases. For these reasons it is better to use soil mix that has been specifically developed for containers. While it is possible to mix your own potting medium at home, it is easier to use a store-bought mixture.

Your choice of soil mix is usually governed not by the plants but by how long you intend your displays to remain in their pots (*see box below*). The exception is containers filled with acid-loving plants, such as rhododendrons, pieris, camellias, and others, which require acidic soil (soil-based and soilless ericaceous mixes are available). Whichever type you chose, buy fresh-looking bags—all growing media eventually lose nutrients and structure if kept for too long.

Good drainage

Free drainage is vital for the health of your plants. Check for drainage holes, which should be at least ½in (1.5cm) across, although plastic pots often have numerous smaller ones. Extra holes can be made, even in terracotta pots, with a small drill on slow speed; cover both surfaces with tape and wear goggles. Many garden centers will drill these holes for you.

Choosing potting mix

There are two kinds of potting mixes, soil-based and soilless. Long-term plantings like specimen shrubs will do better in a soil-based mix, as it holds nutrients for longer, and drains better, an important consideration if plants are to survive outside in winter.

In general, short-term planting, including bedding plants for summer containers, will be fine in soilless mixes. This is lighter and cleaner and has sufficient nutrients for young plants, but as the season progresses, you will have to add more fertilizer.

Soil-based mix is made from sterilized topsoil (loam), with organic matter to hold moisture, grit for drainage, and lime and fertilizer to boost plant growth. It is heavy and holds nutrients well, making it suitable for long-term planting. Many different brands are widely available, as are ericaceous or lime-free types. Ask your garden center staff for recommendations about which type is best.

Soilless mixes are traditionally made using peat moss mixed with fertilizers, plus perlite or vermiculite and, occasionally, sand. They should always be moistened before use (add warm water and leave overnight), being almost impossible to make wet afterward. There are also acidic soil types. These mediums are light and have a high water-holding capacity, making them ideal for hanging baskets.

Ornamental mulches

A mulch is a layer of material used to cover soil mix and is both ornamental and practical. Mulching is less important for short-term plantings since the soil surface is covered by plant growth, but for permanent plants the advantages are many. Mulches help retain moisture while keeping plant stems or crowns dry, stop the mix from splashing up when it's watered, prevent weed seeds from germinating, stabilize the pot, and may deter slugs and snails. There is a wide range available.

Glass beads

Metal blanks

Chipped bark

Colored gravel

Pebbles

Cobbles

Holes alone are not enough to make sure that water drains freely. They can become clogged, causing the mix to become "sour" and leading to rotting roots. Shield holes with bits of broken pot (crocks) or a small piece of screen, or put a 1in (2.5cm) layer of large stones in the bottom of the pot; if weight is a problem, use polystyrene pieces.

Pots can be raised off the ground on "feet" or bricks for better drainage. This is not usually required for short-term plantings or smaller containers, but is important for larger pots with plants that require excellent drainage.

Adding fertilizer

Controlled- or slow-release fertilizers are available as pellets, sticks, or small plugs, which are pressed into the soil mix after the plant has been put in the pot. Alternatively, you can buy granules and mix them into the medium before planting. The fertilizer is gradually released over several months, which is ideal for short-term planting. All forms are useful if you want a low maintenance garden and don't have time to add water-soluble feeds when watering (see p.200), or if you regularly rely on other people to water. Controlled-release fertilizers are also the best option for containers packed full of plants, such as hanging baskets because they remove the need for any other feeding.

Water-retaining granules expand into a gel as they absorb moisture, so don't add too many in case they force the plant out of its pot.

Water-retaining gel is useful for people who may occasionally forget to water and is excellent for hanging baskets, which dry out quickly. The gel stores moisture around the root ball, creating a reservoir for the plant to draw on in dry periods. Add the gel granules to the soil mix at planting time, following the directions on the package.

Creating container displays

Large specimen plants in containers can make instant garden features. You can grow them alone or underplant them with low-growing ivy, lady's mantle, ferns, or herbaceous geraniums to add interest; be careful that underplanting does not overwhelm the growth of the main plant. Containers with mixed plants make attractive displays but tend to be fairly short-term arrangements. Several plants together will outgrow the pot more quickly than one, and more vigorous species can swamp any smaller, slower-growing plants.

Choosing plants for mixed containers

If you mix plants in one container, remember that they must have the same soil, watering, and positional needs. Where plants enjoy the same light levels but need different soil mixes, grow them in separate pots and group the pots instead. Next, decide which season you are planting for.
• Place winter containers near the house, where they are sheltered and easily seen. Try winter pansies (*Viola*), heathers (*Erica*), and hellebores for flowers, and heucheras, evergreen ferns, ivy (*Hedera*), sedges (*Carex*), ornamental brassicas, and conifers for winter foliage color. Mix in early bulbs, such as crocus, winter aconites (*Eranthis hyemalis*), and snowdrops (*Galanthus*). Small plants of evergreen viburnum, aucuba, and euonymus add structure. In larger containers, use cornus

A gap of at least 1in (2.5cm) between mulch and rim of pot acts as a watering reservoir.

Watering is essential from the start. Water freshly planted pots until water starts to drain through the base, then add a layer of mulch, such as bark or gravel, to help keep the soil moist.

and *Rubus thibetanus* for vivid bark, and holly or winter cherry (*Solanum capsicastrum*) for bright berries.
• Spring bulbs, including narcissi, tulips, fritillaries, and, later in the season, alliums, are suitable for containers. Combine them with primroses, lungwort, and shrubs, such as star magnolia, small rhododendrons, and camellias.
• Summer bedding and tender perennials can be bought when the risk of frost passes. A vast range is available, from small, daisy-flowered felicia, silvery lotus with flame-red flowers, purple scaevola, and pink diascia, to exotic canna, bell-flowered abutilon, and trumpet-flowered, climbing ipomoea. Pots with tumbling tomatoes, eggplants, and peppers also look good, as do frilly lettuces and herbs.
• In autumn, choose plants with good foliage tints, such as acers, grasses, winged euonymus , and heavenly bamboo.

Planting mixed containers

Avoid clashes by using foliage and flowers of similar or complementary hues. Silvers, whites, pinks, and blues work well together, as do yellows, oranges, and reds. Alternatively, contrast blue and yellow or purple and orange for striking effects. A mixture of shapes provides interest: combine bold foliage with smaller leaves, and spiky phormiums or grasses with rounded plants. Odd numbers of plants work best. Place larger plants to the back or in the center, smaller ones around the outside, and soften the edges with trailing plants.

For the best arrangement place plants in the container, still in their pots, and work out their positions. Mix bushy, upright plants with tumblers and trailers. Plant up from the center out.

How to plant a container

To make sure that plants grow and perform as well as possible, it is essential to plant them properly. If your chosen container is large or heavy, place it in position first, and then plant it. Check that the drainage holes are sufficient—you may need to fill the bottom of the pot with extra drainage material—and cover with a 1–2in (2.5–5cm) layer of soil mix.

1 Water the plant thoroughly about an hour before planting, then position it—still in its original pot—inside the new container.

2 Add soil mix to raise the plant to 1in (2.5cm) below the rim; this allows space for watering. Add soil mix around the sides.

3 Firm the soil mix well around the pot. Lift out the plant in its pot, leaving a hole in the soil mix. Remove the plant from its original pot.

4 If there is a tight mass of roots around the root ball, tease them out gently. Place the plant back into the hole in the mix and firm in.

5 Check that the plant is at the same depth as it was in its old pot. Then cover the top with a little more soil mix, and water well.

6 Finish off with a layer of ornamental mulch. This helps retain soil moisture and suppresses weeds, as well as anchoring the pot.

Caring for container plants

To keep a container display looking good for as long as possible, regular maintenance is essential. Plants in pots depend on you totally for their food, water, and general care, whereas the same plants in open ground will survive with far less attention. Those planted in the soil in the garden will not need daily watering during dry spells and are more likely to survive the winter unprotected.

Watering

This is the most important job. Containers dry out quickly, especially in hot or windy weather, and particularly in summer. Some plants, like camellias and rhododendrons, will not set flower buds properly if they are short of moisture. Since they are evergreen, they need to be watered all year. Pots close to house walls and fences or under trees will not receive much water from rainfall, and must be monitored closely. The signs of lack of water are obvious—wilting, yellowing foliage, and in extreme cases falling leaves.

Hoses tend to force soil mix out of the pot and fill the reservoir below the lip too fast, wetting only the upper levels of the mix. It is best to use a watering can or a hose fitted with a spray nozzle so that you can moderate the flow of water to trickle, rather than gush, from it. Plants will then receive a thorough soaking, indicated when water flows from the bottom of the pot. Compaction or caking of the surface may prevent water from soaking in at all; push a hand fork into the soil a few times to help remedy this.

When a plant has dried out, the soil mix shrinks away from the sides of the pot and water runs straight through the gap. To alleviate this, submerge the pot in water for up to an hour.

An irrigation system is the most reliable way to keep plants watered. Small-bore pipes with adjustable nozzles are placed in the pots; water can be controlled by a timer on your tap.

Going on vacation

Containers need constant attention in summer, when most people go on vacation; if you don't have an irrigation system, the simplest solution is to ask a neighbor to water your plants. Group pots in a shady site to reduce their water needs. A covering of fine netting or white fleece may reduce water loss, especially in windy sites, but use this only in shade or plants will overheat. If you are away for a short period, soak plants before you go, and most will be fine for a few days. For longer spells, try the "wick method": stand a bowl of water higher than the pot, and run a length of absorbent cloth from the bowl to the pot, pushing it into the soil mix. The cloth draws water from the bowl, and keeps the soil moist.

When to repot

Repot regularly in spring, using a new pot only slightly larger than the original. Potbound plants are often top-heavy and are hard to water, with little space for water to collect on and

Fertilizing

Plants in containers will need feeding from late spring to midautumn if they are to produce healthy growth and a succession of flowers (see pp. 160–61). Feeding is generally done every two weeks, although hungry plants, including tomatoes and angel's trumpet, need food weekly. The simplest method is to add water-soluble fertilizer to the watering can. There are devices that add fertilizer as water passes out of a hose, but they can be fiddly and inaccurate. Controlled-release fertilizers (see p. 197) avoid the need for continual feeding. Adding garden compost to the bottom of the pot when planting or sprinkling pelleted chicken manure on pots in spring are organic alternatives. It is important to follow the manufacturer's guidelines; overfeeding saturates soil with high concentrations of fertilizer that can be fatal to plants.

Prolonging your display

Plants can look disheveled by the middle of summer but may be coaxed into providing a longer display. Dahlias, nasturtiums, and geraniums can be relied on to flower right through until the frosts if you pick off the dead heads regularly. If any plants have died or gone past their prime, remove them and replace with late summer or fall flowers. Move pots around to help plants grow evenly and to uncover slugs or snails hiding beneath them. Wash off any insect infestations or use insecticides.

Deadhead regularly Pick off flowerheads as soon as they start to fade. This stimulates further flower production (*see p.164*).

Remove yellowing and decaying leaves They look unsightly and provide an opening for pest and disease attacks.

Give climbers support, and keep them well trained. They will scramble up wigwams of stakes, obelisks, or trellises.

seep into the soil without spilling over the edge or running down the inside of the pot. Foliage may be yellow, and new growth reduced. If you want to keep an overgrown plant in the same pot, either prune it or divide it and replant in fresh soil mix (*see pp.238–39*). Also, top-dress potted trees and shrubs in spring by removing one third of the soil mix, without damaging the roots, and replacing it with fresh.

Moving heavy pots, even when empty, is not easy. Grow plants that will be moved regularly in light pots with soilless mixes. Plant movers—metal or wooden stands on wheels, and fitted with brakes—are useful for heavy containers.

Winter precautions

The biggest danger to container plants in winter is waterlogging then freezing. In temperate areas move plants against house walls to reduce the amount of rain that gets into the pot. Make sure that evergreens do not dry out. In colder regions, move all plants indoors. Container plants are susceptible to frost because their roots are above ground level, and the sides of a pot offer little insulation. Even hardy plants may need extra protection in extreme cold. When choosing your container it is important to confirm that it is frost-proof; some terracotta and glazed clay pots shatter in cold weather, exposing plant roots. Even frost-proof pots may be damaged if the soil in them is sodden because the water expands as it freezes. Heavy snowfall can also be a problem. Shake excessive snow off foliage to prevent the weight of it from damaging plants.

Wrap pots with bubble plastic or sacking and move them close to the house. Cover more tender plants with straw or fleece to protect them from frost (*see p.167*).When night temperatures are really low, move them inside overnight.

Ideas for container plants

Almost any kind of plant will grow in a container for a short time, but some will provide an effective display for years. There are, however, a few you should avoid:

• Roses rarely thrive in containers because they form deep root systems. With the exception of patio roses, which were bred for this purpose, all are best planted in open ground.

• Plants that grow rapidly and resent pruning, including cistus, ceanothus, and broom (*Cytisus*), are not suitable for pots.

• Vigorous climbers, such as wisteria, are best avoided.

• Some larger shrubs, including most weigela and philadelphus, quickly outgrow containers and look untidy constrained in them.

• In cold regions use woody plants at least 2 zones hardier.

Trees and shrubs

These may eventually outgrow pots, but provide the backbone to a container display. Choose evergreens for year-round structure and foliage, and deciduous plants for seasonal effects.

• **Evergreens** perform throughout the year and are especially useful in winter displays, adding much-needed color and form. Choose compact, slow-growing conifers, like dwarf junipers and pines, for mixed displays. Larger shrubs can stand alone: try *Aucuba japonica* 'Crotonifolia', *Choisya ternata*, *C. ternata* 'Sundance', *Fatsia japonica*, *Euonymus japonicus*, *Viburnum tinus*, pittosporum, and hebes, all of which are easy to care for. Podocarpus, the strawberry tree (*Arbutus unedo*),

skimmia, and viburnum offer both flowers and fruit, as well as foliage. Evergreens with special needs include the tender cypress *Cupressus cashmeriana*, which must have winter protection, and rhododendrons, camellias, *Desfontainia spinosa* and *Pieris japonica*, all of which need acidic soil mix.

• **Topiary effects** can be achieved by clipping small-leaved plants, such as boxwood (*Buxus*), yew (*Taxus*), shrubby honeysuckle (*Lonicera nitida*), or Japanese holly (*Ilex crenata*), into decorative shapes.

• **Deciduous plants** provide a range of effects and by choosing carefully your container displays will perform throughout the year. Use witch hazels (*Hamamelis*),

magnolias, dwarf lilac (*Syringa meyeri*), and hydrangeas for flowers in winter, spring, and summer respectively, coupled with *Corylus avellana* 'Contorta', the corkscrew stems of which drip with catkins in spring. The maples *Acer japonicum* 'Aconitifolium', *A. shirasawanum* 'Aureum', and *A. palmatum* 'Bloodgood', and *Cotinus* 'Grace' provide autumn color. *Cornus alba* 'Sibirica' has bright winter stems, while the leaves of the tiny elm *Ulmus* x *hollandica* 'Jacqueline Hillier' last into winter.

• **Bamboos** are often best restrained in a pot. Use black bamboo, *Phyllostachys nigra*, lime-green *P. aurea*, and large-leaved *Sasa palmata*, but remember that bamboos must be kept moist for the best display.

Hamamelis x *intermedia* 'Pallida' *Phyllostachys nigra* *Pinus mugo*

Viburnum tinus *Cotinus* 'Grace' *Choisya ternata* Sundance *Camellia* x *williamsii* 'Dream Boat'

Climbers

Many climbers, such as the chocolate vine, *Akebia quinata*, thrive in pots and can be trained up obelisks to add height to container displays.

Clematis adapt well to life in a pot; try spring-flowering *C. alpina*, or *C.* 'Prince Charles' for blue summer flowers.

Summer fragrance is offered by *Jasminum officinale*; winter jasmine, *J. nudiflorum*, has unscented yellow flowers.

Evergreens include scented *Trachelospermum jasminoides*, and the tender *Eccremocarpus scaber*, with its long-lasting red tubular blooms.

Annuals for pots are sweet peas (*Lathyrus*), morning glory (*Ipomoea*), canary vine (*Tropaeolum*), and the purple bellflower vine (*Rhodochiton*).

Tropaeolum peregrinum

Akebia quinata

Jasminium officinale 'Argenteovariegatum'

Flowering and herbaceous plants

Most annuals, perennials, and bulbs are at home in containers.

• **For shaded areas**, choose moisture-loving astilbes, winter- and spring-flowering hellebores, and foliage plants, such as heucheras and hostas.

• **Grasses** do very well in containers: try moor grass with its fine autumn tints, bronzy *Chionochloa rubra*, the fluffy spikes of pennisetum, and the small pampas grass *Cortaderia richardii*.

• **Bulbs**, such as narcissi, lilies, tulips, crocuses, cyclamens, alliums, and eucomis, inject seasonal color; remove them when their flowers have faded.

• **Tender bedding plants**, such as impatiens and geraniums, can be over-wintered inside and replanted in pots outside after winter is over and threat of frost passed.

Pennisetum setaceum 'Rubrum'

Hosta 'Francee'

Astilbe chinensis 'Superba'

Fruit, vegetables, and herbs

Keep crops grown in pots well fed and watered, and pick regularly. Good vegetables are eggplants, lettuce, chilies, Swiss chard, French beans, runner beans, and tomatoes. Figs fruit better in pots, blueberries thrive in acidic soil, and strawberries will be protected from snails and slugs. Herbs, such as rosemary, basil, and thyme, grow well, and invasive mint is best kept in a pot.

Strawberry

Lettuce

Variegated mint

Hanging baskets

With careful planning and positioning, hanging baskets can be magnificent, although they are not always easy to plant or maintain, especially in hot, dry weather. Baskets are most frequently used for summer displays, but it is possible to plant them up for other seasons, including winter.

When selecting a spot for a hanging basket, look for a sheltered, sunny area out of the wind. Baskets are heavy once watered, so be sure that the wall bracket or hook is attached properly. Some brackets have pulley systems that lower the basket and make watering and maintenance much easier.

Closed baskets remain more visible than open types, so choose one in a color that complements your planting plan.

Types of basket

There are two types of basket: open and closed. Closed baskets are really hanging pots, usually plastic, with solid sides; most also have an integrated drip tray. They are easier to plant and to look after, requiring less frequent watering than open baskets. Closed baskets are good for individual plants rather than mixed displays, as the sides cannot be planted. Trailing plants can be planted to cover the edges, but displays are seldom as spectacular as those in a traditional open basket.

Both the sides and the top of open baskets can be planted. They require a liner to hold in the soil mix. Traditionally sphagnum moss was used, but this allowed a great deal of water to run off or evaporate. Environmental considerations have resulted in the development of more suitable materials, including recycled wool, plastic sheet, and coir; these are also easier to use.

The advantage of an open basket is that you can achieve a complete covering of plants, although they can be tricky to plant up and do need more water; be prepared to water every day in summer. It is possible to have baskets planted by staff to your requirements at the good garden centers.

Plants for baskets

Brachyscome	Nemesia
Campanula	Osteospermum
Convolvulus	Pelargonium
sabatius	Petunias, such
Diascia	as Surfinas
Felicia	Scaevola
Fuchsia	Spider plant
Glechoma	(*Chlorophytum*)
Helichrysum	Verbena
Impatiens	Viola
Ivy	
Lotus berthelotii	
Million Bells	
(*Calibrachoa*)	

Choosing plants for hanging baskets

Deciding what to plant can be fun. For a simple, elegant basket, you could choose to use a single cultivar to make a ball of white impatiens, or a cascade of scarlet, ivy-leaved geraniums. Color coordinated baskets are also fashionable, and you can extend the color theme to nearby windowboxes and pots by including some of the same plants.

Winter basket

Baskets are usually put out in summer, but they can be used all year if your garden is sufficiently sheltered from strong winds. Winter pansies (*Viola*), heucheras, and hardy ferns and grasses all work well.

Winter baskets can have plants with flowers or fruit, or simply showy foliage. Here, winter-flowering heathers (*Erica*) and variegated ivy lift dark-leaved evergreen skimmia. Small plants of gaultheria and evergreen euonymus are other good winter choices.

Culinary basket

A basket of herbs or summer crops can be both eye-catching and practical. Some of the tumbling tomatoes, lettuces, or strawberries make an unusual display grown this way but do need plenty of water.

A basket of herbs near the kitchen door is convenient, attractive, and fragrant. In this basket basil, chives, and marjoram for culinary use are combined with flowering chamomile. Other suitable herbs include parsley, thyme, and mint.

How to plant an open hanging basket

Summer baskets are usually planted in late spring, but most of the plants are tender, and need protection until any danger of frost has passed. Decide what kind of liner to use, and be sure it is the correct size for the basket. If you are using moss, start with a 1in (2.5cm) layer at the base and put a small piece of polythene sheet on top to help keep water from running through.

1 Sit the basket in a pot or bucket for stability. Put the liner (here of coir) in position and trim it to fit along the rim. Cut a series of slits for planting into the sides.

2 Add a 2in (5cm) layer of soilless mix, mixed with controlled-release fertilizer and water-retaining gel. Remove the plants for the sides from their pots and thread them through the slits. You can use a plastic bag to protect the stems and leaves.

Add more soil mix and build up the planting in tiers until the soil mix is within 2in (5cm) of the rim.

3 Put a pot in the center at the top of the basket to act as a watering reservoir, and plant around it. Use upright plants in the center and trailers around the rim.

4 Firm the soil mix and water the basket thoroughly. Hang your basket in a sheltered spot at a height that you can reach easily to water it. Make sure that the bracket is strong enough to take the weight of saturated soil mix.

Indoor/outdoor plants

In temperate regions, the range of exotic plants we can grow is expanding. Plants once thought of as tender can now survive mild winters, especially in sheltered gardens or in semitropical areas. Elsewhere, it is worth experimenting with exciting new plants that require some protection during winter if they are to be kept from year to year. Many exotics tolerate cool weather and look attractive in a conservatory during cold snaps; some may even be bought inside and treated as houseplants.

Place indoor/outdoor plants outside only after cold weather has passed, usually in late spring, although some can go out sooner. By this time most are actively growing. Remove any yellowing foliage, clean up the pot, and top-dress or repot it if required (*see pp.200–201*). Acclimatize plants gradually to outside conditions; if it is cool at night, bring them in, and shelter them from high winds or heavy rain. If they are left outside with a protective wrapping, such as bubble plastic, remove the wrapping in mild spells to let air circulate and prevent rotting. In warm regions, these exotic plants may need no winter protection. In cold northern and western areas, the plants must be brought indoors.

Echeveria pulvinata Succulents can bring a touch of drama to the garden during summer. Bring them under cover in winter to protect them from wet and temperatures below about 45°F (7°C). They need little attention beyond this.

Phormium plants require free-draining soil. Like cordylines, those with colored leaves are the most tender; the all-green *P. tenax* is tougher. If temperatures fall below 32°F (0°C), cover with fleece, and place in a sheltered spot.

Olea europaea (olive) is easy, given a sunny site and well-drained soil mix. In spells below 23°F (–5°C), bring into a c[o] conservatory or wrap both pot and plant with fleece and move close to the house[...] sheltered from wind and heavy rain.

Musa basjoo (banana) After frost blackens the leaves, remove them and wrap the pot with bubble plastic. Wrap the trunk in burlap, cover with a wire mesh tube stuffed with straw, and put some plastic over the top (*see p.167*).

Nerium oleander needs plenty of sun to flower in summer, and protection from wind, wet, and temperatures below 28°F (–2°C) in winter. Wrap plants with fleece or bring inside; they will thrive in a conservatory or greenhouse over winter.

Agapanthus africanus is evergreen with spectacular flowers and does best in pots. Keep well watered in a hot, sunny position in summer. It tolerates some frost; move into shelter and wrap with bubble plastic or put in a cold frame.

Aeonium haworthii and other succulen[t] are ideal for hot, sunny patios, requiring less water than other plants. Most will n[o] survive outside over winter. They should be kept dry and moved into a cool conservatory or greenhouse.

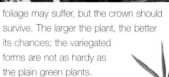

itrus require warm conditions to flower
nd fruit. Bring inside from early autumn
when night temperatures fall below
1°F (5°C). Overwinter in a conservatory,
eenhouse, or on a sunny windowsill at
ound 50°F (10°C), and keep fairly dry.

Agave americana can overwinter
outdoors in pots in sheltered places with
mild winters. Plant in 80 percent gravel to
ensure sharp drainage, and shelter from
heavy rain. Wrap the pot with bubble
plastic and cover with fleece. Some

foliage may suffer, but the crown should
survive. The larger the plant, the better
its chances; the variegated
forms are not as hardy as
the plain green plants.

ordyline australis is vulnerable when
oung. Move to a sheltered spot, tie up
e leaves, and wrap with fleece. Do not
t the soil get too wet. Colored-leaved
pes and *C. indivisa* are more tender;
rotect under glass below 23°F (−5°C).

Canna plants should be brought inside
after the foliage has been blackened by
the first frost. Cut stems to the ground
and keep the soil mix dry until new
shoots appear in early spring. Move
plants outside in late spring.

Fuchsia standards in particular need
frost-free conditions. Bring inside in early
fall and cut the head back by two-thirds.
From midspring fertilize and pinch out
new shoots to keep a bushy shape. Be
careful of brittle shoots when moving.

Phoenix canariensis (Canary date palm)
is tender, young plants especially so. Bring
indoors. In mild areas, wrap the pot, tie up
leaves to protect the crown, and cover
with fleece when temperatures fall below
28°F (−2°C).

rugmansia (angel's trumpet) requires
opious watering and feeding in summer
nd should be kept in large containers,
r the lower leaves will yellow and fall.
he plant quickly reaches 6ft (2m); if this
too large, reduce it to about 3–4ft

(1–1.2m) when you bring it inside. This
pruning should be done in early autumn,
before the first frost. In winter, keep
Brugmansia in a frost-free conservatory
or greenhouse, and make sure that the
soil mix remains moist.

Hedychium (ginger lily) plants are best
treated like cannas. In winter either cut
down and store dry and frost-free ina
garage or basement, or move to a
greenhouse. New shoots will replace
those that have already flowered.

Abutilon tolerates light frosts, but bring it
in if temperatures regularly fall below 41°F
(5°C). At lower temperatures, leaves fall,
and plants are best kept dry. Stems can
be cut back by half. Growth starts in early
spring; pinch out the tips for bushy plants.

Pruning 10

Understanding pruning • Making cuts • Pruning for health, shape, and special effects • How to prune climbers, roses, and wall shrubs

Why do we prune?

Pruning plants serves a wide range of purposes. First, by removing dead, diseased, and damaged wood, it helps to keep plants healthy. Cutting out badly placed stems and reshaping plants by removing shoots that detract from their symmetry and outline also improves their appearance. In addition, some pruning methods manipulate growth and help increase yields of fruit, promote more flowers, increase the size or intensify the color of the foliage, or stimulate the production of young, decorative stems.

Many plants don't need to be pruned every year. If you are unfamiliar with a plant and not sure if it needs pruning, wait for a year and take note of its growth. If, during that time, it produces vigorous shoots, you should prune it very lightly, if at all, since pruning prolongs the period before flowering. If it grows slowly and retains a good shape, it may not need pruning for a few years. Indeed, some plants grow to full maturity and need only dead, awkwardly placed, or damaged stems removed from time to time.

How pruning affects regrowth

The buds at the tips of plant shoots are called "apical buds," and they have amazing powers. They contain chemicals that prevent sideshoots from forming lower down the stem, thus causing one shoot to dominate the others. They also control the development of flowers and fruit, and regulate the flow of nutrients through the plant.

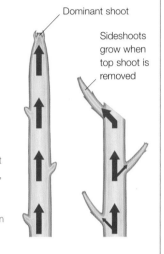

Dominant shoot

Sideshoots grow when top shoot is removed

Removing the apical bud
When you cut off the apical bud, it has a profound effect on the plant, diverting energy to the dormant side buds, which then start to grow. This is why pinching off stem tips stimulates bushier growth.

Pruning for healthy growth

Be vigilant, and remove dead, diseased, or damaged stems promptly, since they can lead to further deterioration in the plant's condition. Cut back diseased wood to healthy growth just above a bud. Then, burn the prunings or consign them to a trash can to prevent the disease from spreading. Wood that has been damaged by frost, wind, or other factors should be removed and can be shredded for composting. Dead wood can also be composted, unless it also shows signs of disease. Also prune out green shoots on variegated plants, since they are more vigorous and will take over the whole plant if left unchecked.

Remove dead stems as soon as you see them; they may be harboring harmful organisms that could lead to disease.

Crossing branches that rub against each other will open up a wound and increase the likelihood of infection entering the plant.

Suckers and unwanted shoots, especially those growing from below the graft union bulge, should be removed as soon as possible.

Predicting a plant's response to pruning

Most plants do not mind losing a few stems and branches, and even hard pruning is seldom fatal if kept within reason. Knowing how plants respond to being cut (*see opposite*) will help you anticipate how your plants will regrow after pruning. Watch to see how quickly they grow in any one season, and the type of growth they put out. For example, do they sprout lots of bushy growth, or produce long upward-growing shoots? This knowledge will help you determine what kind of pruning is needed.

Bushy growth usually indicates apical buds (*see opposite*) that exert weak control over the buds and shoots lower down on the plant. As a result, fewer side buds will spring into life after pruning, and it is less likely that one of these shoots will become dominant. The majority of small shrubs, such as hebes (*right*), behave like this when pruned.

Looser habits develop when a plant has powerful apical buds (*see opposite*). They produce stronger but less numerous branches than plants with weak apical dominance, and have a more open, looser habit. Pruning results in the bursting of a large number of buds lower down the stems, with one soon taking control over the others. Lilac (*right*) is a good example.

Keeping plants small

Although some plants are capable of rapid regrowth after pruning, they will still be shorter than plants that are left unpruned. The disturbed equilibrium between the size of the roots and the top growth following pruning prompts a plant to try to restore the balance. As a result, it sends out more shoots, often from the bottom of the plant, making it bushier rather than taller. The plant may also reduce the extent of its root system. This explains why light pruning results in much less vigorous regrowth than hard pruning. But, despite the reduction in a plant's height after pruning, it is unwise to try to keep a plant small simply by cutting it back. If you find yourself constantly pruning a plant to keep it in check, it is probably in the wrong place.

When to prune

As a general rule of thumb, prune late summer– and autumn-flowering plants, which usually bloom on the current year's stems, in early spring. Spring- and early summer–flowering plants bloom on the previous year's wood and should be pruned after flowering, so that the new stems have time to ripen before winter. To renovate most deciduous trees and shrubs, prune in winter, or after the first hard freeze, when the plants are dormant. For the majority of evergreens, prune in spring, just as the new growth resumes. Pruning deciduous plants in winter results in vigorous regrowth in spring. Pruning in spring and early summer produces much thinner growth, while summer pruning reduces the leafy canopy and the plant's food resources, resulting in relatively weak regrowth.

Masses of young decorative foliage result when plants, such as this cut-leaf elder (*Sambucus*), are pruned hard in winter. Regular pruning also keeps plants compact and neat.

Young dogwood stems make a colorful winter display, lighting up the landscape with fiery shoots. Prune plants hard in late winter to achieve this effect.

How to prune

Before you start, look at the shape of your plant for clues as to how to prune it. First, note where the new wood meets the old. Follow stems back from the tip, and you will see that old wood produced in the previous year looks different (*see opposite*). Because pruning often involves reducing new wood or removing older branches, the distinction is important.

Then look at the habit of your plant, and how it has responded to previous pruning cuts (*see p.211*). Also consider the potential for regrowth. Look for side buds that could take over after pruning, and remember that those closest to the pruning cut are most likely to grow.

The position of the buds is important, too. Try to imagine the direction in which shoots will grow, and make sure that you cut back to buds that point out, rather than to those that point into the middle of the plant. But you should also be aware that many plants have hidden buds that will develop only after pruning. Willows (*Salix*) have these, and it is safe to prune them even if you cannot find any obvious buds to cut back to.

Useful pruning tools

Sharp knife Useful for small tasks.

Pruners The best and safest tool for small cuts.

Shears Good for all-over trimming.

Loppers The best tool for heavy pruning.

Pruning saw Useful where wood is too thick for loppers.

Bow saw A safe and inexpensive alternative to power saws.

Identifying buds

Shoot bud

Flower bud

Buds that produce flowers and those that result in leaves or shoots look different, and it is a good idea to become familiar with each type before pruning.

Flower buds are usually much plumper than other types. When you prune back to a flower bud it won't result in new growth—on the contrary, it is a very good way of reducing growth. By removing the leaf buds beyond a flower bud, you make the flower into a kind of period at the end of the shoot.

By cutting back to a leaf or shoot bud, you remove the apical bud above it, which prevented it from developing (*see p.210*), and this results in a new stem or leaf.

Making pruning cuts

When making any pruning cut, use clean, sharp tools, and always wear gloves—even pruners can cause nasty injuries to unprotected hands. And leave any major pruning jobs, especially tree renovation, to the professionals.

Pruning stems

When pruning stems, try to make clean cuts that do not tear or bruise the plant tissue. Also, make your cuts as small as possible, since they will heal over quickly, thereby reducing the time that the plant is open to infection. Make your cuts either just above a bud, as close to the bud as you can without damaging it, or at the fork of a stem and sideshoot.

Alternate buds Plants with buds that occur alternately along the stem are pruned with a slanting cut. Choose a bud facing in the direction you want a shoot to grow, and position the top of the blade just above the bud, and the bottom just behind it. This sloping cut guarantees that rain runs away from the bud, preventing it from rotting.

Opposite buds When buds are opposite each other along the stem, you cannot make a slanting cut without snipping off one of the buds. Instead, make a square, straight cut just above a pair of buds. This will result in the growth of both buds. However, if you want just one bud to grow, rub out the other one with your thumb after you have made your cut.

Cutting back to a young shoot

There are two reasons for cutting back shrubs to young wood. First, it removes old, unproductive stems. Second, in plants that flower on new, young growth, it makes sure that all their energy is focused on these stems and not diverted into maintaining mature wood.

New wood is usually lighter in color and the stems are thinner and more flexible than mature wood. Young stems grow from side buds, or the top of a shoot.

Remove old wood with a clean cut just above the new stem. Make a slanted cut so that rain water will not collect around the base of the new wood and rot it.

Cutting back to the base

Shrubs that have become congested can be thinned by cutting back some of the old stems to the ground. This will also stimulate new, more productive stems to shoot. Some late-flowering shrubs are pruned to a low framework to encourage new stems on which the flowers will form.

Cut out old weak stems at the base of multi-stemmed plants, such as *Viburnum* x *bodnantense* (*right*). New stems will soon shoot up to replace them. If the plant is overgrown and flowering is poor, cut down all the stems in late spring.

For a low framework on a plant that flowers from midsummer to autumn, such as this *Hydrangea paniculata,* prune all the stems in early spring. This stimulates the growth of new shoots that will flower later in the year.

Sawing a branch

Trees and large shrubs that develop awkwardly placed branches should be pruned with care. If you saw the branch from the top, as you would a smaller stem, the weight may cause it to rip off before you finish the cut.

Instead, make two cuts, starting with one on the underside, and then make a second cut above it. If the branch is heavy, reduce it in stages to lighten the load before cutting it off close to the trunk (*see p.221*).

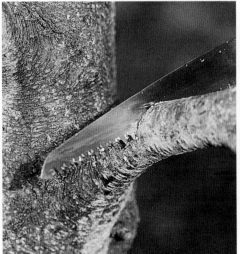

Don't saw flush with the trunk—cut beyond the bulge at the branch base to encourage healing.

1 Make a cut on the underside, close to the collar (the swelling at the base of the branch). Cut a quarter of the way through it. (*To prune heavy branches, see p.221.*)

2 Make a second cut directly above the first, or a little closer to the collar. Be sure that the two cuts meet exactly to achieve a smooth, clean wound that will heal quickly.

3 The final cut should be as small as possible, minimizing the size of the wound through which diseases can enter the plant. Smooth any rough edges with a sharp pruning knife.

Pruning shrubs

Keep an eye on all of your shrubs throughout the year, and cut out dead, diseased, and damaged stems as soon as you see them, whatever the season. Also remove stems that are crossing and rubbing against each other, all-green shoots on variegated plants, and suckers on grafted plants.

Light pruning

If you are not familiar with your shrubs, it is best to prune them lightly at first and see how they respond during the growing season. It's also wise to take a cautious approach for newly planted shrubs, since they need to grow to develop their natural beauty—at most, you should shorten a few stems and encourage a good shape with a little careful pruning. For example, if you want a rounded shrub, you can clip it lightly into a sphere. Other plants, like heathers, just need shearing over to remove spent flowers and to promote neat growth. Tip pruning, where you remove only the shoot tips, can also be carried out on young shrubs to encourage a bushy habit.

Pruning safety tips

- Don't use power saws, especially chain saws. If you need power equipment leave the job for professionals, or use a bow saw—it can be worked by two people and cuts thick wood.
- Avoid pruning above head height unless you are very fit and agile. Leave any pruning that requires you to scale a ladder to arborists, or buy or rent a commercial work platform.
- Use safety goggles to protect your eyes from twigs.
- Wear thick work gloves to protect your hands from thorns and from cuts from pruners or pruning saws—it's easy to slice through a finger by accident when concentrating on pruning.

Remember that many plants that should otherwise be pruned cautiously will respond to renovative pruning when they become too large for their site, their stems have become congested, or flowering is poor. In these cases, cut back the stems to near ground level when the plant is

Pruning young shrubs

One or two years after planting a shrub, you can start to prune a little harder, if required. Young evergreens, such as this mahonia, should be pruned in midspring, when overlong stems can be shortened, or the tips of stems removed to encourage more shoots to sprout father down the plant. This will create a shorter, bushier shrub with more flowers.

1 Mahonias bear scented yellow flowers in autumn and winter, and should be pruned in midspring. This plant has quite a good shape, but more flowering stems are required.

2 Prune off the old flowering stems, cutting just above a leaf or sideshoot. This will stimulate the growth of more flowering stems, which will bloom in the coming autumn/winter.

3 This light prune has left the main structure of the plant and most of the handsome foliage intact, to be enjoyed throughout the summer months until flowering begins.

Pruning shrubs that flower on old stems

Prune lightly shrubs that flower on stems produced the previous year. These mostly include plants that flower in spring and early summer, which are pruned just after flowering, but a few, such as this the mophead hydrangea (*Hydrangea macrophylla*), bloom later in the summer. Remember that if you prune hard in spring before your plant blooms you will cut off the flowering stems.

1 Leave the flowerheads of mophead hydrangeas on through winter to protect the buds below from frost. (*For shrubs that bloom before midsummer, see p.216.*)

2 In midspring, prune the old stems by up to 12in (30cm), down to pairs of fat, healthy buds. These buds will produce the flowering shoots in the summer.

3 Dead or very weak stems should be cut back to ground level, encouraging new stems to shoot up from the base, which will flower the following summer.

dormant, or buds are just breaking, in late winter or early spring. Be aware, however, that such drastic action may result in fewer flowers for a year or two.

Gray-leaved shrubs

Evergreens with gray leaves, such as lavender and sage, quickly become straggly, with hard woody stems. It is tempting to cut them back hard, but they will not reshoot from old wood, and you may either kill the plant, or end up with bare brown patches. The answer is to prune the sideshoots every year in summer after flowering. Cut back to green buds, or to places where you can see leaves emerging.

Moderate pruning

Cutting shrubs back to half their original size works well for those, such as sun roses (*Cistus*), that resent being pruned to a low framework (*see p.213*) but flower on new wood.

Shrubs such as broom that flower on shoots produced the previous year should be pruned after flowering. Remove the old flowering stems and shorten new stems to encourage more sideshoots to develop that will bloom the following year.

Prune a sage bush by cutting back side stems in spring to green buds or healthy leaves. Do not cut back into old stems, as the plant may not regrow from mature wood.

Pruning an early-flowering shrub

Shrubs that flower before midsummer, such as forsythia, kerria, and deutzia (*shown here*), should be pruned after they have flowered. Their blooms develop on stems that were made the year before, so pruning soon after flowering gives the plants time to develop new stems, which will bloom the following year. Deutzias can become tall and leggy if left unpruned, but regular trimming keeps them bushy and compact, and encourages more stems of sweetly scented flowers to develop.

1 This deutzia is five years old and has become too tall, and the stems shooting up from the base are congested. Some flower buds are also suffering from frost damage.

2 After cutting out the dead, diseased, and damaged wood, use sharp pruners to remove one in three of the congested stems, targeting the old and weak growth.

Remove old stems with a clean, straight cut just above a pair of shoots.

3 The remaining stems can be shortened to a pair of strong, healthy buds, or new shoots, as shown here. Pay particular attention to crowded shoots in the center of the plant.

4 Remove any stems that are crossing and rubbing against each other. Also be sure to prune out shoots that are growing toward the middle of the plant.

5 To reduce the height of the shrub, prune the tallest stems down to a more manageable level, cutting them back to healthy, outward-facing shoots or buds.

6 The pruned shrub is shorter, and the congestion has been reduced. New growth will soon appear from the base and below pruning cuts, resulting in more flowers.

Removing entire stems

For shrubs that produce a dense thicket of stems, cut one stem in every three down to the ground. Do this every year in late winter or early spring, and you will gradually replace the older wood with younger shoots that have space and light to develop. New wood is also more likely to flower well than old, congested growth.

If taking out one in three stems will not reduce the thicket sufficiently, you could remove a higher proportion. This will reduce the shrub's size and encourage strong regrowth. On the other hand, if the plant in question is slow growing, or you are not sure whether it is wise to remove a third of its stems, then simply remove fewer each year. Alternatively, you can merely cut back the flowered shoots to strong buds or sideshoots (*see p.215*).

Evergreens

Most evergreen shrubs don't need much pruning, and some need no intervention at all, but if you want to improve their shape, you can remove some outsized shoots in midspring. Shorten the remaining stems to help promote the regrowth needed to fill the gaps (*see p.222 for conifers*). Some evergreens, such as hebes, mahonias, rhododendrons, and garrya, respond well to harder pruning. When these shrubs are pruned more cautiously, the shoots that were not cut take most of the plant's resources, suppressing the regrowth of those that have been pruned. A hard prune in midspring is often the best remedy for established plants. Remove up to half of the old and congested stems, and cut back the remaining stems by half. But be wary of removing too many shoots in any one year because the reduction in foliage, and therefore food, results in weak regrowth. To prevent this, renovate in stages over two or three years.

Treating pruning wounds

Painting cuts with pruning paints, applying tar, or filling cavities with cement or other materials was once common practice, but wounds are rarely treated today. There is evidence that covering pruning wounds inhibits natural healing processes and may provide a humid environment for decay organisms to thrive. It also prevents gardeners from seeing what is going on inside their plants. Therefore, with few exceptions, it is best to let nature take its course unaided after pruning.

Renovating an overgrown evergreen

Some evergreens, especially those with gray foliage, do not respond well to renovation and are best replaced when they become overgrown (*see p.215*). Others, including this mahonia, can be cut back quite hard in midspring. Don't remove all the old stems at one time, since regrowth may be very slow if all of the foliage is cut off, but renovate over two or three years.

Remove congested stems to allow more light into the plant.

1 If your mahonia has become too large, with long and leggy stems, cut it back in midspring to revitalize growth, and to increase the number of new flowering stems.

2 Prune back long shoots that are bare at the base to a strong sideshoot or whorl of foliage. Also cut back crowded stems in the middle of the plant to healthy buds.

3 Cut back about half of the old stems to 12–24in (30–60cm) above the ground. Remove half of the remaining old stems the following year, and the rest the year after that.

Hard pruning

Ruthless pruning is often associated with nongardening spouses, but it can be the best way to treat many plants.

Cutting back to soil level works well with plants that send up shoots from below the ground, such as brambles (*Rubus*). The resulting canes are either colorful, as is the case with *Rubus cockburnianus* for example, or will flower and fruit prolifically, as is the case with autumn-fruiting raspberries.

Unless you are certain that a shrub will regrow from below the ground, it is safer to leave a low framework of stems, say 8–12in (20–30cm) high, from which new shoots can arise. Plants that produce young, colored stems, such as dogwoods (*Cornus*) and willows (*Salix*), should be pruned in this way in late winter.

Foliage and flower effects

Hard pruning can also result in bolder summer foliage on plants such as elders (*see right*). Eucalyptus is also cut back hard to promote the growth of young stems with new foliage, which is an attractive rounded shape and gray-blue in color, while the adult foliage is somewhat dull.

The strong shoots produced following heavy pruning may also bear late summer flowers. Butterfly bush, caryopteris, and California lilac all respond with late blooms when the shoots are shortened as for colored stems (*see above*), but delay pruning until early spring, just before growth starts.

Pruning plants ruthlessly from an early age prevents them from aging, keeping them youthful even if they are very old in terms of years. Be aware, however, that pruning mature trees and shrubs hard carries a risk of fatally injuring them. Older, established plants are not always able to spring back from severe setbacks.

Fuchsia stems killed by frost (*above*) can be cut to just above the ground, and will soon regrow.

Prune dogwoods in late winter to a low framework for colorful shoots the following winter.

Pruning for good foliage

Hazel, elder, willow, and colored-stemmed dogwoods can all withstand hard pruning. When grown for their foliage effects, as with this variegated elder, or for their red or golden shoots, as with many dogwoods and willows, all the old stems should be pruned in late winter or early spring to encourage new growth.

1 Elder is a vigorous plant and most of the growth seen here was made during the previous year. In alternate years all the stems can be pruned back in early spring to a low framework near its base.

Last year's stems are usually smoother and a slightly different color from the older wood.

2 Prune each stem back to two or three pairs of buds above the base of the previous year's wood. Although you will get the best foliage by pruning in this way, you are also removing the flowering stems.

Elder has opposite buds so make each cut straight across the stem above a pair.

3 Old, congested wood in the center of the plant can be cut right down to the ground. Also remove any stems that are badly positioned or growing toward the middle.

4 Make smooth, clean cuts using loppers on all branches that are more than ½in (1cm) in diameter. Use a curved pruning saw on very thick branches, or where you need to make a cut in an awkward spot.

The buds will quickly produce new growth that camouflages all the cuts.

A few months later...

5 Although the finished result looks sparse, pruning encourages vigorous growth. Since the flowering stems have been removed, this spring-flowering plant will not bloom or produce berries this year.

By early summer the elder's stems have grown by 3ft (1m) or more, and the fresh, beautifully variegated leaves have unfurled to make a compact, eye-catching feature in the garden.

Pruning trees

Left alone, most trees naturally form large spreading plants, but in the first few years of a tree's life, removing badly placed shoots, congested growth, and suckers from the base helps to create a well-balanced, attractive specimen.

Assessing your tree and giving it a pleasing shape is very rewarding work, but remember that although it is easy to remove a stem, it takes a good deal longer for it to regrow if you make a mistake, so take your time and cut with care.

Pruning young trees

Conifers and other evergreens, such as hollies, seldom need pruning after planting, and some deciduous trees, including birches, shadbush, and service trees, are best left alone to develop their naturally beautiful shapes. But other deciduous trees should be pruned every year for the first few years.

Inspect your young trees in late summer or late winter, and remove dead, damaged, and diseased wood. Weak or crossing branches are also best cut out. At the same time, loosen ties and remove any weeds growing over the root area. While you're at it, check for any suckers shooting from below the graft union and cut them out too (*see p.210*).

More extensive pruning depends on what kind of tree you want. Many trees sold at garden centers are lollipop shaped, technically known as "standards." These have been pruned by the nursery, and you merely need to continue keeping the trunk clear and pruning back wayward stems.

Younger trees, or "whips," are sometimes available. These usually have a single leading stem and buds that will develop into side stems. These trees are less expensive, and often easier to establish than older trees, and can be pruned and shaped as you wish. For example, if you want a tree with several stems, cut the stem to near ground level, or plant a few whips close together, or even in the same hole.

Competing shoots can occur when the leading stem is damaged or cut off. To form a new leader, prune out all but the most upright.

Pruning a badly shaped tree

It is easy to size up your tree when it is leafless in winter; it's also the best time to prune. Exceptions are trees that bleed sap or are slow to heal, like birches and magnolias, and those prone to disease, such as cherries. Where winters are harsh, prune in late fall or very early spring, but watch out for lots of new shoots.

1 When the leaves of a deciduous tree have fallen, take a look at its overall shape. Look for stems that are badly placed, or those growing too far down the trunk. This tree is misshapen, and has an awkward stem growing from the base that must be removed.

2 Remove any dead and damaged wood. Use a pruning saw to make a straight cut through branches growing from the base of the tree.

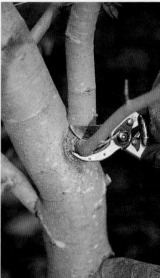

3 Prune out thinner stems with loppers, taking them back to ½in (2cm) from the ring of slight swelling where the stem and trunk meet, known as the "collar."

Cut about a quarter of the way through the underside of the branch.

Do not worry at this stage if the cut snags as it falls away.

4 Thick branches and those that are likely to tear are cut in stages. First, cut under the stem, a short distance from the trunk.

5 Make a second cut above the lower one, and aim to join the two. Make sure your tools are sharp to prevent snagging.

6 Even if you have taken great care, a heavy branch may still snap off, but it doesn't matter at this point, since this is not the final cut.

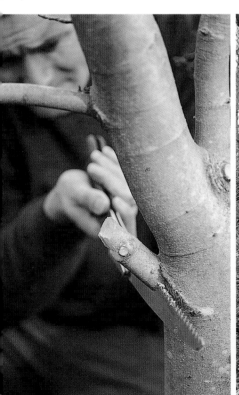

Cut the unwanted leader back to the main trunk.

7 Remove the stub by using the technique outlined in steps 4 and 5. Make your final cut just slightly away from the branch collar.

8 This tree has competing leaders, which must be removed. Choose the most upright, vigorous stem as your new leader.

9 The pruned tree now has a clear trunk, more balanced shape, and a new leading stem, creating a more pleasing outline.

Cutting conifers

Most conifers won't regrow from the old brown wood that forms beneath the outer young green leaves, which means that hard pruning is not usually an option. To maintain a good shape and a bushy habit, young conifers may need their foliage lightly trimmed and shoot tips removed, but many are sufficiently shapely when left to their own devices.

As you might expect from their conical shape, the growing tip of conifers severely restricts the growth of shoots lower down the plant (*see p210*). Cutting off this top shoot stimulates lower buds into growth, leading to a more rounded shape. Unlike many other trees, most conifers don't develop a new leading shoot afterward. Instead, some of the shoots start growing up, rather than out to the side, masking the gaps left by pruning. This is why some conifers that can be clipped regularly, such as yew and cypress,

Remove dead wood and disguise the hole it leaves. First, insert a stake into the gap, and tie it to the trunk. Then tie adjacent shoots to the stake, and when they have grown over the hole, the stake can be removed.

are ideal for hedges and topiary. Dwarf conifers, however, do not respond well to regular trimming.

Renovation

Conifers should not be pruned hard, with the exception of yew (*Taxus baccata*), the stems of which can be cut back to the trunk and will regrow in most cases. Other conifers are best replaced when they get too large or unsightly, or are damaged. At the very least, dead branches should be removed when you see them. Spreading junipers can be cut back to keep them within bounds. Look for a branchlet on the top of an overlong stem and cut back to this. The branchlet will hide the cut and become the new branch.

Pollarding and coppicing trees

Trees that are cut back from an early age can make beautiful garden features. For example, if you want a wildlife area but have little space, you could coppice a hazel, which creates a smaller plant. To do this, cut back all the stems to near ground level every 10 years in late winter or early spring. This results in a clump of nut-bearing stems that will attract a host of native birds and animals. Other trees, such as paulownia (*shown here*), can be cut back annually to promote stems with massive leaves.

1 Coppice paulownias in spring. Left alone, they bloom in late spring, but hard pruning removes the flowering stems.

2 Cut down all the stems to about 12–24in (30–60cm) from the ground. This creates what is known as a "stool."

3 Coppicing results in young stems with large, almost tropical-looking foliage. It also limits the size of this naturally large tree.

Pruning trees that bleed sap

Trees that bleed, such as magnolia (*shown here*), are best pruned in summer; healing is quicker at this time. The regrowth will also be less vigorous, and recovery may be slow, because the tree puts all its energy into healing its wounds. When shaping young magnolias, you can trim them in the spring, but don't cut stems any wider than ⅘in (2cm) at this time.

1 Although it is more difficult to see the outline of a tree in leaf, dead and diseased wood is quite obvious, so remove this first.

2 Take out stems that are growing toward the center of the tree. Be wary of pruning large branches that will heal slowly.

Cut out any crossing stems to prevent a wound that will bleed.

3 It is especially important to remove crossing branches in trees that bleed, since a wound can cause great damage.

4 Prune out weak stems that did not produce flowers or have few leaves, and rub out shoots forming on the lower trunk.

5 Keep the tree in shape by reducing the length of wayward side stems, cutting them back by about one-third.

6 The pruned tree has a better shape and a more open canopy, allowing more light into the center, and promoting vigorous stems.

Pruning climbers and wall shrubs

Climbers stand on the shoulders of other plants to reach the light, and then hog as much of it as they can for themselves. As a result, they tend to grow up out of sight and leave their trailing bare stems behind, which is not a desirable trait in a small garden or where the base of the plant can be seen.

An easy way to remedy this problem is to cut back plants severely, either in late winter as in the case of late summer- or autumn-flowering clematis, or every few years as in the case of honeysuckle. These and other climbers that flower late, such as trumpet vine, can be cut down to two to three buds from the base of the shoots to promote new flowering shoots. The young growth can then be tied in and trained onto the support. Climbers such as climbing hydrangeas that flower earlier in the year and bloom on stems made the previous year should be trimmed after flowering.

Some woody climbers, including Virginia creeper, kiwi vine, and wisteria, are pruned when dormant in winter, although wisteria requires further pruning in summer for the best results (*see opposite*).

When pruning climbers, focus on stems that are growing away from the support, cutting them back to a healthy bud or buds, facing in the right direction.

Training wall shrubs

You can grow most shrubs against fences, walls, and trellises, using the same pruning methods as for free-standing plants, but tying in stems during the summer to guide growth over the surface to be covered. At the same time, shorten shoots growing away from the wall to keep the shrub neat and narrow.

Firethorn, cotoneaster, and lilac make excellent wall shrubs. All flower in spring at the base of stems made the previous year, so if you want flowers and berries, make sure not to cut back too hard into the old wood when pruning. Shorten all new sideshoots in midsummer, leaving two to three leaves to encourage flower formation the following year and to make any berries more visible.

Firethorn berries are formed at the base of stems made the previous year; be careful not to prune them off.

Pruning a wall shrub

Shrubs, such as this evergreen spring-flowering California lilac, resemble climbers when trained onto a wall support. Make sure that the wall is in good condition before attaching a trellis to it, since any repairs will be difficult when the plant is established. Select a young shrub with strong sideshoots that will be easy to train, and prune in summer when the flowers have faded.

1 After planting, tie in the young, flexible sideshoots to the support with soft twine in a figure eight (*see p.137*).

2 After the flowers have faded, cut out any wayward stems that are facing away from the support or crossing each other.

3 Shorten the longest sideshoots by a few buds to stimulate other lateral stems to develop and cover the trellis.

Pruning different types of clematis

Clematis fall into three main groups: those that flower in late winter or spring, those that flower in early summer, and the later-flowering types that bloom from midsummer to fall. For the best flowers, each group should be pruned in a different way.

Early-flowering clematis

These include *C. montana*, *C. armandii*, *C. macropetala*, and *C. alpine*, and all need very little pruning. After flowering, give them a light trim, cutting back overlong or unproductive stems to a healthy bud. Renovation is possible for old, straggly plants: cut back all stems almost to the ground, but do not repeat this for at least three years.

Late-flowering clematis

1 Clematis that flower from late summer to autumn are pruned in late winter or early spring when the buds start to swell. Either prune them down to a pair of plump, healthy buds about 12in (30cm) from the base, or, with more vigorous types, right down to the ground.

2 After a few weeks you will see stems emerge from below ground level, and shoots forming on the pruned stems. Both will produce strong shoots that need to be tied in as the season progresses, and will reward you with a show of abundant flowers later in the year.

Early to midsummer flowering clematis

Clematis that flower from early to midsummer can be left to their own devices, unless the plant needs restricting, in which case trimming after flowering will help. For renovation of old tangled plants, cut back to buds near soil level in late winter. You may lose that year's flowers, or the plant may flower later in the summer.

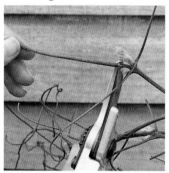

How to prune an established wisteria

Wisteria is a special case, where shortening the sideshoots promotes the formation of flower buds. You need to prune twice: once in summer, and again when the plant is dormant in winter. For large plants, you may need a sturdy ladder to reach the top.

1 In summer, after flowering, prune back the sideshoots to within five to seven leaves of the main stem, and tie in new growth.

2 In winter, shorten the new stems that have formed after you pruned in summer. Take these back to leave two buds.

3 Your pruned wisteria should look like this when you have finished. These short sideshoots will produce lots of spring blooms.

Pruning roses

Roses flower on new shoots, and most are pruned while dormant in early spring to promote strong growth later in the season. Long stems are also pruned back in late autumn to reduce wind damage during the winter.

Pruning shrub roses

Growing shrub roses in a mixed border is becoming increasingly popular. Retain the shape of modern shrub

Prune old-fashioned roses, such as 'Ispahan', in summer after flowering.

roses, including patio types, by lightly pruning them in early spring. You can also stimulate the growth of some vigorous new wood by cutting down to the ground a proportion of the older stems, usually one in three. The new shoots that arise will flower the following year.

Renovating roses

If you have recently moved, and inherited elderly roses that you can't identify, leave them for a season to see how they grow. If you have one in an undesirable

place, it is often best to replace it since mature roses can be tricky to move. If you want to keep an old shrub or bush rose where it is, cut it back hard. In late winter, while the rose is dormant, prune all the stems to 1–1½in (3–4cm) from the ground, sawing out dead and diseased stumps. Drastic action like this may kill very old plants that don't have much life left in them, but you can lessen the risk by renovating over two years, cutting out some old stems and shortening healthy ones each year.

Pruning old–fashioned roses

Old-fashioned roses, such as albas, mosses, and damasks, should generally be pruned lightly in summer after the first flush of flowers (*see steps 1 and 2*). To renovate old specimens, cut back all but the strongest young stems to the ground, and prune those that remain, taking them back by one-third of their length. Renovate after flowering or in the spring—but keep in mind that if you do your pruning in spring, you will lose the forthcoming season's flowers.

Gallica roses are pruned in a similar way to other old-fashioned roses, except that the sideshoots are generally cut back all the way to the main stem, or to a shoot close to the main stem.

1 Remove dead and diseased wood. Then cut back the main stems and sideshoots by one-third to a healthy, outward-facing bud.

2 In the autumn, cut back any extralong whiplike stems that could be vulnerable to damage by strong winter winds.

How to prune bush roses

Cut back both hybrid teas and floribundas hard each year to encourage new growth, but prune floribundas a little less severely to avoid a reduction in flowers. In harsh regions, don't be in a rush to prune. Seemingly dead shoots will often sprout new growth.

Pruning hybrid tea roses

1 Remove dead, diseased, weak, or crossing shoots from the center of the bush to leave an open symmetrical framework from which new shoots can arise.

2 Hybrid tea roses respond well to drastic pruning. Reduce all the main stems to about 8–12in (20–30cm) above the ground, cutting back to a healthy, outward-facing bud.

3 Your rose should look like this when you have finished. After a few weeks you will see new shoots appearing, which will reward you with an abundance of beautiful blooms.

Pruning floribunda roses

Extending the flowering period

Cut the main shoots back to about a third of their length, and trim any remaining healthy sideshoots by about one- to two-thirds.

To keep hybrid teas flowering for a long time, cut back the spent flowers to a healthy sideshoot or strong outward-facing bud.

For floribundas cut back whole trusses of flowers to a healthy sideshoot, leaf, or bud to promote new flowering stems.

Pruning climbers and ramblers

Climbers and ramblers are best pruned in late summer, when you can see the different kind of shoots more easily, although they will respond well to pruning in winter, too.

Pruning ramblers

Each year, ramblers make lots of new growth that flowers the following year. To prevent your rose from becoming a tangled mess, cut out the oldest stems in early fall, near the ground, and retain young stems, tying them in to replace the old ones. On the remaining older wood, shorten the sideshoots to within two to four healthy buds of the main stem. The young stems will then flower the following year, while more new shoots will grow from the base of the plant.

For rambling roses prune the sideshoots back to 2–4 healthy buds from the main stem. Tie in the new growth that arises to wires or other suitable support.

Pruning a climbing rose

After planting a climber, do not prune back the long stems. Instead tie them to stakes and tie the stakes in a fan shape to horizontal wires fixed to your support. Train young flexible sideshoots horizontally along the wires as they grow (*see p.131*). When established, you can start pruning annually to keep the plant neat, and to encourage plenty of flowering shoots.

Cut back dead wood down to the ground.

1 Retain old wood, except for any diseased, dead, or weak growth, which should be cut down to the ground or to a healthy bud.

2 Prune the sideshoots only, reducing them to about two-thirds of their original length, and cutting to a bud facing in the right direction.

3 Tie in the newly pruned stems horizontally to their support. This encourages more flowering sideshoots to form along the stems.

4 Prune back any overlong stems that are protruding beyond the support and sideshoots growing away from it.

Pruning guide

This at-a-glance guide shows a selection of popular plants and how they should be pruned. Note that most shrubs that flower before midsummer are pruned after they have bloomed, while those that flower later are usually cut back in early spring.

Plants to prune cautiously

Picea

Prune these shrubs only when essential for health: *Daphne, Hamamelis*.

Never cut into old bare wood: *Cistus, Cytisus, Lavandula, Salvia,* Conifers, including *Picea, Pinus,* and *Chamaecyparis*, but you can prune *Taxus* back hard.

Shrubs to prune for special effects

Cotinus coggygria

The following shrubs can be pruned hard to stimulate the production of colorful stems: *Cornus alba* and cultivars, *Rubus* (colored cane types), *Salix alba*

Prune for decorative foliage: *Cotinus coggygria, Sambucus, Eucalyptus gunnii, Corylus, Paulownia*.

Shrubs to prune lightly

Spiraea

Abelia, Berberis, Ceanothus, Chaenomeles, early-flowering *Clematis, Cotoneaster, Deutzia, Elaeagnus, Euonymus, Forsythia, Genista, Hydrangea macrophylla, Kerria, Magnolia, Paeonia delavayi, Philadelphus, Photinia, Pyracantha, Ribes sanguineum, Skimmia, Spiraea, Viburnum, Weigela*.

Roses to prune hard in early spring

'Southampton'

Hybrid teas, such as Alexander, 'Blessings', Elina, Fragrant Cloud, Freedom, 'Just Joey', Paul Shirville, Peace, Remember Me, Rosemary Harkness, Silver Jubilee.

Floribundas, such as Anisley Dickson, 'Arthur Bell', Hannah Gordon, Iceberg, Margaret Merril, Mountbatten, The Queen Elizabeth, Regensberg, 'Southampton'.

Shrubs to prune hard

Santolina

Artemisia, Buddleja davidii, Caryopteris, late-flowering *Clematis, Fuchsia, Hydrangea paniculata*, young *Hibiscus, Lavatera, Leycesteria, Perovskia, Phygelius, Santolina*.

Roses to prune lightly in early spring

'Jacqueline du Pré'

Shrub roses, such as 'Buff Beauty', 'Chinatown', Eye Paint, 'Golden Wings', Jacqueline du Pré, 'Penelope', Smarty, Westerland.

Rugosas, such as 'Agnes', 'Belle Poitevine', 'Fru Dagmar Hastrup', Pink Grootendorst, *R. rugosa* 'Alba'.

Miniature roses, such as Angela Rippon, Arizona Sunset, Darling Flame, Minnie Pearl, Snowcap.

Evergreens that tolerate renovation

Choisya

Most evergreens do not respond well to renovation, and old plants are best replaced. The exceptions to this rule include: *Aucuba, Berberis, Choisya, Eucalyptus, Fatsia, Garrya, Hebe, Ilex, Mahonia, Prunus laurocerasus, Prunus lusitanica, Rhododendron, Taxus, Viburnum*.

Old roses to prune lightly after flowering

'De Rescht'

Albas, such as 'Alba Maxima', 'Céleste', 'Félicité Parmentier'.

Damasks, such as 'De Rescht', 'Ispahan', 'Madame Hardy'.

Moss roses, such as 'Capitaine John Ingram', 'Général Kléber', 'Henri Martin', 'William Lobb'.

Gallica roses, such as 'Belle de Crécy', *gallica* 'Versicolor'.

Making new plants 11

Compost and equipment • Raising plants from seed
Dividing and layering • Taking cuttings • Which method to use

Propagation equipment

Almost all plants reproduce by seed, but this can be hampered by several factors in the wild. For example, adverse weather conditions can reduce insect populations, so fewer flowers are pollinated and produce seed. To counter such problems, plants have evolved back-up methods, and most can multiply in other ways too. Perennials often form large clumps made up of many small plantlets that can survive on their own. Other plants can regenerate from a small section of root or stem that is separated from the main plant, and the

Root trainers are ideal for vigorous plants with long roots, such as sweet peas and broad beans.

flexible stems of climbers and some shrubs take root if they rest on the soil. All of these natural traits are exploited by gardeners to make new plants in the garden.

Most propagation techniques are simple once you are familiar with the method. The skills are easy to learn and the results satisfying, allowing you to produce more of your favorite plants for very little cost, or increase the variety of plants in your garden. Plants that are short-lived or of

borderline hardiness can be kept going simply by taking a few cuttings or collecting and sowing their seeds. Old-fashioned, rare, or forgotten plants have often been kept in existence thanks to amateur propagation.

Essential equipment

The simplest plant propagation requires no equipment at all. Stems of impatiens, cornus, or willow (*Salix*) in a jar of water soon produce roots; shake a ripe foxglove or poppy seedhead, and seeds fall to the ground and germinate. For most propagation, however, a few basic items are essential. You will need a pencil or waterproof pen and labels for identifying plants, because many look almost identical at the seedling stage; pruners and a sharp knife for taking cuttings; plastic bags, and elastic bands to secure them over pots; a small sieve for dusting soil mix over seeds; a block or piece of board for firming soil mix before sowing; and a dibber or pencil to make planting holes and lift seedlings.

Trays, modules, and pots

Seed trays are useful for raising large quantities of seeds. The usual size is about 14 × 9in (35 × 23cm); half-sized trays are also available. Module or multicelled trays have a number of internal divisions, each treated as a separate small pot. These eliminate the need to prick out young seedlings (*see p.236*) and are useful for minimizing root disturbance or growing several different plant varieties together. Root-trainers are deep modules with ridged sides to help long roots grow straight.

For single or small numbers of seeds or cuttings, 3–3½in (8–9cm) pots are the most suitable size; for larger quantities 5–6in (13–15cm) pots are more economical. Plastic pots are often easier to use than clay ones, and retain moisture for longer; either type must have drainage holes at the bottom. Biodegradable pots eliminate root disturbance when seedlings are transplanted to larger pots or outside into the ground. As your seedlings grow, they will have to be moved outside to harden off (*see p.236*), so look for pots that fit neatly into trays that can be carried around easily.

Keeping clean

Small plants and cuttings are vulnerable to disease. Make sure all containers are either new or washed and scrubbed thoroughly clean. Always use new soil mix and water with tapwater because rainwater may carry disease organisms.

A "tidy tray" like this keeps the soil mix contained and reduces waste. Before you start propagating, get everything ready, with pots, labels, and other pieces of equipment at hand.

Keeping seedlings covered

Most seeds and cuttings need protection against drying out. Small sheets of glass or clear plastic lids are ideal for seed trays. Enclose individual pots in clear plastic bags held clear of leaves by canes or hoops of wire. Propagators consist of a tray and clear plastic cover and are available in various sizes, some designed to fit neatly on a windowsill. They keep seeds and cuttings warm and the air inside humid. Heated propagators, especially those with an adjustable thermostat, can maintain higher temperatures to speed up rooting.

For propagation outdoors, glass or plastic cloches offer a little protection from low temperatures and bad weather, and are most effective if you can regulate their ventilation and open them easily for watering. A cold frame is indispensable for large-scale propagation. Most can be fully ventilated, and some are also heated, like a mini-greenhouse. Stood on bare ground, you can plant directly into the soil.

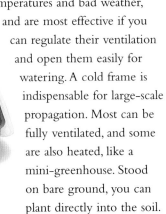

Protect your plants from drying out with a plastic lid designed to fit over the tray.

Cold frames are invaluable for growing seeds or cuttings outdoors and for hardening off young plants grown under cover.

Choosing the right soil or potting medium

You will need a suitable soil mix or other rooting mixture in which to sow seeds or grow plants. Seed and cuttings medium is widely available from garden centers; it deteriorates, so always use fresh medium and buy a small bag if you plan to sow just a few seeds. This is a well-drained soil mix but also sufficiently moisture-retentive to avoid the need for frequent watering. Some plant types need special soil mixes: Alpines, for example, grow best in very sandy or gritty conditions, while acid-loving plants such as heathers and pieris must have a lime-free ("ericaceous" or "rhododendron") soil mix.

Seed or rooting medium is ideal; potting soil is too rich for seedlings. Soil- or loam-based types dry out slowly. Soilless mixes are light and clean, but they can be hard to remoisten once dry.

Horticultural grit on top of the soil mix helps water drain away from stems; in the base of a pot it prevents waterlogging. When sowing water-sensitive plants or rooting cuttings in a cool season, add coarse sand for drainage.

Vermiculite is a sterile, lightweight material that holds moisture and improves aeration. Be sure to choose a grade that is intended for propagation. Perlite is similar and both are added to soil mixes or used on their own for rooting cuttings.

Growing plants from seed

Growing from seed is the most common and often the easiest propagation method. The climax of the growing cycle for most plants is the production of seeds, each containing a safely dormant embryo plant and some stored food. All the seed needs to grow is warmth, moisture, light, and air. If you provide these at the right time, you should be successful.

Buying and saving seeds

Most seeds are sold in a plastic or foil package that preserves them until opened. Seed in paper packets ages more rapidly. Always read and follow the instructions and keep the packet, since it will give growing recommendations and a "use by" date, after which any unused seed will deteriorate.

Homegrown seed is usually worth saving. Always choose healthy plants with the best seedheads: Poor-quality plants may produce poor-quality seeds. Timing is critical: The seeds must be mature, but not so ripe that they are already being shed. Enclose dry heads and capsules in paper bags before cutting them off, then label and store the bags (see also p.96). Spread damp seeds out to dry in a warm, airy place. Dry fruits well and store intact, or extract and dry the seeds.

Seeds from hardy annuals, such as sunflowers, are easy to collect when ripe and usually germinate readily.

Some garden plants do not produce reliable offspring, or "come true" from seed; for example, the plants listed in catalogs as "F1 hybrids" (see p.29). These are specially bred, and if you want more of the same, you will have to buy the F1 seeds again the following year.

Storing and treating seeds

Keep bought seed in its packet (resealed if it has been opened), and saved seeds in envelopes or paper bags marked with the date of harvest. Store in a dark, dry, well-ventilated place, or in cans with one or two packets of silica gel to absorb any moisture. Warmth can dry seeds beyond recovery; aim for conditions that are frost-free but below 41°F (5°C). Some seeds can be stored for years, while others last only months or weeks.

A few seeds need special treatment to speed germination, and this will be detailed on the packet. For example, hard seed coats that are slow to absorb moisture can be nicked with a knife (chipped) or rubbed with sandpaper (scarified), or the seeds can be soaked in warm water overnight. Other seeds may need to be placed in the refrigerator for a period of chilling to simulate winter conditions.

Different types of seed

Some seeds may be sold in a form that makes sowing easier, or treated to ensure successful results. These can be found in seed catalogs or advertisements in gardening magazines.

Pelleted seeds are individually wrapped in a ball of clay so they are easily spaced out; the coating breaks down after sowing provided the soil or medium is kept moist. This is done to make fine seeds easier to sow.

Seed tapes are strips of paper or other biodegradable material with seeds of vegetables or annuals usually sown in rows embedded in them (left). They eliminate the need to thin crowded seedlings.

Dressed seeds are coated with a fungicide, often brightly colored, to help prevent rotting in cool or wet conditions. Always wash your hands after handling.

Primed seeds have been treated to break down any natural dormancy and ensure that they germinate soon after sowing.

Chitted or pregerminated seeds are usually of plants that need heat or special treatment to germinate, and must be ordered. They are delivered at exactly the right stage for sowing, already growing and normally with a tiny visible root. Sow immediately to avoid any delay in their growth.

Sowing in modules

Seeds sown in pots and trays often germinate in large numbers, and then need pricking out while seedlings are still small (see p.236). You can often avoid this additional stage, and the risk of disturbing seedlings, by sowing instead in modules, cell trays, or biodegradable pots (see p.232). Fill these in the usual way with rooting medium, and sow each cell or pot with a tiny pinch of small seeds or two or three larger ones. Cover and germinate as usual. As soon as the seedlings are large enough to handle, pinch off or pull out all but the strongest, and leave this one to grow on.

Sowing seeds under cover

Tender plants and half-hardy annuals and perennials are started indoors since they need artificial warmth or frost-free conditions. The seeds of most hardy plants can be sown indoors too, if you have nowhere outdoors to sow them or you want closer control over their germination and early growth. Remember that seeds sown indoors must be checked regularly to make sure that they are warm and moist. Sow at the recommended depth, because either too much or too little light can prevent the seeds from germinating, and sow sparingly both to reduce the risk of overcrowding and disease and to make pricking out easier.

Sow seed thinly and evenly.

1 Fill the container to the brim with soil mix. Tap it lightly on the work surface to settle the contents and level off any excess.

2 Firm to ½in (1cm) below the rim to eliminate air pockets. Use a presser of wood or plywood or the base of another pot.

3 Pour some of the seeds into the palm of one hand, and use the finger and thumb of the other to sprinkle them over the surface. Never sow direct from the package, as it is hard to shake seed out evenly, and seedlings are likely to end up in overcrowded patches.

Large seeds

Sow large seeds, such as French beans, marigolds, and sunflowers (*Helianthus*), in a large pot or seed tray filled with moist soil mix and firmed to ½in (1cm) space below the rim. Gently push the seeds just below the surface with your finger, about 1–1½in (2.5–4cm) apart. Cover them with a layer of soil mix and proceed as for small seeds

4 If the seeds need darkness for germination, sieve a shallow layer of soil mix over them. Fine seeds needing light, such as begonias, can be pressed gently into the surface or covered with a very thin layer of vermiculite. Label the pot with the variety and date of sowing.

5 Water from below by standing the pot in shallow water until moist patches appear at the surface. Drain and cover with a clear plastic bag, or enclose in a propagator. Keep at the recommended temperature and out of direct sun; cold nights or very hot days can cause failure.

Looking after seedlings

The time it takes for seeds to germinate and produce a visible shoot above the soil varies greatly, ranging from a day for plants like cress and radishes, to a year or more for some shrubs and trees. Germination starts with the appearance of a root, followed by a shoot. Note that the first pair of leaves to develop may look different from those that follow. They are called the "seed leaves."

If you are germinating seeds in darkness, check them regularly and move into good light as soon as the seedlings emerge to encourage sturdy and healthy growth. They will grow tall, thin, and pale if left in the dark, but should also be kept out of bright, direct sunlight, which can scorch tender leaves. Keep seedlings warm, although they usually tolerate lower temperatures than those for germination.

Do not let the seedlings dry out at any stage, but avoid overwatering, which can drown the roots. Use a copper fungicide to reduce the risk of damping off disease. Water small seedlings from below as for seeds (*see p.235*), but more robust kinds, such as lupines and peonies, can be watered gently from above. Use a watering can with a very fine rose, and start and finish with the can to one side of the container to avoid letting heavy drips fall on the plants. Allow containers to drain thoroughly after watering, and never keep them permanently in trays or saucers of water.

Getting ready for the garden

When you have pricked out your seedlings, grow them on at the temperature recommended on the seed packet. Check them daily and water whenever they look dry. Plants in trays can usually remain there until they are planted out, but some vigorous seedlings in pots may need to be moved again into containers 1–2in (3–5cm) wider than their root systems. If planting out is delayed and the foliage starts to turn yellow, use a balanced liquid fertilizer.

Plants raised indoors make soft growth that is vulnerable to wind and cold. They must be acclimatized to conditions outdoors, or "hardened off," gradually. A few weeks before planting out, put plants in a cool spot indoors. Two weeks

Pricking out seedlings

Seedlings in trays quickly fill the available space and become overcrowded, leading to weak growth that is prone to diseases. To avoid this, move or "prick out" seedlings when they are large enough to handle, discarding the weakest if you have too many.

Use new or clean trays, modules, or even small pots for large seedlings, and fill with fresh soil-based potting mix. Make sure the seedlings are moist before starting, and keep them covered to prevent the soil mix from drying out.

Hold by a leaf to avoid damaging the fragile stem.

1 Knock each end of the container on the work surface to loosen its contents. Use a dibber or pencil to separate seedlings, and lift out each seedling carefully by its leaves.

2 Make a hole for each seedling in the new soil mix, in the center of pots or modules, or in a grid pattern in trays. Full trays hold 5×8 small plants, or 4×6 larger ones.

3 Transplant a seedling into each hole, at the same depth as before or slightly lower. Firm around each one very gently. Pat the sides of the pot or tray to level the soil, and water well.

Store-bought seedlings and plug plants

Flowers and vegetables can be bought, where available, as seedlings or plug plants, which are a useful alternative if you do not have the time or facilities to raise plants from seed. The most popular kinds are sold through garden centers or specialty nurseries. Seedlings are supplied in small trays and need pricking out in the usual way as soon as they are large enough. Plugs are individual plantlets started in tiny cells and supplied ready for potting up to a larger size.

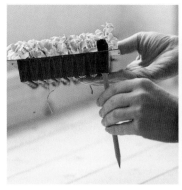   

1 Water the plugs as soon as you can and fill module trays with soil mix (*see p.235*). Use the blunt end of a pencil to push the plug plants out of their modules.

2 Using a dibber or the end of a pencil, make a hole in a module large enough for the root ball. Move the plug into the new module, handling it by the leaves.

3 Place the plug in the hole, slightly deeper than it was in the module tray in which it arrived. Firm lightly around the stem and continue with the rest of the tray.

4 Keep the young plants in a light, airy place to grow on. Water from below by placing the module in a tray of water, or use a watering can fitted with a fine rose.

later, stand them outside for a few hours each day in a sheltered, shady place, covered with a double layer of horticultural fleece. Bring them in at night. Leave them out for a little longer each day and remove a layer of fleece. About a week before planting out, remove the fleece during the day, and leave them out at night covered by the fleece.

If you have an unheated cold frame, place the containers of plants in this instead of using fleece, keeping the lid shut for a few days. Gradually increase the ventilation, opening the lid just a crack to start with but eventually leaving it fully open, at first during the day and then at night too.

Planting out

Plant out as soon as the young plants are hardened off and the weather is suitable: Mild, damp conditions are best. Wait until all threat of frost is past before risking half-hardy plants outdoors. Prepare the site thoroughly in advance, and water the plants well and leave to drain before planting.

Tap each side of a tray sharply on the ground to loosen the soil mix, then slide it out in one block and separate the plants carefully with your fingers or a trowel. Release plants from modules by pushing on the base of the cells; some modules are torn apart. Check the seed package for planting distances. Plant out as for perennials, but in smaller holes (*see pp. 94–95*). The roots will not need any teasing out and should be firmed in by hand, rather than with your heel.

Care tips

Plants are at their most vulnerable at the seedling stage. Take care to give them the right conditions consistently and keep an eye on their development to achieve the best results.

Tiny seedlings, such as lobelia, are best sown in rows in shallow drills or grooves marked across a seed tray or pan with a stick. The seedlings will appear like miniature hedges, which are easy to separate into small clusters of 4 or 5 for pricking out into trays.

Avoid bright sunlight since young leaves scorch easily in hot sun, especially when grown under glass. Avoid windowsills in direct sunlight, or shade seedlings on very sunny days with sheets of newspaper, horticultural fleece, or fine net. Remember to remove it on cooler days.

Slugs and snails often target the soft, juicy growth of seedlings and young plants. Ideally, make sure they cannot reach trays and pots, and check underneath them, where these pests often hide. Protect young plants once they are outside by using a suitable treatment (*see p.260*).

Encourage bushy growth on young plants, such as dahlias, by pinching out the tips of each stem (*left*). This encourages sideshoots to form lower down, producing bushier specimens that will carry more blooms.

Pinch out tips

Dividing plants

Division is both the easiest method of making new plants and the usual way of increasing most herbaceous perennials (*see p.247*). Many hardy plants mature and fatten into fairly bushy clumps. These can be divided by digging them up and splitting them into smaller portions to make new rooted plants that are ready to grow as soon as conditions are favorable.

Unlike growing from seed, division uses an existing plant to produce more plants that are exactly like the original. It is also a reliable way to rejuvenate perennials that are old and no longer flowering well.

Choosing plants to divide

The plant you choose to divide must be healthy in every respect. Whereas few ailments are passed on through seeds, a diseased plant will usually result in diseased new plants if used for either division or cuttings (*see pp.242–244*).

When buying new herbaceous perennials, look for particularly large plants: These are an economical option if you can divide them into two or three portions before planting. In choosing a suitable clump of plants for division, check that the roots are healthy. They should be flexible and

Multiplying bulbs and corms

Dividing bulbs and corms (*see pp.100–101*) reinvigorates plants and provides extra for planting elsewhere. Many bulbs, such as narcissi, tulips, and snowdrops (*Galanthus*), form offsets, or new bulbs, within the same outer papery skin. They can become overcrowded and fail to flower if left undisturbed.

Some bulbs, especially alliums and lilies, form bulblets on stems or flowerheads; plants with corms, like crocuses and gladioli (*left*), develop smaller cormels around the base. Grow them on, several to a 5in (13cm) pot, until big enough to plant out.

Offsets can be detached when bulbs (here, narcissi) are lifted, or, for permanent bulbs, after the foliage has died down. Plant a little shallower than full-size bulbs at the usual time. Split snowdrops (*see p.102*) while leaves are still green, just after flowering.

Dividing herbaceous perennials

Select a healthy-looking plant and water it a few hours before lifting to be sure that the roots are moist. Incorporate well-rotted manure or compost into the soil in the new location where you will be planting your divisions, and some all-purpose fertilizer if needed. If replanting is delayed, dip the divisions in water and keep in a plastic bag in a cool place so they do not dry out.

Lever plant from ground with a fork.

1 Cut down old stems so you can see the crown clearly. Dig around the clump and lever it out with a fork. Shake off surplus soil to reveal the roots, and wash out any weed roots.

2 If you cannot tease the clump apart by hand, insert two forks back to back and work the handles together to split it. Repeat until you have enough good-sized segments.

3 Replant segments in fresh, well-prepared ground before the roots dry out. Check that the plants are at the same depth as before, firm in and level the soil, and water well.

Dividing bearded irises

Plants such as bearded irises and bergenias can produce thick horizontal stems, or "rhizomes", at soil level. Lift these with a fork, inserted well away from the clump to avoid damaging the fleshy rhizome. Take the entire clump out of the soil and shake off any soil and weed roots. Divide them with a knife into short rooted segments, each with at least one growth bud.

1 Split the rhizomes into sections by hand, ensuring that each has several healthy shoots and good roots. Trim off the older shriveled sections farther away from the leaves with a knife. Dust cut surfaces with fungicide.

2 Trim back long roots by one third. Cut the leaves of irises to approximately 6in (15cm). This will help reduce rocking by the wind, keeping the replanted section more stable until it develops strong anchoring roots.

3 Replant the sections of rhizome in well-prepared ground. Space them about 5in (12cm) apart, and check that they are at the same depth as before; iris rhizomes should be half buried. Firm in, level, and water well.

undamaged, and most healthy roots have numerous short, pale, hairlike side roots growing along them. Discard plant segments that look dry or withered, with dark roots that crumble or break easily, since these may be symptoms of disease. Discard the tired, old parts of the plant, which are usually in the center of the clump, and select the young, vigorous sections toward the edges for replanting.

Dividing techniques

Herbaceous perennials may develop solid, woody crowns, clusters of smaller crowns, or simply a mass of fibrous roots. Chop through solid crowns with a spade, or cut them with a knife. Make sure each segment has plenty of healthy roots and several strong growth buds. Divide looser clumps with garden forks, or hand forks if they are small (*see left*). You may be able to simply tease them into smaller portions with your fingers. Some plants, such as alpines, produce "offsets," complete young plants alongside the parent. Loosen these with a hand fork, separate them from the parent plant with a sharp knife or pruners, and replant.

Divisions that fit comfortably in one hand are the best size for replanting, but you can use larger ones for more rapid establishment. Grow on smaller fragments with one or two buds in a nursery bed without any competition for a season before planting them out.

When to divide

Most perennials can be divided at any time while they are dormant and unlikely to suffer any impairment in growth, but different times of year are better for different divisions.

Most perennials, especially fleshy-rooted types, are best divided in early spring. The worst weather is usually over, and growth resumes quickly. Some plants will already have buds, which can help you distinguish the strongest parts for replanting.

Very early flowering plants, such as doronicum, pulmonarias, and *Primula denticulata* are best divided after flowering. Iris clumps can be divided after flowering or in late summer or fall.

Marginal and aquatic pond plants are usually divided in late spring to early summer, as their growth revives.

Some perennials, such as hostas, often make new roots in late summer, and can be divided then. Most of the growth is over and divisions will quickly settle in. To be on the safe side, keep late divisions in a cold frame or nursery bed to protect them from harsh winter weather, and move them to their final positions in spring.

Avoid early or late winter, since wet or very cold weather can sometimes cause divisions to rot.

Early shoots show vigor

Layering plants

Many shrubs and climbers (*see p.247*) will naturally develop new roots on low branches if these come into contact with the ground or are buried for any length of time, and you can use this phenomenon to produce new plants. Known as layering, it is a particularly attractive method, because the stem used is left attached to the parent plant until it has rooted, so nothing is lost if the attempt fails. This is a useful way to fill a low gap in a mature hedge (*see also p.147*).

How layering works

You can simply bury a stem to exclude light and it should then start to root, but the chances of success are often increased by cutting or twisting it to damage some of the tissues. This interrupts the normal flow of hormones and other sap-borne chemicals, encouraging them to become concentrated at the injury site and stimulate root formation. The section of stem beyond the wound will become slightly water-stressed, and this also promotes root growth as the plant struggles to survive. Applying a rooting hormone powder or solution to the wound accelerates the process further. Rooting takes a variable amount of time, depending on the species and when you layer the stems: If you do this in early spring, most layers will have rooted by the fall.

Mound layering and dropping

Also known as "stooling," mound layering is an easy way to make new plants. Instead of burying a single stem, rooting is stimulated by creating a mound of soil around the bottom of many stems. This works well with low-growing shrubs such as gaultheria, heathers, and woody herbs, including rosemary, thyme, and lavender. Prune back the stems of young plants to 3–4in (8–10cm) in late winter. When the new shoots are about 6in (15cm) long, cover them to half their height with a mound of free-draining soil (add grit or

Simple layering

This easy method can produce new plants within a few months. Once you have layered a shoot, it needs very little attention, because it is still receiving most of its water and nutrients from the parent plant while it forms new roots. Only after you have severed that connection do you need take extra care that the new plant does not dry out.

1 Select a vigorous, healthy shoot that can be bent with little effort to touch the ground. Trim off any sideshoots and make a shallow, slanting cut on the underside of the shoot about 12in (30cm) from the tip. If you wish, you can apply a rooting hormone compound.

2 Carefully bend the stem to the soil. Weight or peg it down to keep the wound in contact with the soil, and tie its tip to an upright stake. If the soil is poor, bury the wounded area in a shallow hole filled with moist soil mix. Firm in gently with your fingers and water well.

Tie the shoot to a supporting stake.

3 When the layered shoot is well rooted and the tip has started to grow new leaves, you can transplant it into a pot or its new position. Sever it from the parent plant close to the new roots.

Other simple layering techniques

Serpentine layering is a form of layering in which the long, flexible stems of climbers like clematis, honeysuckle, grapevines (*Vitis*), and wisteria are pegged down several times between leaves, to produce several new plants. Tip layering is used for blackberries, brambles, and other *Rubus* that naturally produce roots from their stem tips.

Serpentine layering Make several wounds along a young stem, each just behind a leaf joint or bud. Peg down the wounded sections, leaving the stem between them exposed to the light. Roots will form on the buried wounds, while buds on the exposed sections will develop into new shoots. When well-rooted, separate and transplant sections.

Tip layering In summer, select a healthy, vigorous young stem and simply bury the shoot tip in a hole about 3–4in (7–10cm) deep. A new shoot will appear from the stem tip after a few weeks, at which point you can sever it from the parent plant. Allow the new plant to grow on where it is, and transplant it the following spring.

sand to clay soil). Repeat in midsummer, again covering the stems to half their height. In autumn, carefully scrape away the soil and you should find rooted stems that you can cut free and transplant into new positions.

An alternative method for older, straggly shrubs with bare stems is "dropping." Dig up the plant with minimal root disturbance in spring and replant in a deeper hole, mounding up as well if necessary so that just the top 1–2in (2.5–5cm) of the stems are showing. Leave it until fall.

The stems of this thyme will each produce roots when buried in soil, providing many new plants from the original one. The rooted sections can be potted in fresh soil in autumn.

Self-layering climbers

Some climbers, such as ivy and honeysuckle, naturally take root where their stems bend down and touch the soil. You can sever rooted sections in the autumn, or in spring if they have not formed a strong enough root systems in autumn. Choose a rooted section with new leaves beyond the roots, and lift it out of the soil with a hand fork. Then trim off all other parts of the stem, except for those with new roots and leaves. Remove the lower leaves on the rooted section of stem, and then plant it in a pot or in its final position.

Growing plants from cuttings

Taking cuttings is perhaps the most popular propagation technique after sowing seed. As the name implies, cuttings are portions of plant stem or root (occasionally leaves or a bud) cut from a strong, healthy parent plant and encouraged to develop their own roots. It works for the majority of plants and produces exact replicas of the donor. Unlike divisions or layers, cuttings are dependent on your care and a supportive environment until they are self-sufficient. Some are quicker to root than others, and different types will be more successful if taken at a particular time of year.

You can take cuttings from roots and shoots. Those taken from shoots are distinguished by the age and maturity of the shoots used. Root cuttings are fairly easy to take, and, as the name suggests, they are sections of root, normally taken from the parent plant when it is dormant in winter (*see opposite*). Hardwood cuttings are taken from midautumn on, when shoots are woody and the leaves have fallen. Although the slowest of the stem cuttings to root, most are simple and can be grown outdoors (*see box below*). Softwood cuttings root quickly and are best taken in spring and summer, using the soft, new tips of the current year's young shoots before they start to become woody (*see p.244*). Semiripe cuttings are taken from early summer to early autumn, when the base of the shoot is firm, or "ripe," but the tip is still soft and green. Because the cutting is firmer, they are often easier to deal with than soft cuttings (*see p.245*).

Taking hardwood cuttings

These are the easiest cuttings, simply inserted into good garden soil and left undisturbed for at least a year. Use this method for deciduous trees, shrubs, roses, climbers, and fruits (*see also p.247*). Choose strong, straight, well-budded stems of the current year's growth after the leaves have fallen, and trim to size just before planting. For trees, leave a single bud above the ground; for multistemmed bushes, allow 1–2in (2.5–5cm) of stem above ground so that several buds develop into shoots.

1 Make a V-shaped trench by inserting the spade about 8in (20cm) deep, and pushing it forward a little way. If drainage is poor, add horticultural sand at the bottom. Cut a long stem, leaving the tip intact.

2 Cut the stem into lengths of about 9in (23cm), pruning the bottom below a bud and the top just above another bud, with a sloping cut to distinguish it. Remove any leaves and sideshoots.

3 Insert the cuttings upright and about 4–6in (10–15cm) apart along the trench, with enough buds above the surface to form one or several shoots. Backfill around the cuttings with soil and gently tread firm. Label the cuttings and water well.

4 Root plants that are less hardy, such as Russian sage, hibiscus, and rock rose, in pots kept in a cold frame or cold greenhouse until spring. Trim cuttings to 3–4in (8–10cm), insert with the top bud just above the surface, and keep moist.

Taking root cuttings

This is a very easy and reliable way to produce good results. It is the best way to multiply perennial border phloxes, because it does not transmit nematode, a pest that infests top-growth. Root cuttings of variegated plants will produce all-green plants.

Cuttings are normally taken during the plant's dormant period in midwinter, to minimize disturbance and injury. Always choose a healthy plant. Lift small plants out of the ground completely with a fork and replant immediately after taking the cuttings. With larger plants, scrape away enough soil to expose the roots, and then replace and firm the soil at once to avoid destabilizing the plant. Never remove more than a few roots from each plant.

Most plants propagated this way (*see p.247*) have thick roots, which are planted upright. Plants such as phlox and drumstick primrose have thin roots, which are rooted horizontally in trays.

Select fat, healthy roots.

1 Remove 3 or 4 whole roots from each plant, cutting them off close to the crown. Choose moist, pliant, healthy material with no blemishes; avoid thin, withered, brittle, or woody roots. Keep roots fresh in a plastic bag until you are ready to prepare them.

2 Cut roots into 2–3in (5–8cm) segments, trimming the top ends of the sections—those closest to the stems—straight across.

3 Cut the bottom of each section at an angle so you can tell the top from the bottom when planting. This is not necessary for thin roots.

4 Insert cuttings vertically in pots or trays of rooting medium, with the flat end at surface level. Lay thin cuttings flat in trays on a 2in (5cm) layer of medium. Space both 2in (5cm) apart. Cover with ½in (1cm) of coarse sand or grit, water well with a dilute solution of fungicide, and label. Keep in a cold frame or covered with fleece in a sheltered area until well rooted.

A few months later...

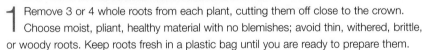

Leaf growth may appear before plants have made good root systems. Wait until you see roots near the holes at the bottom of the pot before transplanting.

Softwood and semiripe cuttings

Softwood cuttings are taken from very soft, new growth at the tips of nonflowering shoots, produced in abundance in spring and early summer. They have few defenses against pests and diseases. In a closed, warm environment most should root quickly, within six to eight weeks or even faster.

Semiripe cuttings are taken later in the year, when the stems have had time to firm up at the base, or ripen. They are generally larger, easier to handle, and more robust than softwood cuttings, and are less likely to wilt or rot. Their disadvantage is that they take longer to produce roots; six to ten weeks is average, and some, especially those taken in late summer, may even take until the following spring.

Essential equipment

You will need both pruners and a knife; clean them before taking each batch of cuttings and keep them sharp (*see p.153*). Use fresh medium and new or sterilized containers.

Cuttings must be spaced out when planted, so that their leaves do not touch. Small pots, about 3½in (9cm) diameter, are ideal for single cuttings; a 5–6in (13–15cm) pot will accommodate several cuttings. Larger quantities can be rooted in a module or cell tray at least 2in (5cm) deep. Use a rooting medium, which is blended to be free-draining, or mix your own from equal parts soilless seed medium or sieved leaf mold and sharp horticultural sand or grit.

Natural warmth will often be sufficient for root cuttings in summer if pots are enclosed in plastic bags or trays are kept covered with lids (*see p.233*). At cooler times of year, or if you produce a lot of new plants from cuttings, a propagating case on a heated tray or a heated propagator fitted with a thermostat will alleviate uncertainty. Hormone rooting preparations speed root initiation, and usually contain a fungicide; use them sparingly. Buy a fresh supply at the start of each season and store it in a refrigerator.

Taking softwood cuttings

Softwood shoots wilt quickly, so take cuttings from suitable plants (*see p.247*) early in the day, before the sun gets hot. Prepare containers in advance, so that you can get to work at once. Delphiniums and lupines can be increased both by stem-tip cuttings and also from basal shoots – the soft shoots that sprout from the solid crown of the plant in early spring. Cut them when they are 2–3in (5–8cm) long, with a portion of the crown at their base, and root them in the same way.

1 Using a sharp, clean pair of pruners or a knife, cut sections 3–4in (8–10cm) long from the tips of healthy, young, nonflowering stems. Place in a plastic bag, and keep this closed and out of the sun as you work.

2 Trim your cutting just below a leaf joint. Remove the leaves from the lower portion of the cutting so that only 2 or 3 remain at the top.

Dip ¼in (5mm) of stem in hormone rooting powder and tap off excess.

3 Dip the end of the stem in hormone rooting powder. Push the lower half into the medium, around the edge of the pot when there are several cuttings. Gently firm in, water thoroughly with tap water, and label. Enclose in a plastic bag or propagator. Most softwood cuttings root best at 59–70°F (15–21°C).

Taking semiripe cuttings

This method is commonly used for propagating shrubs that do not grow well from hardwood cuttings (*see p.247*), especially broad-leaved evergreens such as aucuba and mahonia. It is also effective for climbers, conifers, and tender perennials such as fuchsias. Gather strong, healthy sideshoots, about 6in (15cm) long, at any time from midsummer until midautumn. Some plants root more successfully from sideshoots pulled off with a short strip or "heel" of bark from the main stem, rather than cut. Long year-old stems can make several cuttings, each trimmed below a node at the base and just above one at the top. Cuttings are usually rooted indoors, but hardier plants will succeed outdoors in a cold frame or in the ground under a cloche or low plastic-covered tunnel. If you use a propagator with a heated base, set the thermostat at 64–70°F (18–21°C).

1 Choose a current season's shoot that is slightly resistant to bending at its base but still soft and green at the tip, and cut it just below a leaf joint.

2 Using a sharp knife, trim off the soft top portion of the cutting just above a leaf and discard it. This is done to reduce moisture loss through the soft leaves at the tip.

3 Make a shallow cut ½in (1–2cm) long on one side of the stem base to encourage rooting. Remove the leaves and sideshoots from the lower half of the stem.

4 Dip the bottom ¼in (5mm) of the cutting in hormone rooting powder, and tap or shake off any surplus. Make sure that the entire wounded area is dusted with the powder.

5 Insert the cutting up to its lowest leaves in rooting medium, or 3in (8cm) apart in the soil in a cold frame. Firm in place, label, and water thoroughly with tap water.

6 Place the pot in a lidded propagator, or cover with a plastic bag. Make sure the bag does not touch the leaves by inserting sticks into the sides of the pot to hold it clear.

Aftercare of cuttings

Check your cuttings regularly for signs of rooting – when you can see new leaf growth and roots at the bottom of the container. It is important to be patient and bear in mind the different times cuttings can take to root. If the cutting looks healthy, without any rotting, wilting, or leaf loss, leave it alone to root in its own time. Don't be tempted to pull up cuttings early to see if they have rooted: this can be fatal.

Hardwood cuttings, root cuttings, and semiripe cuttings in open ground or cold frames standing on the soil can be left to grow until you are ready to plant them. Those rooting in pots have little or no food, so as soon as new leaves and roots at the base of the pot indicate successful rooting, carefully pot them up individually in multipurpose soilless medium or peat or a soil-based potting mix. Hardwood cuttings and some semiripe cuttings, such as boxwood or other hedging, can be planted in their growing positions once grown to a reasonable size, but most will need to grow on in a pot for a year before they are sufficiently robust.

Indoors and under cover, softwood cuttings should root in 6–8 weeks, and semiripe ones in 6–10 weeks (occasionally longer). During this time, make sure that they stay consistently moist and in a humid atmosphere by keeping them covered; check them frequently, and water them lightly if the soil mix shows signs of drying out. If the cover mists over, ventilate so that the excess moisture can evaporate. Lift off plastic lids and dry them, or turn plastic bags inside out, otherwise drops may fall on the cuttings and cause them to rot. Immediately remove leaves that fall, or any foliage showing signs of mold or yellowing; these are usually signs that the atmosphere is too cold or damp, or too dry. If the cuttings need warmth, make sure the temperature is maintained, but shade them from direct sun. Once cuttings have rooted, let in some air by opening vents in the propagator lid or propping it open, or cutting a slit in plastic bags. After a few days you can remove the covering and pot up the cuttings individually. Keep them warm at first, away from cold draughts and direct sun, and make sure that you do not overwater.

Planting out

All cuttings rooted indoors, under cloches, or in a cold frame will have to be acclimatized to the open air or hardened off before they are planted outside toward the end of spring (*see box*). Tender bedding plants such as geraniums and verbenas raised from softwood cuttings indoors, on a windowsill or in a greenhouse, are more vulnerable and need extra care in the early stages of acclimatization (*see pp.236–237*).

Cleaning up

Hygiene is important for success with cuttings. Always water with tap water rather than stored rainwater, and either add a diluted fungicide to the water or spray weekly with a fungicide as insurance against rotting. Promptly clear away any leaves that fall from cuttings because they can harbor rot, and remove any cuttings that start to show signs of decay.

Hardening off

Cuttings raised with protection will need to be acclimatized before planting out, or all your work will be wasted.

• Hardening off in spring can take two or three weeks for plants that have been protected under cloches or low tunnels (*see right*) or in a cold frame outdoors, and six or seven weeks for those being moved from indoors.

• Wait until hard frosts are passed, and increase the level of protection again if there is an unexpected cold snap.

• Do not rush the process. The plants need time to develop thicker and tougher leaves.

• Remember that hot sun will scorch soft growth, and young plants will need shading.

A low polythene tunnel or cloche is the simplest and most cost-effective way of hardening off plants. Raise and lower the sides to adjust the ventilation.

A cold frame is a worthwhile investment if you have young plants to harden off every year. Prop open the lid for progressively longer periods each day.

Plants to propagate

Most plants can be grown from seed and at least one other method described in this chapter. Different plants respond better to some techniques than to others, and the lists below show the most successful. The time of year is also important. Taking cuttings in early summer means that supplementary heating may not be necessary, and they will have rooted and be well on their way before winter. Hardwood cutttings, layers, and divisions can be left to more or less look after themselves, apart from watering in dry weather, whereas seeds need plenty of attention.

Seed (see p.234)

Suitable plants Look through any catalog and you will see that most plants can be grown from seed as long as you provide the right conditions. If you collect your own seed you may not get what you expect. Double flowers may be sterile; variegated plants have all-green offspring; cultivars and F1 hybrids (see p.234) may disappoint.

When All year round

Division (see p.238)

Suitable plants Achillea, aconitum, aster, astilbe, bergenia, brunnera, campanula, coreopsis, erigeron, ferns (some), geranium, geum, helenium, heuchera, hosta, kniphofia, liatris, ligularia, lysichiton, miscanthus, pampas grass, primula, pulmonaria, rudbeckia, saponaria, sidalcea, snow-in-summer, solidago, thalictrum, tiarella, trollius, veronica

When Spring • Autumn

Layering (see p.240)

Suitable plants Amelanchier, celastrus, clematis, cornus, cotinus, cotoneaster, daphne, euonymus, fatsia, ficus, grapevine, hamamelis, hazel, hibiscus, holly, honeysuckle, ivy, jasmine, lapageria, lilac, magnolia, passion flower, pieris, skimmia, viburnum, weigela, wisteria

When Spring • Autumn

Root cuttings (see p.243)

Suitable plants Acanthus, anchusa, campsis, catananche, crambe, dicentra, drumstick primrose, eryngium, gaillardia, garden phlox, globe thistle, hop, Japanese anemone, macleaya, mint, Pasque flower, physalis, romneya, stokesia, symphytum, verbascum

When Winter

Hardwood cuttings (see p.242)

Suitable plants Actinidia, buddleja, celastrus, cornus, deutzia, ficus, flowering currant, elder, forsythia, grapevine, honeysuckle, jasmine, kerria, laburnum, leycesteria, mulberry, perovskia, philadelphus, populus, privet, rose, santolina, spiraea, symphoricarpos, tamarix, viburnum, weigela, willow, wisteria

When Autumn • Winter

Softwood cuttings (see p.244)

Suitable plants Argyranthemum, aubrieta, begonia, calceolaria, caryopteris, catmint, centranthus, chrysanthemum, dahlia, evening primrose, fuchsia, geranium, hebe, lantana, lobelia, malva, mimulus, mint, penstemon, philadelphus, rhododendron (deciduous types), spiraea, thyme, veronica

When Spring • Summer

Semiripe cuttings (see p.245)

Suitable plants Abutilon, anthemis, artemisia, aucuba, berberis, boxwood, broom, bupleurum, carpenteria, choisya, cotoneaster, deutzia, elaeagnus, escallonia, garrya, heather, holly, honeysuckle, lavender, lilac, mahonia, olearia, pieris, prunus, rosemary, sarcococca, skimmia, weigela.

When Summer • Autumn

Troubleshooting 12

Protecting your plants

All gardens, however carefully nurtured, will harbor some pests and diseases, but plants' natural defenses are usually able to fend off these foes. Even when defenses are down, most plants can tolerate some damage and will survive a minor onslaught.

Some plants, most notably fruit and vegetables, are more prone to damage from pests and diseases, and although they may not necessarily die, yields will be reduced. Ornamental plants, on the other hand, are seldom very seriously affected. Exceptions occur when large numbers of susceptible plants are grown close together, in rose borders for example, or in conditions that favor pests and diseases, such as hot, humid greenhouses. Plants growing in conditions to which they are not suited are also less able to resist attack. Hollyhocks planted in poor, dry soil, for example, are more likely to be affected by the fungal disease rust than those growing in moist conditions.

Early detection

Some damage is a normal part of gardening, and you can manage problems by being vigilant, and avoiding plants that are unsuited to the conditions in your garden. Take a few minutes to stroll through your garden every day, or as frequently as you can, and look under leaves and keep an eye out for signs of trouble—swift action usually prevents the need for more prolonged measures.

Recognizing what you see is essential for good pest and disease control. Plants have only a limited number of responses to put forth when they are attacked or injured, and several different problems can cause very similar symptoms, which means that some investigation is often needed before you can make a diagnosis. Also, to prevent overuse of pesticides, be wary of jumping to hasty conclusions.

Despite the bewildering number of potential plant problems, there are just a few that account for most of the

Spotting beneficial garden creatures

Many creatures in the garden offer great benefits by eating pests. Some birds, such as chickadees, eat aphids, while others consume slugs and snails. Although the birds are unlikely to completely eliminate these pests in summer, they are still to be encouraged. Similarly, adult and immature ladybugs can reduce the severity of an aphid attack but will not prevent one. Their efforts are usually enough to protect trees and shrubs, but be ready to take further action to protect young plants and shoots.

Earthworms eat dead plants and other organic matter, and their feces contain soil conditioners and plant nutrients. Worm tunnels also help to aerate the soil and increase drainage.

Ladybugs and their larvae feast on green- and blackfly, which suck the sap from plant leaves and stems, causing them to distort. Take note of the larvae (*left*), since they bear little resemblance to the adults and could easily be mistaken for a garden pest.

Ladybug larva

Some birds like to snack on slugs and snails. Attract them into your garden with a pond for them to drink from, and leave a few rocks or large pebbles around the garden, which they will use to crack open snail shells.

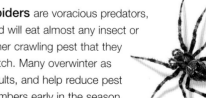

Spiders are voracious predators, and will eat almost any insect or other crawling pest that they catch. Many overwinter as adults, and help reduce pest numbers early in the season.

Keeping plants healthy

Plants that are under stress are more open to attack from pests and diseases than those in good health. Keep your plants in tip-top condition by growing them in the conditions they like, and make sure they are well watered and fed. Pay particular attention to plants in containers, which are especially vulnerable to drought. Remove any damaged stems quickly—infections can enter through wounds—and collect dead or diseased leaves from the ground since these can spread problems to other plants.

Overwatering can do as much damage as underwatering. Make sure your soil has good drainage to prevent the roots from drowning.

Container plants are vulnerable to drought if they are not watered regularly. Remember to water the soil, not the flowers and leaves.

This large wound increases the plant's vulnerability to attack

Broken branches, snapped off by wind or children playing, must be cut off neatly with loppers or a pruning saw (*see p.213*).

damage in gardens, and the majority of others can be grouped into categories that require similar remedies.

Getting a good balance

To prevent a buildup of pests and diseases, aim to grow a wide range of plants. Ideally, avoid too many of each kind, and those that don't thrive in your soil. If a plant's leaves turn yellow, it may mean that it is suffering from a deficiency in iron and manganese, which occurs when plants that like an acidic soil are grown in alkaline conditions. Test your soil with a pH kit (*see pp.38–39*) to check. Likewise, growing moisture-loving plants on dry soils can lead to outbreaks of powdery mildew and magnesium deficiency, while planting drought-lovers in soggy ground leads to root rots and stunted, dying plants.

Friend or foe?

Most little creatures and fungi found in the garden are harmless, and many are actually beneficial, improving soil fertility and preying on your plants' enemies. For example, woodlice, centipedes, and millipedes do minimal damage to plants, and by disposing of dead and decaying material they help to increase soil fertility. Other insects, such as ladybirds and their larvae, munch through hordes of sap-sucking aphids that cause serious damage to plants.

Fungal growth often shows up as a white mold in the soil, and although it can look unsightly, fungus plays an important role in breaking down organic matter, turning it into plant food and soil-conditioning compounds.

Lichen and moss may look alarming but they don't harm your plants. You may find them growing on the shady, damp side of tree and shrub stems.

Yellowing leaves often indicate an iron and manganese deficiency in acid-loving plants, such as rhododendrons, when they are grown in alkaline soil.

What causes plant stress?

Plants that look as if they are troubled by an infestation of pests or have a disease but don't seem to be actually under attack may be suffering from a disorder. Disorders happen when a plant lacks sufficient nutrients or water, or is growing under adverse conditions, such as excessive cold or warmth. They can also occur if plants are subjected to more wind or sun than they can handle, are growing in shade when they prefer sun, or have a poor root environment. Disorders are very common, and if the underlying problems are not rectified quickly, they often lead to an outbreak of disease or attack by pests, which take hold of the weakened plant.

Scorched foliage may be the result of cat urine. Deter cats with prickly stems laid on the soil close to vulnerable plants.

Nutrient and water deficiencies

Insufficient nutrients are less common than you may think. Most tended garden soil has been fed over many years, replenishing levels of potassium and phosphorus. Nitrogen may be lacking, however, since it is easily washed out of the soil. Deficiencies lead to pale leaves and sickly growth, and can be remedied by applying a nitrogen-rich fertilizer, such as dried chicken manure pellets or sulfate of ammonia, and watering well. Organic matter, such as compost or manure, dug into the soil before planting or used as a mulch will also boost nitrogen levels.

Insufficient water is the most common cause of disorders, and leads to poor growth and flowering, a deficiency of nutrients, and powdery mildew attacks. Without an adequate supply of water and vigorous root growth, plants find it hard to grab enough nutrients, such as magnesium, which they take up in solution from the soil.

During prolonged dry spells, plants may develop autumn tints and lose their foliage. Well-established woody plants have enough roots to ride out these dry spells and recover when rains return. Lawns turn brown, but the buds at the

Disease or disorder?

Plant disorders are not diseases, although the symptoms can look similar. Adverse weather, such as drought or unusually low temperatures, can affect plant health, although mature, hardy types usually recover quickly when more favorable conditions return. Young plants, or those that have recently been planted, are more vulnerable, and you will need to keep a close watch on these and protect them against extreme weather. Increase their resistance by growing them in a suitable site and soil.

Drought The leaves of perennials, such as this primrose, may develop brown edges if the roots are suffering from a lack of moisture.

Sun scorch Japanese maples prefer a shady site and moist roots. A site in full sun may result in scorched, brown leaves.

Frost damage The flowers of plants that bloom in early spring, such as magnolias, may suffer frost damage, even if the plant is hardy.

Flattened, ribbonlike growth, known as "fasciation," is thought to be caused by early injury to the buds, and although it looks peculiar, it rarely affects the overall health of the plant.

base of the leaves remain alive, and they quickly regrow when rehydrated. But plants with limited root systems, such as annuals and herbaceous perennials, are more vulnerable and may require emergency measures. First, cut back wilted stems and remove dead leaves, and then give the plant a good watering. Continue to water regularly, and you should soon see new buds and stems emerge.

Root problems

Newly planted plants, especially trees, shrubs, and climbers, are particularly vulnerable to drought and a lack of nutrients. To prevent problems, water new plants well and regularly, and keep the area around the roots free of weeds.

More insidious is root damage. Roots suffer when soils are waterlogged, dry, or airless. They are also more likely to contract fungal diseases when stressed by these conditions.

The first signs of root problems may be symptoms in the foliage. When roots are too dry, the leaves farthest from the roots, which are most vulnerable to moisture loss, turn brown, especially at the edges. Drought often causes the bark at the base of the stem to rot and die too, although this is also a symptom of the root disease honey fungus (*see p.257*). If the base of the stem is sound, check for dead roots that appear red or brown and brittle. If the root system is dead or damaged, the plant's chances of survival are slim, but if roots are healthy, watering may save the plant.

Poor light levels

Growing plants in shade when they prefer a sunnier site will lead to pale or yellow leaves and stems, and poor growth. Plants and seedlings may grow tall and spindly and lack vigor. The only cure is to move the plants to a location where they will receive the right amount of light.

Lack of light causes plants and seedlings to grow tall and thin, and leaves to turn yellow. This is known as "etiolation."

Chemical damage

Sometimes gardeners are responsible for plant disorders. Weedkillers are useful, but they can do great damage when they come into contact with valued plants. Unless scrupulously cleaned, watering cans and sprayers can hold traces of

weedkillers, which may end up killing your favorite plants if they are then used to apply fungicides, or for watering. Suckers of roses and other plants can also pick up traces of weedkiller used on nearby lawns, and great care must be taken when spraying weeds close to ornamental displays. Severe damage results, often the following spring when the weedkiller has had all winter to permeate the plant.

Weedkiller damage

Scorching due to salt spray

Salt used to prevent icing on paths and roads can harm the roots of plants growing close by, either killing them or stunting their growth. Near the coast, sea salt is often carried on breezes and can scorch the foliage of susceptible plants,

leaving brown patches on the leaves. In this case, salt damage is relatively easy to diagnose, since it will be much worse on the windward side of the plant. The same applies to sun scorch, wind damage on evergreens from winter gales, and the effects of summer storms on deciduous foliage. In all these instances, the symptoms will be worse where the foliage is most exposed to sun or wind.

Salt injury to a choisya

What is a pest?

Pests are creatures that prevent gardeners from enjoying their garden, usually by damaging cultivated plants. Soiling by cats and dogs, and furniture and paving spoiled by sticky honeydew are other forms of damage. Pests may be mollusks (such as slugs), mammals, birds, mites (such as spider mites), or, most commonly, insects.

Picky eaters

Many pests stick to one host plant. Most beetles and caterpillars are picky about what they will eat. Viburnum and lily beetles, for instance, stick to their respective hosts. Greenfly and blackfly, officially called aphids, also have a limited range of host species. The trouble is that there are so many different kinds of aphids that one type or another

Lily beetles at work

will attack most plants at some time. These insects obtain nutrients by sucking plant sap through their thin, hollow mouthparts. Other sap-suckers include thrips, scale insects, and capsid bugs. To aid feeding, sap-sucking insects inject materials that regulate plant growth, and induce severe distortion and curled foliage that hides and shelters the insects. Their hollow mouthparts also spread viruses.

Garden gluttons

Some pests are happy to tuck into anything tasty that you have grown. Slugs and snails eat most plants, except trees and shrubs. Seedlings, herbaceous plants, and climbers are

Leaf miners are quite common, if not especially harmful pests. There are many different kinds; those found on primroses (*left*) are different from those that attack holly (*right*).

Sooty mold (*above*) is often the result of an infestation of aphids (*right*). These pests secrete sticky honeydew, which provides an ideal growing medium for the black sooty fungus.

most affected. Holes appear within the leaves as well as at the edges, and you may notice telltale slime trails. Slugs and snails also mine bulbs and tubers. They feed in mild, humid weather, mainly at night, hiding out during the day beneath garden waste and under the soil. When slugs and snails damage soft growth, other problems often follow.

Vine weevils also attack a wide range of plants. The adult insects, almost all female, cannot fly, and crawl around the garden from midspring to midautumn, usually after dark, laying eggs. They feed on leaves, mainly of herbaceous plants and shrubs (especially evergreens such as rhododendrons), notching the leaf edges only, as their mouthparts are not adapted to making holes within leaves. The eggs, too small to be easily seen without a microscope, hatch into grubs, which feed on roots. The grubs are young and vulnerable and yet they do much damage in late summer and early autumn, which is when you should apply controls.

Friend or foe?

Some insects, such as ladybugs and hoverflies, are completely benign, others are pests, and others are somewhere in between. In a humus-rich garden, earwigs are just a nuisance, taking bites out of petals and infesting lawn furniture; if humus is lacking they eat many plant parts and can devour a row of seedlings in a night. Ants farm aphids for their honeydew so that they build up into large colonies, but also kill plants by excavating the soil beneath them when constructing their nests.

Earwig on a buttercup

What pest damage looks like

Pests are often only identifiable by the damage they cause. Many are elusive; some, like mites and nematodes, are almost microscopically small. Others fashion hiding places for themselves within leaves, while pests such as gall formers secrete chemicals that induce the plant to "grow" them a home. Many pests cover themselves with protective coatings, such as webbing or the "cuckoo spit" that surrounds froghoppers, which render pesticide sprays less effective.

Leaf nematode distorts foliage and spreads in water on leaves. Clearing away dead foliage reduces their spread. Replace badly affected plants.

Leaf rolling sawfly grubs cause rose leaves to roll up around them. Picking off and destroying affected leaves before mid-July may limit attacks the next year.

Galls may be unsightly but cause no serious damage to plants. Destroying affected leaves and fallen foliage may reduce subsequent attacks.

Pollen beetle populations surge in midsummer. They do little damage to plants but are unsightly on cut flowers; they can simply be shaken off.

Slug damage is most common on vulnerable plants like hostas (*above*), which need to be protected with slug control materials, or biological controls.

Caterpillars often strip leaves bare. Some are obvious, living in colonies, often beneath webbing. Others feed on plant roots or work at night, hiding under foliage by day. Use contact insecticides when picking off is inadequate, and dig out soil-dwelling caterpillars when they reveal themselves by killing plants.

Capsid bugs are seldom noticed until it is too late. Insecticides applied when the damage is in its early stages may help, as can good weed control.

Vine weevils feed on the leaves of many plants, including rhododendrons (*above*). They are particularly common where "wild" rhododendrons grow.

Vine weevils can be introduced into your garden in the roots or top growth of newly bought plants. Always check plants and rootballs before planting.

Vine weevil larvae in roots often kill potted plants. Control in late summer with insecticides watered onto the pot, or use soil mixes with insecticides.

Snails' shells make them less dependant than slugs on moist cover, and you may find them in climbers, or on bulb leaves and flowers, such as this hyacinth.

What is a disease?

Most plant diseases are caused by fungi, while others are caused by bacteria, viruses, or other microorganisms. They often enter a plant through a wound; once inside, they grow and multiply and the plant sooner or later shows visible symptoms, and may die. Gardeners often spread plant diseases inadvertently when they acquire infected material, so always refuse offers of suspicious plants.

How diseases spread

Fungi that infect plants consist of microscopic threads that can grow together to form structures that are visible to the naked eye. But the first signs of infection you will notice are usually spots, rots, or stem dieback; these are then followed by the distinctive mildew, mold, or other evidence of the fungal disease.

Fungi cannot produce their own nutrients and are sustained by the plant host. Typically, fungi produce spores that spread by air currents, rain or watering splash, or, less significantly, on insects or on seeds. Spores need moisture to germinate, which is why fungal diseases—mildews and molds for example—are so much worse in wet weather. Many fungi also produce resting bodies that sit out dry or cold periods. These persist in the soil until better conditions or the presence of a susceptible plant is "detected," and then release spores that start the disease cycle over again. Fungi also persist in infected plants. Dieback diseases carry over from year to year in infected shoots and rose blackspot will lurk in fallen leaves ready to reinfect roses in spring.

Bacterial infections can cause a wide range of symptoms, depending on the bacteria. Rots of soft tissue, such as bulbs and rhizomes, with a distinctive nasty smell are often caused

Diseased fruits and berries can persist on trees or the ground over winter, ready to release spores in spring. To prevent this, put them in the trashcan, on a bonfire, or in a deep hole.

by bacteria. Cankers, such as bacterial canker of cherries, is also widespread. Another common bacterial disease is fireblight, which affects plants in the apple and pear family, including mountain ash and cotoneaster. Symptoms include dieback of branches, and leaves that hang as if scorched by fire. Fireblight is spread by insects that carry the bacteria from flower to flower; other bacterial diseases are spread by air currents, or by rain or watering splash. Many need help to enter plants, and gain access through insect pest damage, pruning wounds, or even the scars left at leaf fall in autumn.

Viruses are even less able to gain access to plants without help. Insects carry them from plant to plant. Greenfly or aphids are the most effective carriers, but thrips, whiteflies, and occasionally other insects play their part. Viruses are very widespread in weeds as well as most mature garden plants, where their effect is usually not noticeable.

Rose blackspot is a fungal disease that is prevalent in wet weather, spreading by water splash in wet, windy conditions. Regular treatment with a fungicide is required, but removing infected leaves and pruning out diseased wood also helps. Catalogs list roses that are more resistant than others to this disease, and these are worth considering, but no rose is completely immune.

Rose rust symptoms in spring. The spots shed fungal spores later in the summer, soon followed by leaf loss. Rusts are a large group of diseases, characterized by orange spots or "bumps."

What diseases look like

The four ailments in the top row are extremely serious, and there is no chemical "cure"; all that can be done is to cut away the affected parts or remove the plant. Similarly, seedlings will not recover from damping off disease, and an affected batch must be disposed of. Virus-affected plants may also have to be removed, although they often produce surprisingly healthy seed. Other diseases may be treatable, but in all of these cases, never add any affected plant material to the compost pile.

Canker Shrunken, cracked rings of dead bark in apples and pears, including crabapples, caused by a fungus. Cut out all affected wood as soon as seen.

Honey fungus Destructive, incurable fungus that spreads from plant to plant by dark strands, seen here beneath the bark. Affected plants must be removed.

Coral spot Causes pink/red spots that dot the bark of dead wood, but it can invade healthy shoots of many trees and shrubs. Must be cut out.

Bacterial canker on cherry tree This bacterial disease has no chemical control. If you cannot cut out all infected wood safely you will have to remove the tree.

Powdery mildew This thrives on plants growing in the dry soil close to walls, such as clematis (*above*). Mulching and watering reduces plants' vulnerability.

Gray mold Affects rose buds. Not readily controlled by fungicides, but promoting free air flow by pruning out crowded growth in and around plants can help.

Gray mold Damaged plants are especially vulnerable to this fungus, also called botrytis. Careful handling and good slug control minimize the risk.

Damping off Fungus that affects seedlings at soil level, causing them to collapse. Copper-based fungicides give effective protection but won't cure it.

Hollyhock rust Like other types of rust disease, this disfigures rather than kills plants. Choose resistant plants, and keep in good health to resist attacks.

Powdery mildews These are all specific to their host plants and are worse in hot dry weather. Fungicides are effective at controlling mild attacks.

Rose mosaic virus Viruses often attack a number of plants, causing different symptoms in each. Badly affected plants have to be replaced.

Gray mold Crowded plants, such as this geranium, which are grown indoors in a stuffy atmosphere are at risk. Remove affected material and improve conditions.

Preventing problems

Plants, like people, are much less susceptible to disease when they are doing well than when under stress. This means that the best gardening techniques will help plants to shrug off troubles. Many problems occur because of poor gardening methods—not only neglect of the plants but also factors such as inadequate soil preparation. These are physiological disorders caused by factors such as insufficient light, nutrients, or moisture, or even waterlogging. But problems also arise when plants are simply in the wrong place.

Choosing the right plants for conditions

First, select plants that are suitable for the general climate in your area and conditions in your garden. Acid-loving plants, for example, are useless where the soil is alkaline, or even neutral in some cases. Similarly, plants that thrive in alkaline

Damp, shady woodland gardens look lush when planted with big-leaved, deep green foliage plants that like the moisture. Plants that hanker for sun and whose roots resent being wet would soon fade away and succumb to pests and diseases.

Garden hygiene

It's important to keep your tools and equipment clean to reduce the risk of any problems spreading.

Scrub out pots

- **Wash tools** and boots with garden disinfectant after handling potential diseases and pests.

- **Scrubbing pots**, stakes, posts, and wires will help prevent carry-over of spores and eggs to new areas of planting.

- **When taking cuttings** and pruning, before moving to a new plant wipe the blades of cutting tools with a rag soaked in garden disinfectant to help prevent the spread of problems.

Clean pruner blades

- **Greenhouses** and cold frames should be cleaned thoroughly in both spring and autumn.

Golden-leaved plants may turn green when planted in shade. It doesn't hurt them, but they are not giving you the intended effect in the garden. The yellow leaves will return if you move the plants into better light or remove foliage that's shading them.

conditions seldom give their best on acidic soil, although they may well survive.

You also need to find plants to match all of the different microclimates that exist in your garden (*see p. 60*)—a sunny spot, a shady area, a cold wall, or a patch of damp ground, for example. When plants are not battling with conditions that they don't enjoy, they will give you a much better show in the garden. This may sound restrictive but, with so many plants to choose from, you can actually grow a beautiful display anywhere and on any soil.

Of course, there is much that the gardener can do to ameliorate very poor growing conditions—cutting back large plants to let light through to those beneath, for example, or increasing water retention in dry soils. And where pests and diseases are very damaging, a tactical retreat to using less susceptible plants (*see Resistant plants, right*) makes more sense than continual vigilance.

Good gardening for good health

• Plants are especially vulnerable when newly sown or planted and should be protected against the cold, wind, and drought. Spread out roots and carefully secure them in well-prepared soil, avoiding excessively deep planting. Faults here may be fatal but not before years of disappointing growth.

• Plant rotation may be something you have only heard about in relation to vegetable growing, but it also makes sense for bedding plants to avoid carry-over and buildup of pests and diseases. Introduce variety by not planting pansies or wallflowers, for example, in the same place in consecutive years.

• Conscientious weeding helps reduce pest and disease problems. Clean up fallen leaves, fruits, and dead wood. Do not compost or recycle infested material; remove it by burning it or putting it in the trash.

• You can inadvertently damage plants with mowers and weed trimmers, or by pruning, opening up the way for diseases and rots. Make use of tree guards, and edging strips on lawns.

• Good airflow to lower humidity levels within plantings can help reduce molds and rotting. Control very dense planting and thin crowded growth by pruning. Indoors, too little humidity is more likely, encouraging red-spider-mite and whitefly attacks. It can be countered by misting and dampening plants frequently, and by standing plants in trays of moist gravel or inside larger pots of damp moss.

• Permanently wet roots can lead to root rots and dieback, after which even mildly harmful fungi, such as coral spot (*see p. 257*), can cause great damage.

• Conversely, dry roots and irregular watering weaken plants, allowing powdery mildew and aphids to have a field day.

Resistant plants

Plants that resist problems make gardening a pleasure. Rabbits are less likely to eat lupines and hellebores than other herbaceous plants. Slug-infested areas are bad news for hostas and delphiniums but robust epimediums and monks-hood (*Aconitum*) will remain unspoiled. Delphiniums and Michaelmas daisies are martyrs to powdery mildew; monkshood and Korean chrysanthemums, with their later summer color, are more resilient alternatives.

Benign creepy crawlies

Most insects are not pests and some, often seen in the vicinity of damaged plants, only take advantage of damage that has already been done by the weather or another pest.

Ant

• **Ant's delvings** are a nuisance in lawns and may loosen your plants' grasp on the soil, but this can be countered with watering, raking, and soil firming.

Woodlice

• **Woodlice, centipedes, and millipedes** are excellent "recyclers" of plant debris, but might occasionally nibble at holes made by slugs and other pests, or damage delicate seedlings. Encourage them to go elsewhere by clearing away debris.

Honeybee

• **Bees are vital for pollination**, and therefore are among the creatures that should always be spared—even the leaf-cutting bees that take an occasional bite from plants. Wild bumblebees are not quite as numerous as they once were, while honeybees are the source of beekeepers' income.

Wasp

• **Wasps can be a nuisance** throughout late summer, but before that they will obligingly prey on other insects. You should only destroy their nests if you really have to—for example, in a family garden.

Targeting pest problems

Natural predators, such as ground beetles, ladybugs, and spiders, consume vast numbers of pests. Any control, including many pesticides, that reduces the number of these helpful creatures inadvertently increases pest problems in the garden. Although there are times when tough remedies are called for, gardeners are often uneasy about using pesticides for minor problems because many products, both chemical and natural, act indiscriminately. (Exceptions include slug pellets which, used according to the instructions, affect only slugs and snails.) However, traps and barriers that do not harm friendly wildlife offer valuable protection for plants.

Traps and barriers

Although traps and barriers require some effort to install, in many cases they provide full protection against pests, including deer, rabbits, gophers, and birds. To prevent deer from entering your garden, erect fences at least 6ft (1.8m) high all around the garden; rabbit barriers must be 4ft (1.2m) or more high and sunk 1ft (30cm) more beneath the ground to prevent the rabbits from burrowing under them. Fruit cages or nets will stop birds from feasting on your fruit trees and bushes. Although these barriers can be costly, they can provide peace of mind.

Trapping small mammals is a job often best left to the professionals. It is possible, although not easy, to trap moles, squirrels, and rabbits, but you have to be competent to deal with the catch. Trapping mice is straightforward, but rats are wilier, and poison bait, carefully placed to avoid harm to pets, wildlife, and children, is the best option.

Pots can be protected by a band of Vaseline around the side or rim to help keep out insects, and bands of copper help to deter slugs and snails. Slugs and snails find crossing

copper very uncomfortable; however, they will soon seek out any leaf or other bridge across the barrier, so you need to be watchful. In beds and borders, rings of sharp materials that slugs and snails may find scratchy to cross can be used around vulnerable plants. Grit, crushed eggshells, and cocoa shell mulch give some protection; however, they are far from foolproof, and commercial granule barriers may be more effective. Again, a leaf bridge will undo all your work.

Ants and other pests can be prevented from climbing prized plants by collars of aluminum foil turned outward, but these need to be refreshed as the plants grow. Bands of a

Natural protection

Traps for slugs and snails range from the homemade—a hollowed-out potato, or the rind of half a grapefruit upended on the soil—to this high-tech version of the beer trap (*far left*). Companion planting (*left*) is a very old but largely unproven method of natural pest control. Traditional companion plants such as these marigolds may deter flying pests, including whiteflies, and their root secretions are thought to inhibit soil pests and weeds.

special plant-friendly grease can be applied to the stems of trees to prevent pests from climbing them. Apple trees (*Malus*), including crabapples, are most likely to benefit from this. If the tree is staked, you must grease the stake too, or it will provide a bypass for pests up into the crown of the tree.

Some plants are said to help protect adjacent plants. Although consistent evidence is hard to come by for the effectiveness of "companion planting," it can't be completely discounted and may work well for you. Marigolds are said to keep flying insect pests off plants such as roses, and their root secretions are thought to help prevent soil-borne diseases and pests, such as nematode worms.

Natural allies

Encouraging natural helpers, such as predatory insects and spiders, insect-eating birds, bats, snakes, and frogs, will have some effect in keeping plants trouble-free. Bird boxes and feeding stations, organic mulches, and water features help sustain the gardener's friends. But they cannot cope at all times of the year, especially when pests are abundant—in spring, for example, before predator numbers have built up, or in years when a pest's population surges. However, it is likely that damage would always be a lot worse without natural allies, and doing everything you can to encourage them makes sense.

A garden pond will encourage beneficial wildlife. Make a "deep end" 24in (60cm) in depth to help aquatic creatures to escape freezes, and a "beach," so small animals and birds can approach the water safely.

Encouraging pest predators

Attract beneficial creatures into your garden by providing them with food and shelter. Features to encourage wildlife are generally inexpensive, many are attractive, and those that are less so are fairly unobtrusive. Gardeners can also create a wild corner of the garden where grasses and plants are left to grow unrestrained and allowed to stand over winter. Also include a range of native species, and use pesticides only when absolutely necessary, targeting them carefully to avoid harming helpful organisms.

Nesting boxes are far more likely to attract occupants if you also provide a feeding station nearby to help birds supplement scarce natural resources.

Attract butterflies and bees with flowers rich in nectar, such as sedum and butterfly bush, and with open blooms that insects can get into easily.

Lacewing houses can be purchased for these helpful insects, whose larvae prey on a range of harmful garden pests, including aphids.

Old logs stored in a cool, undisturbed area of your garden will provide an excellent hiding place for many helpful creatures, such as toads and beetles.

When to take action

Acting swiftly when problems arise greatly eases their control. Take frequent walks around your garden to enjoy the results of your work, and to keep an eye out for signs of trouble. You will soon become aware of the plants that are especially vulnerable to pests and diseases, and need regular inspection.

Often, pruning out diseased shoots or removing cover for harmful pests will put an immediate halt to any damage. At other times, pesticides may be needed.

Although their use is not obligatory, pesticides are useful tools when other measures prove ineffective. If a problem is detected early and dealt with quickly, you will need to use just a small amount of pesticide. A colony of pests or a patch of infected plants can be carefully treated and the chemical can be confined to the place where it is needed. Ready-to-use packs are very convenient and particularly useful for small infestations. They spare you the burden of mixing a limited quantity of pesticide solution in a sprayer. A hand-pump sprayer is cheap and handy, but for larger gardens a pump-up sprayer will save you a lot of work. Ideally, you should have two: one for weedkillers and one for other sprays, such as fertilizer.

All pesticides sold to gardeners are carefully tested and licensed for use. However, many people are uneasy about using them. Organic gardeners are only willing to use those that are derived from natural sources rather than manufactured chemicals. Fortunately, there are many natural products available, such as derris, which may be less effective

Protective copper bands on pots of hostas help to protect these vulnerable plants from slug and snail attacks.

than synthetic products but are good enough for all but the pickiest gardeners. In fact, when used in the early stages of a pest or disease problem, they are usually all that you need to stop the trouble before it gets out of hand.

For good results it is sometimes necessary to use chemical pesticides frequently as a preventative measure. Unless you are prepared to do this in rose borders, for example, you need to find other ways of growing roses.

How controls work

• Controls can be absorbed into the plant's sap (described as "systemic"), killing fungi within the plants, and sap-sucking insects, such as aphids, as they feed. Thorough coverage with a spray is less important with these pesticides than with contact-action controls.

• Contact insecticides include all the naturally derived materials, as well as some synthetic pesticides. Here, the chemical has to touch the pest to do its job, so coverage of upper and lower leaf surfaces is necessary. Once foliage becomes distorted and curled it is difficult to get contact materials where they are needed, so take action promptly.

• Contact fungicides work by forming a protective layer that prevents spores from getting into the plant, but they will not cure infections. Again, aim for full coverage, before the disease gets a grip on the plant.

• Dusts are contact materials and must be applied early. Puffer packs are not very satisfactory applicators, and sprays are usually preferable to dusts.

Recycled plastic bottles with the bottoms cut off protect vulnerable plants from slugs and birds. They also warm the soil, helping to get seedlings off to a good start.

Biological controls

Instead of using chemicals, you can release insects or mites that prey on certain pests. These "biological controls" are most effective in greenhouses and conservatories, because outside they can dissipate. You shouldn't combine these natural controls with synthetic insecticides, and ideally you should only use those based on fatty acids or oil that leave no residues.

Biological controls for vine weevils and slugs are watered onto the soil or compost. For slugs, apply from spring to early autumn. The control for vine weevils is best used in containers in later summer before the grubs do much damage. Both work best on open-structured soil. Controls for spider mite and whitefly are effective as long as they are used before the pests become too numerous.

It's usually best to buy biological controls by mail order. A few garden centers stock them, but since they're living creatures, they aren't easy to store. Check the AHS website or ask your garden center for suppliers. Follow the instructions carefully.

Using chemicals

Reading and following the instructions on the label is vital for safe, effective, and legal pesticide use. Calculate how much you need. If in doubt, make less; you can always mix more, or, if only a few plants remain untreated, add a little water to the dregs and use this to treat the last few plants. Take care to avoid spills and never allow pesticide to get into drains, ponds, streams, or ditches. Set nozzles to give a fairly fine spray that neither drifts nor drenches, and apply evenly over the affected plants. Foliar sprays should not be applied so heavily that dribbles occur, but just enough to evenly wet the target.

Spray both upper and lower surfaces of foliage. Keep pets and children away from the sprayed area until the material has dried onto the leaves. Wash any skin that has come into contact with the spray.

Store pesticides in a secure, locked cabinet, and be sure they are clearly labeled; never keep them in food or drink containers. Only use government-authorized facilities to dispose of old or surplus chemicals.

• Pellets and baits, such as slug pellets, have a bad reputation and are certainly harmful if misused. But if applied at the exact rates specified on the packaging, and stored safely and securely, they are a useful and safe last resort.

Protecting seedlings

Applying insecticides and fungicides promptly is especially helpful in protecting young plants. Older plants can shrug off disease, or at least come back from a bad attack. Young plants frequently succumb or are so slowed up in growth, or "checked," that they never make good plants. Inspect young plants as often as you can.

Insects—aphids, for example—are often fine-tuned to recognize the pale foliage of young plants. They head for these because young plants are less well defended and richer in protein than tougher, older plants.

Fungal diseases thrive on the soft tissues of young plants as well. And viruses affect all plants but do most damage to young specimens. They take time to multiply, so infection later in a plant's life rarely affects its growth and flowering, and does little damage; robust mature plants are able to stand up to their effects. Viruses are most commonly spread by insects, so controlling insects also suppresses these diseases.

Gather up spent vegetation and move it to the compost pile to deprive slugs of cover. Diseased material is best burned or, in more populated areas, consigned to the garbage can.

Planning your gardening year

To make life easier, this garden planner shows you at a glance what jobs need to be done and when. Simply look at the season and follow the advice given—you will find more information on each subject in the relevant chapters in the book. For example, early spring is a good time to start preparing your soil for planting, and there are further details on soils in the chapter starting on p.34.

Early spring

This is the beginning of the gardening year and is a busy period for gardeners, but keep off lawns and soil if they are frozen or wet, and don't attempt to dig until the weather improves.

- Start weeding—pull small seedlings by hand but dig out the roots of perennials such as dandelions, or use a glyphosate weedkiller.
- Prepare the soil for planting by forking it over and digging in organic matter.
- Sow seeds of marginally hardy and tender bedding plants indoors in a frost-free place.
- Plant summer-flowering bulbs and perennials.
- Prune bush roses.
- Prune deciduous shrubs and climbers that flower later in the summer, such as butterfly bush.
- Lift and divide oversized clumps of perennials; discard dead or unproductive sections in the middle of the clump.
- Prepare soil for planting in fair weather.
- Rake the lawn, removing leaves and other debris, and brush off worm castings if you need to mow.

Prune butterfly bush

Dig organic matter into the soil

Mid- to late spring

Stake tall perennials as growth emerges

The garden is changing daily now, with plants shooting up and buds bursting into life.

- Apply a general-purpose fertilizer around established shrubs and roses.
- Mulch the soil after rainfall or watering.
- Stake herbaceous perennials as growth emerges.
- Sow seeds of less hardy and tender annuals inside, or buy plug plants and grow in a frost-free place.
- Harden off bedding plants sown earlier in spring.
- Sow hardy annuals *in situ*.
- In late spring, thin hardy annuals sown outside.
- Plant evergreens, and move any in the wrong place.
- Prune early-flowering shrubs and climbers after they have bloomed.
- Cut back ornamental grasses as they start to grow.
- Make new shrubs and climbers by layering.
- Start taking softwood cuttings from new shoots.
- Sod or sow new lawns, and repair worn-out lawns.
- Apply weedkiller and a spring fertilizer to lawns.
- Cut the grass with the blades set low.
- Keep weeding.

Thin seedlings of hardy annuals

Early summer

Rising temperatures coax roses and peonies into bloom, while plants whose spring flowers are already spent need to be pruned.

- Feed flowering shrubs and roses with a rose fertilizer to promote flowering.
- Weed carefully to avoid damaging nearby plants.
- Buy bedding plants and plant out after the frosts.
- Fill hanging baskets and summer pots with plants.
- Plant out less hardy and tender bedding plants when the frosts are over.
- Prune late spring-flowering shrubs and climbers after they have bloomed.
- Trim vigorously growing hedges, such as privet.
- Remove suckers from roses.
- Tie in climbers regularly to their supports.
- Divide congested clumps of primroses and irises after they have flowered.
- Continue to take softwood cuttings.
- Mow grass regularly, increasing the cutting height as days grow warmer.
- Water new plants in dry spells.

Fill hanging baskets

Weed beds and borders

Mid- to late summer

Water containers regularly

The work in the garden gradually eases off as summer progresses, leaving you free to sit back and enjoy the fruits of your labor.

• In dry spells continue to water new and establishing plants, and new lawns.
• Deadhead flowering plants to promote new blooms.
• Water and feed baskets and containers regularly.
• Continue to weed regularly.
• Mow lawns regularly, keeping increased height so longer grass shades roots and reduces evaporation.
• Cut back herbaceous plants after flowering for a second burst of foliage and flowers.
• Plant daffodil bulbs in late summer.
• Trim evergreen and conifer hedges in late summer.
• Prune rambling roses after they have flowered.
• Take semiripe cuttings of shrubs.
• Prepare the soil for a new lawn or border.

Trim hedges

Autumn

As rain returns and the weather cools, get ready for a season of activity—planting, and lifting and dividing before winter sets in.

• Remove dead or dying stems and foliage from perennials, but you can leave a few to protect the roots of your plants over winter.
• Plant hardy perennials and hardy evergreen shrubs early in the season.
• Plant deciduous shrubs and trees in late autumn when the leaves have fallen.
• Remove and compost summer annuals.
• Plant spring-flowering biennials, such as wallflowers.
• Plant spring-flowering bulbs.
• In late autumn, transplant deciduous shrubs.
• Lift and divide hardy perennials.
• Lift and store, or insulate, tender perennials and shrubs before the cold weather. Wrap pots and cover vulnerable plants with fleece when frost is forecast.
• Lift and store dahlias and cannas after the first frosts.
• Take hardwood cuttings of deciduous shrubs.
• Check tree ties and loosen if tight.
• Cover ponds with nets to keep out falling leaves which contaminate the water as they decompose.
• Apply an autumn lawn fertilizer.
• Lay sod or sow new lawns, or repair if ncessary.
• Mow lawns, reducing cutting height back to spring level to reduce risk of snow-mold damage.
• Rake leaves and debris from lawns.
• Aerate lawns using a fork and top-dress to stimulate root growth and prevent moss.

Rake autumn leaves

Plant spring bulbs

Winter

Brush heavy snow off branches

Cold winter months are a time of rest for most plants, but there is still plenty to do in the garden, and venturing out in the brisk air can really raise the spirits.

• Dig organic matter, such as well-rotted manure or garden compost, into clay soils.
• Protect slightly tender perennials by covering them with straw or compost.
• Brush heavy snow off trees, hedges, and shrubs to prevent the weight from snapping branches.
• Plant deciduous trees, shrubs, and hedges on dry, frost-free days, unless the soil is very wet.
• Prune trees (except for plums and cherries) and wisteria, and renovate any old or overgrown deciduous shrubs.
• In late winter, coppice shrubs for special effects like colorful stems or bold foliage.
• In windy gardens, prune back the top growth of tall roses and other shrubs to prevent wind rock.
• Check stored dahlias, cannas, and gladioli, and remove any that show signs of rotting.
• Continue to take hardwood cuttings of deciduous shrubs if you want to make new plants.
• Take root cuttings of perennials.
• Continue to rake up leaves from lawns.
• Keep off lawns and soil when waterlogged or frozen.
• Check and repair garden tools. Service and sharpen mower blades.
• Make plans for next year's planting.

Renovate deciduous shrubs

Plant index

The index below will guide you to specific or detailed information about the plants mentioned in the text, such as their height, color, or other features. You will also be able to find information on techniques including planting and pruning using the General index starting on p.268. Page numbers in **bold italic** refer to the captions for the illustrations.

lily tree *see Magnolia*
Liriodendron tulipifera
    'Aureomarginatum' 117
Lonicera
    L. nitida 'Baggesen's Gold' 148
    L. periclymenum 139

M

magnolia, pruning 223
Magnolia
    M. denudata 122
    M. x *soulangeana* 39
mahonia 214
    pruning 217
Mahonia x *media* 'Charity' 128
Malus
    'Butterball' 122
    M. x *moerlandsii* 'Profusion' 117
maple *see Acer*
medlar 111
morning glory *see Ipomoea*
mulberry 111
Musa basjoo 206
muscari 102

N, O

Nerium oleander 206
Nyssa sinensis 123
oak *see Quercus*
Olea europaea 206
olive *see Olea*
orchids, roots 19

P, Q

Pachysandra terminalis 39
Papaver orientale 105
Parthenocissus tricuspidata 139
Passiflora caerulea 138

pear *see Pyrus*
Pennisetum setaceum 'Rubrum' 203
Perovskia 'Blue Spire' 129
Phoenix canariensis 207
Phormium 206
Phyllostachys
    P. aurea 140
    P. nigra 140, 202
    P. vivax f. *aureocaulis* 140
Pleioblastus pygmaeus 141
pieris 39
Pinus mugo 202
poppy *see Papaver*
Potentilla 149
Prunus
    P. cerasifera 'Nigra' 117
    P. laurocerasus 149
    'Okame' 123
    P. serrula 116, 123
Pulsatilla vulgaris 38
pyracantha 139
    pruning 224
Pyrus salicifolia 'Pendula' 117, 123
Quercus ellipsoidalis 123
quince 111

R

Rhodiola rosea 62
rhododendron, watering 155
Robinia pseudoacacia 'Frisia' 123
rock rose *see Cistus; Helianthemum*
Rosa
    'Alba Maxima' 132
    'Baby Love' 133
    'Bonica'
    'Buff Beauty' 133
    'Cider Cup' 132
    'Climbing Iceberg' 133
    'Félicité Parmentier' 133
    Fragrant Cloud 133

    Gertrude Jekyll 133
    'Gloire de Dijon' 133
    Handel 133
    Little Bo-peep 132
    'Lovers' Meeting' 133
    Pheasant 132
    'Roseraie de l'Haÿ' 133
    R. rugosa 149
    Valencia 133
    Warm Welcome 132
rosemary *see Rosmarinus*
roseroot *see Rhodiola*
roses
    choosing 132–133
    climbers 134, *228*
    deadheading 164, 165
    designing with 112, 130–133
    in exposed gardens 71
    feeding 160
    planting 130, 135
    pruning 226–229
    ramblers 228
    shape and foliage 131
    training 131
    types 130
    see also Rosa
Rosmarinus officinalis Prostratus Group 129
Rubus cockburnianus, pruning 218

S

sage, pruning 215
    see also Salvia
Salix alba 'Britzensis' 128
Salvia officinalis 'Tricolor' 105
Sambucus, pruning 211, 218–219
sasa 140
scabiosa 38
Sedum spectabile 105
Sisyrinchum striatum 'Aunt May' 105

skimmia 39
Sorbus
    S. aria 38
    S. commixta 123
    'Joseph Rock' 123
Spanish broom *see Genista*
spindle tree *see Euonymus*
star jasmine *see Trachelospermum*
syringa 38, 211
Syringa vulgaris 'Katherine Havemeyer' 129

T

Taxus baccata 149, 222
Thamnocalamus crassinodus 'Kew Beauty' 140
Thuja plicata 149
Trachelospermum jasminoides 139
Trachycarpus fortunei 123
tree ferns, protection 167
Tropaeolum peregrinum 203
tulip 102
tulip tree *see Liriodendron*

V, W, Y

verbascum 38
Viburnum
    V. x *bodnantense* 212
    V. x *bodnantense* 'Dawn' 128
    V. opulus 129
    V. plicatum 'Mariesii' 124
    V. tinus 202
Virginia creeper *see Parthenocissus*
Vitis coignetiae 139
willow *see Salix*
wisteria 135
    pruning 225
witch hazel *see Hamamelis*
wormwood *see Artemisia*
yew *see Taxus*

General index

Page numbers in **bold italic** refer to the captions of the illustrations.

Acknowledgments

The publisher would like to thank the following for their kind permission to reproduce their photographs. On pages where several images are shown, the grid to the right will help you locate them.
Illustrations on other pages may be identified using the key: a=above, b=bottom, or below, c=center, f=far, l=left, r=right, t=top.

tl	tcl	tc	tcr	tr
cla	cal	ca	car	cra
cfl	cl	ca	cr	cfr
clb	cbl	cb	cbr	crb
bl	bcl	bc	bcr	br

7: Andrew Lawson/Morville, Shropshire. Designer: Kathy Swift (bl); Clive Nichols/Hampton Court 98 (br); 8: John Glover (t); 9: John Glover (tc); Clive Nichols/White Windows, Hampshire (b); 22: Photos Horticultural/MJK (bc); 25: DK Images/Steven Wooster (bl), (br); 28: Oxford Scientific Films/Photolibrary.com (bl); 30: DK Images/Jacqui Hurst (b); 55: DK Images/Steven Wooster (tr); 59: Garden Picture Library/Howard Rice (tr), (tc), (bc), (br); 60: Garden and Wildlife Matters/John Feltwell (bcr); 67: Garden and Wildlife Matters (bcl); Holt Studios International/Bob Gibbons (bcr); 69: Garden Picture Library/Neil Holmes (br); 70: Garden Picture Library (tr); 73: DK Images/Steven Wooster (tr); 74: John Glover; 75: Andrew Lawson/Patrick Wynniatt-Husey, & Patrick Clarke, Hampton Court Show, 2000 (tl); Clive Nichols/Keukenhof Gardens, Holland (tr); Clive Nichols/Nyewood House, Hampshire (b); 76: Jerry Harpur/Design: Judith Sharpe (tr); Marcus Harpur/Design: Justin Green for Holly Oldcorn (bl); 77: Jerry Harpur/Diana Ross (t); Clive Nichols/Designer: Lucy Huntington (br); 78: Jerry Harpur/Design: Luciano Giubbilei, Kensington (tr); Marcus Harpur/Design: Brian Cross, Lakemount, Ireland (bc); 79: Clive Nichols (tr); Clive Nichols/The Nichols Garden, Reading (bl); 80: Jerry Harpur/Huis Bingerden, Holland (tr); 81: Clive Nichols/Chiffchaffs, Dorset (bl); Clive Nichols/Hadspen Gardens, Somerset (bcl); Clive Nichols/Pettifers, Oxfordshire (bcr); Clive Nichols/Designer: Elisabeth Woodhouse (tr); Jo Whitworth/© Rob Whitworth, RHS Garden, Wisley (br); 82: Jo Whitworth/Sheila Chapman, Essex; 83: Jerry Harpur/Design: Tom Stuart-Smith (tr); Jerry Harpur/© RHS Chelsea 1997, Design Stephen Woodhams (tl); Clive Nichols/© Chelsea 2002/Marston & Langinger (br); Clive Nichols/Pettifers Garden, Oxfordshire (cr); 84: Jo Whitworth/Sheila Chapman, Chelmsford, Essex (bl); 85: DK Images/Eric Crichton (bcr); DK Images/John Fielding (cbr), DK Images/C. Andrew Henley (bcl); DK Images/Andrew Lawson (cr); 88: Clive Nichols/Keukenhof Gardens, Holland (tc); Clive Nichols/Design: Pamela Woods (bc); 89: Clive Nichols/White Windows, Hampshire (br); 90: John Glover (tr); Clive Nichols/Design: Rupert Golby - Chelsea 1995 (bl); 91: DK Images/Andrew Lawson (cbr); DK Images/RHS Garden Wisley (cr); Clive Nichols/Lady Farm, Somerset (tr); 96: Garden Picture Library/John Glover (tr); 98: Clive Nichols/Lady Farm, Somerset (bl); Clive Nichols/The Old Vicarage, Norfolk (tr); 100: Jerry Harpur/Chiffchaffs, Dorset (bl); Clive Nichols/Little Court, Hampshire (tr); 101: DK Images/Eric Crichton (tcr); DK Images/Steven Wooster (bcr); 104: Andrew Lawson (bl); Andrew Lawson/Designer: Penelope Hobhouse, Bettiscombe (crb); 105: DK Images/Eric Crichton (tcl); DK Images/Dave King (cr); DK Images/Juliette Wade (bcl); DK Images/Dave Watts (ccl); 109: Clive Nichols/White Windows, Hampshire (tl); 110: Garden Picture Library/Jerry Pavia (tc); 111: John Glover/Chelsea '02 Design: Roger Platt (t); Marcus Harpur/Design: June Shave, Jo'Burg (br); 112: John Glover/Design: Fiona Lawrenson (tr); Clive Nichols/Joe Swift (bl); 113: Andrew Lawson/Bosvigo House, Cornwall (b); 115: DK Images/Fleurmerc (tr); 116: Clive Nichols/Lakemount, Cork, Eire (bl); Clive Nichols/White Windows, Hampshire (br); 117: Garden Picture Library/John Glover (br); Clive Nichols (tr); Clive Nichols/The Anchorage, Kent (tl); 118: DK Images/Peter Anderson (bl), (bc), (br); 122: DK Images/Andrew Butler (cr), (br), (tr); DK Images/Courtesy of the Cambridge Botanic Gardens (tcr); 123: DK Images/Andrew Butler (cl), (bl); DK Images/Andrew Lawson (tr); DK Images/Juliette Wade (cfl); DK Images/James Young (tc); 124: Clive Nichols/Beth Chatto Garden, Essex; 125: DK Images/Juliette Wade (bl); Clive Nichols/Designer: Sarah Hammond (tr); 128: DK Images/Clive Boursnell (cr); DK Images/Jonathan Buckley (bl), (cfl); DK Images/John Glover (br); DK Images/Howard Rice (bcl); 129: DK Images/Jonathan Buckley (tr); DK Images/John Fielding (bcr); DK Images/Juliette Wade (tcl); DK Images/Steven Wooster (cr), (cfr); 130: DK Images/Clive Boursnell (bcl); 131: John Glover (br); 132: DK Images/Clive Boursnell (bc); 133: DK Images/Andy Crawford (cr); DK Images/Andrew Lawson (tr); 134: DK Images/Jacqui Hurst (t); Andrew Lawson (bl); 135: DK Images/Neil Fletcher (tfl); Clive Nichols/Little Coopers, Hampshire (br); 138: DK Images/Jonathan Buckley (br), (cfr); DK Images/Steve Hamilton (bl); DK Images/Howard Rice (bc); John Glover (cal); Andrew Lawson (cla); 139: DK Images/Andrew Butler (br); DK Images/Neil Fletcher (c), (cr); DK Images/National Trust (Erddig) (tcl); DK Images/Howard Rice (tr); 140: John Glover (bcr); Andrew Lawson (bl), (br), (bcl); 141: John Glover/Lois Brown. Pasadena, California (t); Andrew Lawson (bc); 143: Andrew Lawson (tr); 144: Photos Horticultural (bl); 148: DK Images/Juliette Wade (bl); 49: DK Images/Savill Garden, Windsor (cfr); 157: Photos Horticultural (br); 159: Clive Nichols/Claire Matthews (bc); 171: DK Images/Steven Wooster (br); 174: Photos Horticultural (tl); 178: Holt Studios International (cr); 179: Science Photo Library/Pam Collins (bcl); Science Photo Library/Maurice Nimmo (tr); Garden World Images (tcr); Holt Studios International (cr); Photos Horticultural (tl); 180: Garden World Images (bcr); Holt Studios International (cfr); Photos Horticultural (cr), (bl); 187: Garden Picture Library/Howard Rice (tr); 190: John Glover; 193: Marie O'Hara/Planting Design: Paul Williams (tl); Science Photo Library/Bjorn Svensson (br); 197: Garden Picture Library/Mark Bolton (cla); Garden World Images (tr), (tl), (tcl), (cra); Photos Horticultural (tcr); 204: Photos Horticultural (tl); 206: Jerry Harpur (bcr); 237: Brian North (cla), (cra), (cal), (car); 248: Photos Horticultural; 249: Garden World Images (b), (tr); 250: Photos Horticultural (cb); 251: Garden World Images (cla), (ca), (bc), (br); 252: Garden World Images (tc), (bl), (bc), Garden World Images/Jacqui Dracup (br); 253: Garden World Images (tl), (bcr), (cr); Holt Studios International (bl); 254: Garden World Images (tc), (tr), (bl), (bcl); Photos Horticultural (cl), Premaphotos Wildlife/Ken Preston-Mafham (br); 255: Garden World Images (c), (bl), (br), (bcl), (bcr), (cl), (cr), (tcr); Garden World Images/Jacqui Dracup (tl); Holt Studios International (tr), (tcl); 256: Garden World Images (bl), (br); Holt Studios International (tc), (tr); 257: Garden World Images: (cla), (cra), (bcl), (tcl), (tcr), (bcr), (cfr); Holt Studios International: (cl), (cr), (bl), (br), (cfl); 258: DK Images/Steven Wooster (b); 259: DK Images/Steven Wooster (tl); 260: Photos Horticultural (bl); 261: DK Images/Kim Taylor (bl); DK Images/Steven Wooster (tr).

All other images © Dorling Kindersley. For further information see: www.dkimages.com

ILLUSTRATIONS
Antbits Illustration: 56, 173, 182
Deborah Maizels: 18, 64, 101, 102, 131, 135, 210
Sandra Pond and Will Giles: 35
Gill Tomblin: 85

DK PUBLISHING WOULD LIKE TO THANK:
Jeni Kubba, Dean Peckett, Colin Crosbie, David Hide and the many staff at RHS Wisley and Hyde Hall Gardens for their invaluable and patient help with photography.
All the staff at the Royal Horticultural Society, especially Barbara Haynes, Susanne Mitchell, and Susannah Charlton at Vincent Square and Mike Grant at Wisley.

EDITORIAL ASSISTANCE: Louise Abbott, Chris Dyer, and Annelise Evans

DESIGN ASSISTANCE: Ursula Dawson, Vanessa Hamilton, and Stephen Josland

PICTURE RESEARCH ASSISTANCE: Carlo Ortu

INDEX: Michèle Clarke